Covering the
Campus

A History of
the *Miscellany News*
at Vassar College

Covering the Campus

Brian Farkas

iUniverse, Inc.
New York   Bloomington

Covering the Campus
A History of the Miscellany News at Vassar College

Copyright © 2009 by Brian Farkas

All rights reserved. No part of this book may be used or reproduced by any means, graphic, electronic, or mechanical, including photocopying, recording, taping or by any information storage retrieval system without the written permission of the publisher except in the case of brief quotations embodied in critical articles and reviews.

iUniverse books may be ordered through booksellers or by contacting:

iUniverse
1663 Liberty Drive
Bloomington, IN 47403
www.iuniverse.com
1-800-Authors (1-800-288-4677)

Because of the dynamic nature of the Internet, any Web addresses or links contained in this book may have changed since publication and may no longer be valid. The views expressed in this work are solely those of the author and do not necessarily reflect the views of the publisher, and the publisher hereby disclaims any responsibility for them.

ISBN: 978-1-4401-2683-3 (pbk)
ISBN: 978-1-4401-2939-1 (ebk)

Library of Congress Control Number: 2009923353

Printed in the United States of America

iUniverse rev. date: 3/20/2009

Cover Image:
Springtime at Vassar, 1940
Lucille Corcos. American, 1909–1973
Tempera on board
Gift of Steven and Susan Hirsch, Class of 1971
The Frances Lehman Loeb Art Center, Vassar College,
Poughkeepsie, New York
2003.43.1

To the tireless
editors of the *Miscellany*,
past, present and future

and to Vassar's
History Department,
for teaching me
to go to the source.

Contents

Foreword

Those of us with boxes of snapshots laying about the house know that the pictures that matter most are the ones that capture people—and that those are also the ones most likely to be saved when it comes time to sort through the boxes that are handed down from previous generations in the family. What's the point of holding on to a picture of Mount Rushmore unless grandma and grandpa are tastefully grouped with George, Abe, Tom and Teddy?

So too it is with old letters. The ones to treasure are the ones that give us a sense of people's lives, not just a factual record of how and where they lived. Is there a better insight into history than to read the first-person perspective of a participant, be it Abigail Adams or your Aunt Alice?

For any college, student newspapers are those personal pictures and letters from an eyewitness. As a category of historical record there is no substitute—produced contemporaneously with the history it reports, written by participants with a consistently fresh perspective, and designed to provide insight as well as information. Other published materials produced by and about a college—catalogues, yearbooks and promotional material—have their roles as well, but their content is much more processed and filtered. Digging in college archives for internal reports and committee minutes can give a somewhat less managed perspective, but one seldom finds the sense of time, place and spirit that one finds in a college newspaper.

Even as a record of events, the college newspaper is often the best source for something like finding out who spoke on campus and what the topic was. But when I pick up an issue of a college newspaper—old or new—I am particularly drawn to the opinion pieces and the letters. It is there that the issues of the campus come alive and the feelings of the community regarding the major topics of the day are revealed.

To absorb fully the insight that the *Miscellany News,* or any college newspaper, gives to the historical record, I suppose there is no substitute for reading the paper itself. This admonition to "go to the source" attributed to Vassar history professor Lucy Maynard Salmon rings in every Vassar student's ear. But short of that, a book about the paper, say one written by a Vassar history major and *Miscellany News* editor, is surely the next best thing.

Catharine B. Hill
President, Vassar College

Acknowledgements

*C*overing the Campus is the product of tremendous collaboration. Over 100 former *Miscellany News* editors and writers were interviewed, ranging from the Class of 1936 to the Class of 2007. These alumnae/i were so generous with their time, spending hours on the phone to relive their experiences in the *Miscellany* newsroom—"a room filled with constant chaos, unimaginable stress and god-awful aggravation, but just the most wonderful memories," as one former Editor in Chief described it.

Tracking down these scores of editors and writers would have been impossible without the assistance of the Alumnae and Alumni of Vassar College (AAVC), which certainly lives up to its mission of facilitating communication among the College's tremendous body of graduates. I especially appreciate the assistance of Willa McCarthy and Nancy Wanzer, whose careful records on the College's 36,000 living graduates proved invaluable. Samantha Trautman Soper '91 and Tom Hopkins have also been instrumental in allowing me to communicate with alumnae/i about the *Miscellany News*'s recent endeavors.

Vassar has a number of individuals dedicated to preserving and perpetuating the College's history. College Historian Elizabeth Daniels '41, of course, is the ultimate treasure trove of information for anyone researching Vassar. Her many publications on the school's complex past are unparalleled, and have given me a broad context for appreciating the *Miscellany News*. I thank Special Collections Librarian Dean Rogers for his willingness to share original source material and guide me through the vast archives. I have also been inspired by the steadfast interest of

Ronald Patkus, Associate Director of the Vassar College Libraries for Special Collections, in archiving and preserving local heritage. Ron is thoroughly committed to the exhilarating—albeit massive—project of digitizing the *Miscellany*'s archives. His knowledge of digital databases and research standards will prove invaluable as we translate a century of newspapers into their new online home.

Vassar President Catharine Bond Hill showed tremendous enthusiasm to support my work on this project. That the College president cleared her frenzied schedule to write alongside me is living proof of the close and collaborative relationship between students and faculty members—a quintessential hallmark of the Vassar education.

The editors of the *Miscellany News* inspire me each day with their dedication, cleverness and incisive reporting. Our Editorial Board is comprised of a uniquely talented pool of student journalists. The strong personalities and well-informed opinions of our editors ensure the veracity and voice of our publication. In particular, I want to thank our Design and Production Editor Eric Estes '11, the most gifted graphic designer one could ever hope to work with. His artistic vision and technical skills are unmatched. Online Editor Molly Turpin '12 has risen to the challenge of directing our recently redesigned Web site. With flair and vigor, she has ensured that that the *Miscellany* continues to prosper in the age of 24-hour, fast-paced, multimedia journalism. And of course, the paper's recent progress would have been unimaginable without my Senior Editors, Alexandra Matthews '11 and Emma Mitchell '09. Their constantly watchful eyes, critical minds and outstanding management skills keep the *Miscellany* running like clockwork, even under the unbelievable pressures of the production cycle.

On a personal note, I am so very grateful for my friends, who put up with my endless chatter about "Farkas's ridiculous newspaper," as they have rightfully taken to calling it. Because of this project, I have skipped many dinners, many conversations and many of our usual adventures. Nevertheless, they have been understanding and indulgent despite my time constraints. Emma has seen me through this venture from the beginning, encouraging me every step of the way. I could not have done this without her, nor would I have wanted to. She has been ever supportive of my archival digging—and ever skillful at luring me away from it.

Finally, I must also thank my family for their strong support. My father's myriad of wisdoms has taught me judgment and determination. My mother's loving encouragement and analytical eyes have pushed me never to settle for anything but my best—and even then, to keep trying harder. My parents have been very understanding this past year; I have spent too many long days in the Poughkeepsie archives, and too few at home with them. In so many ways, they have made my work on this project possible.

Introduction

"Here is the living disproof of the old adage that nothing is as dead as yesterday's newspaper. This is what really happened, reported by a free press to a free people. It is the raw material of history; it is the story of our own times."
—*Henry Steele Commager*

The Alumnae House Library is a cramped rectangular room, found at the end of a snaking hallway. The dimly lit collection would more accurately be described as a reading room than a library, complete with Victorian furniture, thick air and creaky wooden floors. Books are stacked every which way on shelves and cabinets. None of the items—which range from old yearbooks and brochures to novels by Vassar graduates—are catalogued, nor are they arranged chronologically or alphabetically. This made my search all the more difficult.

I sat there on the hardwood floor for hours, pouring over these yearbooks, admissions materials, and stacks of novels. It was almost seven o'clock and I was just about to give up my quest in favor of some dinner. As I turned to collect my papers, despondent that my search had been fruitless, something caught my eye. From across the room I made out a small wooden hatch below the bookcase on the back wall. A mahogany table blocked it. I hurried to the other side of the room, and once I shifted the heavy piece of furniture, the hatch fell open. There was no light, so I reached my hand into the pitch-black compartment and blindly felt around. After a few seconds of groping, I pulled out the first item I touched. It was a small book, no more than six inches tall and four inches wide. The front and back were fashioned out of reddish leather, and the interior pages were yellowed and torn. The binding was falling apart and the pages were coming loose from the spine. Dust flew off of its jacket and onto my lap as I opened up the to the title page: *Vassar Stories, 1907*. Bingo.

Just above the title was a penciled name, written in cursive—Louisa Brooke. I opened to the center of the book. As my eyes glanced across the pages, I was awestruck at the story in front of me—the one that I had read about in a 1908 book review in Vassar's student paper. And after a long search, I now held it in my hands. "The Molders of Public Opinion," read the title of the chapter. The story it told was a familiar one.

"We've got to put the *Miscellany* to bed, you know," nagged one Vassar student to another.[1] "Hang the *Miscellany*!" responded the other girl with a gloomy rage. "I'm tired as a little dog. I want to go to bed. Let's send it off to-morrow!" The first girl, the Editor in Chief, would have none of it. "No sir! We've never been late to the printer yet. We're not going to break our record now. We've got to take an all-nighter," she insisted.

The conversation gave me a sharp twinge of déjà vu. It was a conversation I have lived through myself during my time on the Editorial Board of the *Miscellany News*. Each Tuesday night is production night, the occasion when editors gather to put together the final draft of the weekly paper. It begins at about 5 p.m. and often extends to 4 or 5 a.m. the next morning. Inevitably, someone wants to go home. Someone whines about a biology exam the next day. Another person complains of being exhausted from a baseball game. A third protests that he has a job interview first thing in the morning. But no one ever leaves. A combination of adrenaline, anticipation and caffeine—along with an abiding dedication to the paper—keeps all editors in their seats until the last round of copyediting is complete. This is as true today as it was for these two editors at the turn of the 20th century.

As I examined the tiny book, I had the distinct feeling that I was the first person to read it, or even look at it, since Ms. Brooke herself read from its pages more than a century ago. This sense of discovery, of being the first set of eyes in a very long time, has followed me through more than 200,000 pages of newsprint. I feel humbled by the history of Vassar

College, which I have learned about through its campus newspaper. The *Miscellany News* speaks volumes about life at the College, and about the lives and beliefs of American students in the 19th, 20th and 21st centuries.

Newspapers are key historical sources for two reasons. First, they recount the events of a particular region, state or institution. They can tell us the who's, what's, when's and where's of history. But beyond these factual bare bones, they also give us a glimpse into the values and ideals of their writ-

At Vassar nearly everyone reads the Miscellany News . . .

ers and editors. Sometimes these ideals are easy to interpret, such as an editorial running in Fall 1942 complaining that students were too ignorant of World War II.[2] Other times, they require more subtle examination. Which stories were placed on page one? What national and international issues were relevant enough to students to slip into the *Miscellany*? What was going on at Vassar or in the world that did *not* make it into the newspaper?

The *Miscellany News* serves both functions—as a recorder of historical facts and a barometer of values—for Vassar. The paper literally spans the College's history. Vassar was founded in 1861, but with the disruption of the Civil War, instruction did not begin until Fall 1865; the predecessor to the *Miscellany* debuted in Spring 1866, and included pieces written by students since their arrival on campus the previous September. With few interruptions, students have continuously written and read some form of the paper ever since. This makes the *Miscellany* one of the oldest college publications in the United States and, by my count, the second oldest of its kind in the State of New York.[3]

The paper is significant for more than its impressive longevity. Equally important, the original *Vassar Miscellany* was the first student publication of its kind to be produced independently by women. This milestone is as symbolic as it is practical. Vassar's founding as America's first endowed college for women shocked many across the country. How much would these girls be taught? Some worried that this "disturbing venture of educating women" to the same level as their brothers at Harvard and Yale could forever shred the fabric of American society.[4] A number of smaller female seminaries had sprouted up earlier in the century—notably Emma Willard's seminary in Troy, New York (1821) and Mount Holyoke (1837), which did not become a degree-granting college until 1888. But the curricula of these early seminaries were often limited to "female arts" such as conversational French, piano and embroidery.[5] Mathematics, chemistry and logic were usually ignored. Vassar was the first to deliver women a full liberal arts education at the college level.

The classroom experience was only one source of national anxiety. What would the Vassar women do outside of academics? Would they have the same freedoms as the Amherst boys, for example, who were known for their "late night wanderings"?[6] Extracurricular activities indeed drew as much attention from the growing national media as intellectual activities. In a column entitled "What the Girls are Doing," the *New York Times* regularly reported on daily life at 19th-century Vassar.[7] In addition to noting the newly elected student government officers each year, the column announced plays, recitals and other extracurricular endeavors.[8] The *Times* also gave short biographies of the incoming *Miscellany* editors, as if to keep a watchful eye on Vassar's student press. The tradition of announcing the paper's editors continued on and off between 1867 and the mid-1940s.

Clearly, independent student publications were a source of concern in the College's early days. Could these female students publish whatever they chose? Could they really manage the editorial and business sides of a publication? Such questions must have plagued the *Miscellany*'s first editors. Although there were certainly periodicals written by women in the United States—*Ladies Magazine* (founded 1827) and *Godey's Lady's Book* (founded 1830) were the most popular—there was not a strong tradition of *student* publishing among American women.

This tradition was already well entrenched within several prominent male colleges. The *Gazette* appeared at Dartmouth in 1800, and a host of other student publications were printed at institutions such as Harvard and Yale. It was the monthly *Yale Literary Magazine*, founded in 1836, which set the standard for student writing. Though it began as a collection of essays on education and philosophy, a section approximating news quickly increased in popularity. This section focused on "the doings at Yale, written in a terse and graphical style."[9] Moreover, election to the "Lit. Board" constituted one of the greatest undergraduate honors. The five or six student editors of the magazine were among the smartest and most respected in their class. Later in the century, the years surrounding Vassar's founding saw the birth of many other all-male publications across the country. The *Maroon-News* of Colgate University, founded as *Madisonesis* in 1868, is the oldest college weekly in the United States.[10] The *Bowdoin Orient* was established in 1871 as the joint newspaper and literary magazine of Bowdoin College.[11]

Starting an independent student publication by young women was a risky business—more risky than we can understand today. In the same way that reporting and editing gave these male students a sense of authority and importance, so too would their early publication give Vassar women a sense of significance. Reporters from the *Miscellany* have sat down with some of the nation's most important political, social and intellectual figures, usually when these figures came to speak at Vassar. Students writing for the *Vassar Miscellany*, the 19th-century literary magazine that preceded today's conventional newspaper, were influenced by encounters and conversations with Ralph Waldo Emerson, Mark Twain and Walt Whitman. These men all lectured at the College and spoke with numerous students who went on to contribute poetry and prose

to the *Miscellany*.[12] Since the transition to a more traditional weekly newspaper in 1914, *Miscellany* writers have interviewed Woodrow Wilson, Franklin D. Roosevelt, Eleanor Roosevelt, Katherine Ann Porter, Max Lerner, T.S. Elliot, W.H. Auden, W.E.B. Du Bois, Frank Sinatra, Meryl Streep '71, Tom Hanks and David McCullough, just to list a handful of recognizable names. Additionally, the paper has interviewed every sitting president of Vassar College, with the exception of Milo P. Jewett who resigned from the post in 1864 before students arrived on campus.

The immense responsibility of conceptualizing and creating a newspaper, along with the chance to interview so many movers and shakers and shape campus opinion, inspired the female students in 1866 as strongly as the coeducational students of today. As the *Miscellany* approaches its 100th anniversary of weekly publication and its 150th anniversary of publication altogether, the moment is ripe to step out of the newsroom and into the archives room. As historian Henry Steele Commager reminds us, newspapers are the "raw material of history" in modern society; they tell the "story of our own times."

But telling the story of a newspaper's times is an unusual genre. After all, newspapers are histories unto themselves. No broad description of the *Miscellany News*, or any newspaper for that matter, can do justice to the thousands of individual stories that they recount. Often, my words do little more than describe the incisive commentary of generations of writers and editors. At other times, though, I hope to provide some useful analysis and historical background to illuminate their coverage. This background is sometimes national—for example, the change over time of college newspapers across the country—and at other times very local to Vassar and its history.

Three disclaimers: First, it is important to understand what this project is *not*: it is not a comprehensive history of Vassar College or of its students. Though the *Miscellany* certainly tells both stories, fascinating stories at that, my subject is the development of the paper itself as a student medium. When I go into depth on a particular area of coverage (the Great Depression, for example) I do so only to illustrate the *Miscellany*'s response to such an event. My goal is certainly not to encapsulate 150 years of news between two covers; rather, it is to describe the process by which that news was written, produced and understood by the College community.

Second, I have relied on the accounts of over 100 former *Miscellany* editors and writers. While I do not always quote them directly, each decade's staff has informed my understanding of the paper's character and added a deeply human dimension to the archives. Generations of editors have put tremendous time and energy into the paper; to describe each of their contributions would take volumes. Rather than summarizing the work of each Editorial Board, I instead try to identify the broader eras of development.

Finally, it is unusual that the author of a work of history is concurrently a participant in that history. In addition to researching the history of the *Miscellany News*, I am also its current Editor in Chief. While my voice and stance remain as neutral as possible throughout the first four chapters, which trace the paper's history from 1866 through 2004, I use the first person in subsequent chapters to give a first-hand account of the contemporary paper as I have experienced it. I also describe projects planned for the coming years and the particular problems and place of the paper at this moment in Vassar's history. Like many editors, I have poured endless time into the paper; consequently, I have strong opinions about the goals of the *Miscellany* and the directions that it should take. To correct for these biases, I include a chapter discussing my own personal background and experiences on the *Miscellany* and at Vassar. Although it is admittedly problematic to place the present in a historical context, it would be equally impractical to cut this history short, rather than trace the paper's recent developments and exciting plans for the future.

A Note on Names: At various points, the newspaper has had seven different titles, all variations of "the *Vassar Miscellany News*." When trying to understand the paper's history, these names quickly become a source of confusion.

To simplify this narrative, I use "the *Miscellany News*" (or "the *Miscellany*" for short) as general terms referring to the student paper of Vassar College, though I use the correct chronological name when referring to a specific moment in the paper's history. To refer to the *Vassar Miscellany Monthly*, I will sometimes use its common nickname, "the *Monthly*." Similarly, I will often shorten "the *Vassar Miscellany News Supplement*" or "the *Vassar Miscellany Weekly*" to "the *Weekly*." Throughout the paper's history, many Vassar students have simply called the paper "the *Misc*," which briefly became the publication's official title in the early 1970s and again in 2001.

The name of Vassar's student government—which has maintained a strong relationship with the student paper—has also shifted over time.[13] The Student Association began in 1868, but in 1947 renamed itself the College Government Association. In the 1970s, it shifted to the Student Government Association. Finally, in 1982, it adopted its current title of the Vassar Student Association, or VSA.

A Note on Notes: In order to make this project as navigable as possible for researchers, all sources are carefully cited. The final bibliography records every book, article and encyclopedia entry consulted during my research. Chapter notes provide details on specific pieces of information, as well as direct references to the paper's archives. Because much of this history is based on personal interviews, I will often discuss the person I interviewed to introduce the quotation, rather than citing interviews individually and repeatedly.

A Note on Dates: Vassar's student newspaper has a history that is as complex as it is nonlinear. Unlike many other newspapers that can trace their first issue to a single publication date, Vassar's paper has developed in several iterations. Looking through the archives of the *Miscellany News*, dates become a quick source of confusion. Beginning in 1954, the paper has printed "Since 1866" on its first page. Simultaneously, it printed the volume number as LIV (54), indicating that the paper began in 1915. The practice of printing the seemingly inconsistent founding date and volume number on the front page continued until 2008. To further complicate matters, the Bylaws—the 20-page document outlining the paper's operating procedures—opens by saying that "the *Miscellany News* is the College's oldest publication, beginning in 1914." However, the full title "the *Miscellany News*" did not even come into use until 1973.

So which is it? 1866? 1914? 1915? 1973? When did the *Miscellany News* begin? In some ways, all of these dates are correct. But all of them are also misleading, making the generations of confusion understandable. Each chapter will explain the different names as they develop. For convenience, the following page includes a reference chart of the most significant dates and name changes in the publication's history.

1866 • The *Vassariana* publishes first and only issue in June, becoming Vassar's first student-run publication.

1867 • The *Transcript* replaces the *Vassariana* as the College's annual year-in-review publication.

1871 • For the first time in the College's history, no June publication appears following bitter disputes with College administration.

1872 • The *Vassar Miscellany* debuts in April as a quarterly.

1876 • Editors gain the right to publish monthly instead of quarterly, further increasing the paper's frequency. The *Vassar Miscellany Monthly* is born.

1914 • First issue of the weekly *Vassar Miscellany News Supplement* appears in February.

1916 • Paper becomes bi-weekly, coming out on Wednesdays and Saturdays.

1917 • Editors shorten title to the *Vassar Miscellany News*.

1924 • Following several years of lackluster student interest, the *Miscellany Monthly* finally folds, leaving behind the weekly newspaper

1942 • Under the pressure of the three-year plan surrounding World War II, the paper returns to weekly publication.

1970 • In the hopes of sparking student interest following the social strains of coeducation, paper changes title to the *Misc*.

1971 • Title changes once again to the *Miscellany News*, which it has remained ever since.

1994 • The *Miscellany*'s first Web site launches at misc.vassar.edu.

1995 • Printing process becomes entirely digital.

2008 • Web site completely overhauled with new design and features.

Covering the Campus

1 Grace Margaret Gallaher, *Vassar Stories*, (Boston: E.H. Bacon, 1907), p. 38.

2 "Students Lacking Engagement," *The Vassar Miscellany News*, October 13, 1942.

3 Based on founding dates of the college and university student publications in New York. The *Miscellany* is one of the state's oldest publications, but *not* the longest running weekly, since weekly publication did not begin until February 1914. The argument could be made that the *Miscellany* cannot even be considered a newspaper at all between 1866 and 1914, since its primary focus was literature. However, because the publication always printed snippets of campus news (increasingly so during the 1880s and 1890s), it is still comparable to contemporary 'real' college newspapers. Also, the paper has been "continuously published" since 1866 only in the sense that it continues to exist to this day. There have been three brief occasions when the paper skipped issues—once in 1870, again in 1970, and then most recently in 2001. The causes of these gaps were faculty pressure in 1870, and then a combination of financial troubles and student disinterest in the two later cases.

4 Maryann Bruno and Elizabeth Daniels, *Vassar College*, (London: Arcadia, 2001), p. 99.

5 "Troy Female Seminary," 2008. *Encyclopedia Britannica Online*. August 31 2008, http://www.britannica.com/EBchecked/topic/606900/Troy-Female-Seminary.

6 Theodore Baird, *English At Amherst: A History* (Amherst: Amherst College Press, 2005), p. 25.

7 "What the Girls Are Doing," *The New York Times*, October 22, 1894.

8 "Vassar College Activities," *The New York Times*, October 30, 1892.

9 Charles Franklin Thwing, "College Journalism," *Scribners Monthly: An Illustrated Magazine for the People* (Scribner and Son: October 1878): p. 808.

10 *The Colgate Maroon-News*. "General Information, Policies and Procedures." 2008. http://www.maroon-news.com/home/generalinformation/ (accessed July 20, 2008).

11 *The Bowdoin Orient*. "About the Orient." 2008. http://orient.bowdoin.edu/orient/about.php (accessed July 20, 2008).

12 This conclusion can be drawn by closely examining student essays in the *Miscellany* that describe these writers' visits. The writers do not merely quote the public lectures, but describe extended, seemingly private conversations—conversations that we might today label as interviews.

13 Vassar College, *Guide to the Vassar Student Association Records, 1868-2004*. 2006. http://specialcollections.vassar.edu/findingaids/vc_student_assoc.html (accessed June 1, 2008).

A Brief History of
Early Vassar College

Before plunging into the origins of the *Miscellany News*, a short outline of Vassar College's early history will prove useful. Like any good college story, the story of Vassar begins with ale.

Matthew Vassar was born in Norfolk, England in 1792. Transplanted to America at the age of five, his family began a life in the mid-Hudson Valley. Matthew was a sickly boy, constantly battling typhus and other illnesses. His formal education was meager; he would later recall in his autobiography that his father James had always prioritized "learned experience" and business over "academic instruction."[14] In this spirit, Matthew began to work in his father's small brewery. Matthew was always careful with money; at the age of 14, he ran away from home to the nearby town of Newburgh. When he returned four years later, he had saved some $150—a sizeable amount for an 18th-century teenager. After his escape from family life, he returned more mature and ready to take a position of leadership in his father's business.

Unfortunately, a severe fire in 1811 crippled the brewery and took the life of Matthew's oldest brother. His father was bereft, seeing his life's work destroyed in a cloud of smoke. Matthew, in an effort to restore his family, took control of the Vassar enterprise. Through a series of partnerships with wealthy investors, he raised enough money to rebuild the brewery in the Town of Poughkeepsie. For two decades, M. Vassar & Co. thrived. By 1836, he shed his unnamed financial partners and prepared for further expansion, commissioning a newer building on the banks of the Hudson River. This new brewery was the largest in the United States at the time, producing some 50,000 barrels of beer annually.

After years of success, Matthew became increasingly active in the Poughkeepsie community. He became a village trustee in 1819, a position roughly equivalent to a city council member.[15] He volunteered at various governmental and charitable organizations, and even played a role in establishing the Poughkeepsie Savings Bank.

By the 1850s, the middle-aged brewer had accumulated a substantial fortune. After a trip to Europe where he saw Sir Thomas Guy's endowed hospital, he began to think of his own historical legacy. Always self-reflective, Matthew wanted to ensure that he would be remembered for generations after his death. He went after immortality in several ways, initially through art and charity. First, he commissioned a Roman sculptor to create a statue in his likeness. Realizing the bust was too small a gesture, he purchased Springside, a 50-acre garden estate that he hoped to open to the public. But even then, he sought to fashion a more lasting, institutional legacy like Guy's. "It is the plague of my life," he said of his quest to be remembered, "What shall I do?"[16] In many ways, Matthew was a man looking to burn his place into the history books; he was a man in search of a cause.

It was Lydia Booth, Matthew's step-niece, who first introduced the idea of founding a school for women. Booth taught at a female seminary, and saw first-hand the urgent need to expand women's education in the United States. Milo P. Jewett, a clergyman and educator who had experience in girls' secondary schools, echoed Booth's idea.[17] "If you establish a real college for girls and endow it," he wrote to Matthew, "you will build a monument for yourself more lasting than the pyramids."[18] That was all that needed to be said to convince the brewer that the cause was worthy of his legacy. With this guidance, Vassar began organizing the College, chartering it officially on January 18, 1861 with the "object and purpose... [promoting] the education of young women in literature, science, and arts."[19] He also gave to the College a sizeable endowment. Famously, on February 26, 1861, he bequeathed a small tin box to his assembled Board of Trustees containing $408,000—half of his savings—along with a deed for 200 acres of land.[20]

Walter Scott Shinn's 1842 photograph of Matthew Vassar was one of several attempts by the brewer to immortalize himself. *Archives and Special Collections Library, Vassar College.*

And those acres would soon be filled with the voices of nearly 400 students who enrolled for the 1865-1866 academic year. In the early years, some of the students were as young as 15. Requiring applicants to pass a challenging entrance exam, Vassar College was an academically demanding institution from its founding. Many of the girls still required more secondary-level education, so the College maintained a "Preparatory Department" for more than a decade. This extra coursework allowed the students to transition into a more strenuous college-level curriculum. The curriculum was modeled closely on all-male colleges. As Matthew had insisted, two of the eight original professors were female, giving the students living examples of sophisticated intellectual women. "I wish to give one sex all the advantages too long monopolized by the other," he said at a June 1864 meeting with the Board of Trustees.[21] "We are… defeated if we fail to express by our acts [of hiring female professors] our practical belief in her pre-eminent powers as an instructor of her own sex." Eschewing gender stereotypes, the College proudly taught the natural sciences— astronomy, chemistry, physics, botany, zoology and mathematics were all present in the early curriculum. Maria Mitchell, famed astronomer, was the director of the school's observatory, the second largest in the United States at the time.[22] The student body rose to the challenge; in the first year of instruction, 40 percent elected at least one science course, while 21 percent selected a course in classics—both subjects that were limited almost entirely to men.

Key to this initial success was John H. Raymond, who served as president after Milo Jewett resigned in 1864, before the arrival of the students. During his 14 years at Vassar, he fashioned the College's administrative structure and shaped the first curriculum. Combating popular Victorian opinion, Raymond was "a firm believer in including scientific principles, mathematics, and modern languages into a young woman's education."[23] Yet Raymond also believed in domestic preparation for women, offering courses in "interior decoration, flower arrangement, and telegraphy." Nevertheless, under Raymond's leadership, Vassar became known around the country as a daring example of women's higher education in action. When he died in the summer of 1878, John L. Caldwell was asked to take the helm as Vassar's third president. Like the two men before him, Caldwell was a Baptist minister who believed firmly in women's intellectual capabilities. But unlike his predecessors, he was unable to navigate the College's politics to accomplish much. After struggling with student and alumnae criticism and a poor relationship with the Board of Trustees, he resigned in 1885.

The next year, James Monroe Taylor was appointed. Under Taylor's long and steady leadership (1886-1914), the College underwent physical expansion and ideological renewal. He began by focusing the College's mission by abolishing the preparatory school in 1890. At that point, Vassar took the form of the four-year liberal arts college that exists today. Over the course of his 28-year tenure, the student body tripled in size to more than 1,000 and the campus grew to match the increase. "Endow the college" was Taylor's motto as president. He raised over one million dollars and ventured on constant public speaking tours to "solidify Vassar's reputation."[24] With the additional flow of money, Taylor constructed many significant buildings including Strong House (1893), Rockefeller Hall (1887), the Chapel (1904), the Thompson Memorial Library (1905), and the Student's Building (1913). The curriculum expanded as well. Taylor increased the number of faculty in the social sciences, allowing dramatic growth in history, economics, political science and sociology courses.

Vassar's first four presidents all had something in common: though fierce advocates for women's education, they maintained fairly conservative social values. Even Taylor, often heralded as Vassar's "first modern president," was uncomfortable with the burgeoning progressivism among the students that he saw at the tail end of his tenure.[25] According to Henry Noble MacCracken, Taylor's successor, Taylor hoped that Vassar graduates would "be cultured but human, not leaders but good wives and mothers, truly liberal in things intellectual but conservative in matters social." MacCracken continued, "Throughout Taylor's term Vassar was a college for women developed by men."

Perhaps there is no better description of Vassar during its first 50 years—a college for women developed by men, a school that both encouraged and constricted social and intellectual independence. Maybe it was the prevailing social norms, or the fact that the 19th century students were younger and less educated in secondary schools than their 20th century counterparts. Whatever the reason, the men at the helm of the College were almost solely responsible for the school's policies, mission and identity.

Matthew Vassar was chief among these architects. Far beyond simply financing the venture, Matthew had a strong hand—the strongest hand—in establishing the spirit and character of his school.[26] Even if he began as a wealthy man in search of a place in history, he fell deeply in love with the school that he created. "My dearest mother," wrote Martha Warners, Class of 1868, "I wish you could see old Mr. Vassar. His face is a perfect sunbeam, he seems entirely happy and contented to walk over the buildings and nod at all the girls. Every pleasant day his carriage is here." Indeed, Matthew paid much attention to his College in its first years, creating a unique identity and "strong sense of place," as Vassar's ninth president Frances Fergusson would later say.[27] For example, he believed that art should be central to the liberal arts, declaring that it should stand "boldly forth as an educational force." Matthew endowed the College with his massive collection of American and European artwork to found the Vassar College Art Gallery, a teaching museum. This made Vassar the first college in the country to include a museum as part of its original plan. The College's museum, which has grown significantly, remains central to the 21st-century curriculum. In very clear ways, Matthew's visions set the tone for the school's future. In addition to art, he pushed the faculty to "engage [their] students fully not only in the study of great literature [but] in learning to write it themselves." This command almost certainly resulted in the first student publications, which featured students' poetry and short stories. The Founder thus played a key role in shaping the Vassar experience, both inside and outside of the classroom.

And this brings us to an uncertain legend—a legend once well known on the *Miscellany* staff, that lives now only in the memories of editors from the 1930s. The story, as best it can be pieced together from these alumnae/i, begins on a chilly evening in November 1865. Four students sat in the drafty dining hall in Main Building. A tattered American flag flew over their heads as they sipped hot soup from the bowls in front of them. Out of the corner of their eye, a dark figure wearing silky suit, black snow boots and a top hat approached. The figure, barely more than five feet tall, was Mathew Vassar. The four girls quickly rose from their chairs out of respect and inquired about his evening.

"How are you faring in this cold weather, sir?" one of the students asked.[28]

"Not well," replied Matthew. "All day, I have been looking at the students magazines of Harvard and Yale." He pulled several copies out of his sack. "Just look," he said as he sat down at their table. The girls nervously returned to their seats beside him. "Each year," Matthew continued, "the affairs of their schools are immortalized in these publications. They contain important news, wonderful stories and all sorts of memories. We will have no comparable publications to document out first year."

"And they are written by the students themselves?" asked one of the girls.

"Yes," replied Matthew. "Their students record the events of their schools, allowing them to be widely known and later remembered. Our College should produce documents like these!"

"But the students couldn't do this," said one of the girls, who had been quiet up to this point. "Mr. Vassar, these publications are produced by men at male-colleges. They can write and publish all they like."

"And why can't our students do the same?" asked Vassar pointedly.

"Because we are merely girls," replied the girl sheepishly, as if remembering this hard truth all over again.

"Nonsense!" screamed Vassar, banging his hands on the creaky wooden table and spilling soup every which way. The American flag waved above his head as he roared. "You are not just girls, nor are you women. You are Vassar students. And Vassar students will not be weak, or timid, or acquiescent to the boys of Harvard and Yale. And we will not be outdone by any other school." He stood up indignantly and donned his top hat, then leaned down slowly on the table. "By the end of this year, you will produce a student magazine," he whispered. "A publication even stronger than those of these other schools, with its own unique character that will mark the events and development of our college. Do I make myself clear?"

The girls, not knowing whether to apologize or agree, simply nodded. The man walked out of the dining hall and back into the shadows. The girls were left at the table in silence. After a few moments of quiet reflection, they began to discuss the business of this new publication—its size, its scope and its contents. After hours of vigorous debate, the four students were overflowing with ideas. One suggested that they return to their rooms to commit their discussion to paper and begin work on the publication.

And off they went.

14 Elizabeth Hazelton Haight, ed, *The Autobiography and Letters of Matthew Vassar*, (New York: Oxford University Press, 1916), p. 3.

15 Carl Degler, "Vassar College," in *American Places: Encounters with History*, edited by William E. Leuchtenburg, (New York: Oxford University Press, 2002).

16 As quoted in "Vassar College Celebrates its Semi-Centennial," *The New York Times*, October 3, 1915.

17 *Ibid.*

18 Elizabeth Hazelton Haight, ed, *The Autobiography and Letters of Matthew Vassar*, (New York: Oxford University Press, 1916), p. 3.

19 "The Charter and Amendments, An Act to Incorporate Vassar Female College," Passed January 18, 1861 by the Senate and Assembly of New York, as quoted in the Governance of Vassar College.

20 Edward, Linner, Vassar: *The Remarkable Growth of a Man and His College*, Edited by Elizabeth Daniels, (Poughkeepsie, NY: Vassar College, 1984), p. 19

21 Karen Van Lengen and Lisa Reilly, *Vassar College:* The Campus Guide, (New York: Princeton Architectural Press, 2004), p. 5.

22 *Ibid.*

23 Lila Matsumoto, *John L. Raymond*, edited by Elizabeth Daniels, 2005. http://vcencyclopedia.vassar.edu/index.php/John_H._Raymond (accessed December 3, 2008).

24 Lila Matsumoto, *James Monroe Taylor*, edited by Elizabeth Daniels, 2005. http://vcencyclopedia.vassar.edu/index.php/John_H._Raymond (accessed December 3, 2008).

25 *Ibid.*

26 Indeed, Matthew Vassar held a strong influence over the school from its early days through the 20th century. Generations later, the Founder and the founding continued to influence the Vassar community's self-conception. When the College became coeducational in 1969, the *Miscellany News* described it as Vassar's "second founding," and fully "in keeping with Matthew's original vision for equality between the sexes," according to a December 3, 1969 staff editorial.

27 Karen Van Lengen and Lisa Reilly, *Vassar College*: The Campus Guide, (New York: Princeton Architectural Press, 2004), p. 19.

28 This conversation is fictionalized and pieced together from the memories of the *Miscellany* alumnae. These four students might correlate to the four original editors of the *Vassariana*, H.A.L. Mason, H.A. Johnson, H.A. Warner, and M.L. Dickinson.

Chapter One:
Poetry and Prose, 1866-1914

The legend of Matthew Vassar inspiring the first foray into student journalism is dubious at best, but the story does contain several grains of truth.[29] In speeches and personal communications, he persistently used Harvard and Yale as yardsticks for his own institution. Vassar was highly conscious of his image, and demanded that his school be seen as first-rate in the eyes of the world. He was known for obsessively collecting each week's press clippings and monitoring public opinion.[30] As we have already seen, the radical venture into women's education raised many eyebrows. Public opinion would shape the founding of the student newspaper just as it shaped the College itself.

In the Beginning: Foundations in Rough Stone

Vassar's first publication, the *Vassariana*, debuted on June 27, 1866 as a student-written retrospective of the College's first year of operation.[31] This issue was four pages in length, and was more of a yearbook than any sort of newspaper. The tone was purely retrospective: "The first year of Vassar College will long be remembered by those who have shared its pleasant scenes," read the sycophantic first editorial. This issue included no critical analysis of college life, no forum for dialogue, and no 'new' information for readers—all defining facets of a modern newspaper. Instead, the first page blandly listed the titles of administrators and faculty. On the final page, the publication records the members of each student organization, such as the Floral Society, the Organ Voluntary and the Light Croquet Club. Additionally, it catalogued the officers of the Philaletheis Society, which began as a literary club and served as a catchall organization for various extracurricular activities. A calendar of important lectures and concerts was printed to remind readers of all that had taken place since Vassar opened its doors in September. The *Vassariana* also showcased several short student essays and flowery reminiscences.

Although the paper included no bylines, it did have a small staff box listing the four students involved: H.A.L. Mason, H.A. Johnson, H.A. Warner, and M.L. Dickinson. Dickinson was also the first student president of Philaletheis, suggesting that the number of unique students heavily involved in extracurricular activities was limited during the first few years of instruction.

Despite their small numbers, the "editresses" seemed to be very aware of their own pioneering role in creating the College's first publication. "Now, we lay down the editorial pen," they wrote at the conclusion of their first editorial, "believing it will be taken up by those who will carry on the work we have begun; who, although the foundations are of a rough stone, will build above with polished marble, and who will maintain the *Vassariana* in the front ranks of the college papers in the land."[32]

Their early sense of legacy building is extraordinary. The newspaper, indeed the entire College, had only been operating for a single year. Yet these girls allude to crafting monuments in polished marble, as if they were constructing as lasting a legacy as the Parthenon. Their sense of competition with other college papers is also noteworthy. That final line suggests that these editors looked to some of the more entrenched collegiate periodicals as models, and aimed to match or even surpass them—an extraordinary idea, given that virtually all of those competing publications were assembled by men. Indeed, there seemed to be a great sense of heritage and pride growing on the young Editorial Board. "We are conscious that [the *Vassariana*] is surrounded by many difficulties," they noted. "But no well trodden path is prepared for its journey… We send forth to clear the way for more favored ones which may follow in years to come."

Sure enough, a "more favored" attempt arrived the following when the *Transcript* debuted.[33] Although the name was different function and design of the year-end publication was very similar— essentially a recap of the most important events of the past nine months of school. However, the *Transcript* showed some growth over the *Vassariana*, both in physical size and in the scope of the coverage. The 1867 issue was six pages, compared to the *Vassariana*'s four the previous year. By 1868, the *Transcript* had increased to eight pages. From a fairly mundane listing of calendar notices in the 1866 publication, the 1867 publication introduced more newsy tidbits in addition to poetry and personal

This 1866 wood engraving of Main Building by German artist A. Aarland hints at the College's relative insularity. Students both lived and learned in Main. Understanding the parochial nature of the College sheds light on the equally parochial coverage in the *Vassariana* and *Transcript*. The Frances Lehman Loeb Art Center.

stories. For example, it briefly mentioned a book by a professor and a newly established scholarship fund. Also included were longer academic essays; the 1870 issue sported lengthy ruminations on "Individual Sovereignty" and the value of "Women's Education."

The increased depth of items in the *Transcript*—renamed the *Vassar Transcript* in 1869—suggest not only a growth in the College publication, but in the College itself. The student body bloated from 353 in 1865 to about 475 just three years later; the number of campus events grew concurrently. The calendar on the back of the newspaper indicates a total growth of about 22 percent in the combined number of plays, recitals and lectures between the 1865-66 academic year and the 1868-69 year. An 1869 editor's note indicated a rise in circulation from 150 copies to 270 "to match growing student demand for our words."[34]

The popularity of the periodical led the staff and community

to take it more seriously; as Vassar's fourth President James Monroe
Taylor noticed, the staff of the *Vassariana* referred to themselves as
"editresses," whereas the staff of the *Transcript* referred to themselves as
"editors."[35] The shift in gender seems hardly accidental; students began
to view themselves as the editorial executives of their publication,
just like those in charge of publications at male institutions. Many of
their articles were written sharply, particularly those on the subject of
women's rights. In reviewing an 1869 speaker who considered marriage
mandatory for women, the editors had sharp words: "Had we not long
since made sufficient advancement in the intellectual life to decide
that man is not our author and disposer, we might have been more
consumed by… Dr. Holland's [talk]."[36]

But besides these occasional barbs, the publication's general tone
was "overly idyllic" according to editors looking back in the 1940s.[37]
"The staff editorials concerned themselves [mostly] with flowering praise
for our dear mother [Alma Mater]," these later writers complained.
They objected to the obsequious sentiments expressed by the *Transcript*
editors, like that students "are unworthy children of our dear Mother
school's knowledge."[38] The publication was far from being investigative
or critical of the College, as the Yale and Harvard papers tended to
be.[39] Indeed, the header of the *Transcript* showed a young girl being
dramatically directed toward Main Building by the goddess Athena
with the rising sun behind them. The design was essentially student-
produced publicity material for Vassar. Although the articles were
relevant to student life, the paper clearly lacked any sort of independent
editorial muscle. The publication was too lauding of the College and too
removed from day-to-day life to capture many students' imagination
for long. There seemed to be a growing ennui with the *Transcript*, as the
staff shrunk significantly between 1868 and 1869.

Fighting for editorial control was a central issue. While the
original *Vassariana* was heavily controlled by College administrators,
the *Transcript* was understood by many to be the official voice of the
Students' Association, the student government. As Mary Mallon '15
noted in her 50-year retrospective of student publishing at Vassar, the
Students' Association appointed *Transcript* editors, changed the paper's
title and advised on content.[40] In its early days, the student government
itself was fairly weak and heavily influenced by the faculty. As such,

the *Transcript* was likely shaped directly or indirectly by professors' judgments and sensibilities—and also shaped by administrators' control over budget and advertising revue.

Despite its impotent editorial voice and ambiguous student control, the annual publication had become an expected end-of-year tradition. At the suggestion of the editors, the Students' Association petitioned the faculty in 1869 for permission to publish the paper once every two months rather than only once each year. The faculty refused. In 1870, the Students' Association tried again, this time advocating for a quarterly paper. This too was quickly refused. It is not clear exactly why the faculty were so set against increasing frequency. Perhaps the additional cost would have eaten too much into the relatively modest student activities budget. More likely, though, the faculty was wary of giving these women additional independence, particularly with all of the media attention surrounding Vassar at the time. Despite the growing number of female journalists in major cities like New York and London, Victorian-era propriety remained a barrier for Vassar students.[41]

In any case, June 1871 saw no student publication to document the year—the only such year in Vassar's history. Fortunately, this absence seems to have caused much discontent. The next fall, the faculty quickly changed its collective mind and approved plans for a new quarterly publication during its first meeting of the year. Whether this was due to student pressure or simply an enlarged activities budget is not clear. But there was hope for the future of student publishing.

Volume I, Issue 1: The Birth of the *Miscellany*

Not only did its increased frequency make it more omnipresent, but the new publication's content was more dynamic. The uncertain scope of the *Transcript*—with its pithy news, assorted descriptions of old events and occasional poetry—would now be more clearly defined. Initially, though, there was disagreement on exactly what shape the new publication should take. According to Mallon, even the name of the quarterly was the source of much debate.[42] The *Vassar Voice*, the *Vassar Cycle* and the *Vassar Quarterly* were all advocated as potential titles. But in April 1872, a strange-sounding title, the *Vassar Miscellany*, emerged from the fray.[43] A miscellany, a collection of writing by different authors, was a common term for an anthology in the 19th century deriving from the Latin word *miscellanea*—a mix of written works. This new title fit the *Vassar Miscellany* well, since unlike the two preceding publications, it would serve mostly as a literary review that combined various genres of student writing. The faculty pushed for a focus on literature, rather than news, in order to ensure a gentler, more academic tone.

Sarah Riane Harper '09, who researched the *Miscellany News* for the *Vassar Encyclopedia*, drew a connection between this chiefly literary publication and the young College's reputation.[44] "In many ways," Harper concluded, "the caliber of the literary sections served as a bulletin on the status of Matthew Vassar's 'great experiment.'" Vassar students were fairly accustomed to national attention. Since 1861, Matthew Vassar himself had collected news items about his pioneering school and greatly enjoyed the notoriety that came with his revolutionary project. Indeed, the editors hoped that the *Vassar Miscellany* might "be a permanent literary influence in the College… and that Vassar should stand where it ought to stand in the field of college literature."[45] Predictably, the *Miscellany* received much attention in its first two decades of publication. According to Mallon, the *Yale Literary Magazine* and the *Cornell Era* were impressed by the *Miscellany*'s literary merit, and wrote about its success.[46] Editors also had a sense of competition with these all-male publications. "Let us work with [all] our might to place the *Miscellany* in the first rank of college magazines," they declared in an 1874 piece, rallying Vassar's most talented writers to join the staff.[47] The eloquent prose in the *Miscellany* thus served as concrete evidence of the intellectual abilities of Vassar women. Although the Founder died in 1868, he surely would have been proud of the positive attention that the *Miscellany* received.

Given the attention paid to the publication, the level of censorship exercised by the College administration on the *Miscellany* is uncertain. Censorship certainly existed to some degree; Vassar had a Press Committee comprised of faculty and employees to regulate student communications with outside newspapers. "Before any student can send out a line for any newspaper, her manuscript must be examined and edited by authorities," wrote a reporter seeking a comment in vain for the *Poughkeepsie News Press* on April 16, 1896.[48] But it is unclear how much the *Miscellany* itself was affected. On one hand, some evidence suggests that faculty members reviewed a draft before publication, but it is ambiguous whether students asked for advice, or whether such intervention was required. To be sure, members of the faculty wrote articles relating to school policies and their own research as early as 1873, and by the 1880s the faculty authored a regular column entitled "Faculty Notes."

Yet some of the items that crept into the *Miscellany* in its first two decades suggest incomplete or half-hearted censorship. Many editorials, poems and essays took subtle positions against the College administration. Thus, if there was a system of censorship in place, it seems that it was exercised only occasionally. Beyond its public relations role, the young *Miscellany* aspired to be a mouthpiece for student voice. In the publication's initial editorial, the editors complained that "We have had, heretofore, no means of expressing our opinions, and much that we have often considered unfairness in our instructors has been, probably, ignorance of our real wants."[49] They desired, in other words, a forum to make their voice as students heard. The annual format of the *Vassariana* and the *Transcript* were simply unworkable as tools for sustained campus dialogue. But this new quarterly forum was now frequent enough to maintain a conversation—and for students to make their "real wants" known.

Writing a New Chapter in Women's History

The idea of a group of young girls demanding a public forum to express "unfairness" would have been radical, even comical in the 1860s. The Victorian sensibilities that required women to be "soft, Bible-reading [and] prudish" in England were also manifested in the United States—especially for the predominately wealthy Protestant girls at Vassar.[50] Although American women were hardly expected to be as docile as they had been at the beginning of the century, social norms ensured that most did not complain about the status quo. Those who did were usually wealthy and well connected. Though the families of the elite Vassar women tended to have both qualities, the students themselves did not; parents expected "heightened docility from their daughters" as preparation for womanhood.[51] For their academic activities alone, female college students were often regarded with suspicion and unease.[52] Further questioning of authority to make their "real wants" known would have completely broken with Victorian gender roles that required "girls to dwell in quiet homes amongst a few friends, to exercise noiseless influence, and to be submissive and retiring."

It was groundbreaking not just that *Miscellany* women expressed themselves, but that they did so on paper. From the beginning, the *Miscellany*'s editors were very aware of their unique place in society. As the staff of 1873 believed, "A new quarterly, no matter how brilliant, if issued by the students of Harvard or any other university for men, would cause not the slightest ripple on the sea of criticism outside of the little bay of college literature."[53] But their own publication from "the first college for women" was far more significant. "That we have succeeded in winning so much honest and kindly criticism is a good omen," they assured themselves. "Time was when the very fact of a woman having wrought a work was sufficient to cause it to be ridiculed." The staff felt a profound sense of accomplishment, having entered into the field of publishing "untrammeled by prejudice."

One cannot underestimate the significance of a publication managed by women in the 1860s and 1870s. Many Vassar parents, even those who encouraged their daughters to receive an education, were puzzled at the idea that their girls could participate in activities such as publishing or student government. "If I were you, I would be very retiring and ladylike whenever there is any voting to be done, and avoid having anything to do with a party that savors women's rights," counseled Mrs. Mary Elinor Poppenheim in a February 1884 letter to her daughter Mary.[54] If Mrs. Poppenheim objected to something as seemingly benign as voting ballots in a student government election, she surely would have objected to her daughter penning a fiery editorial against the College administration.

The Poppenheims, a useful case study, were a wealthy South Carolina family that sent all four of their daughters to Vassar—the "Harvard for women." [55] They likely looked toward "Yankee country" because the South lacked the academic muscle of the North; also, Vassar was preeminent among women's colleges. Vassar was also appealing because, although their academics rivaled those of male institutions, the girls' social lives were severely curtailed. The students' manual during the years that Mary and her sister Louisa attended indicates a very strict schedule: morning bells rung at precisely 7:00 a.m. and lights-out came at exactly 10:00 p.m.[56] Classes ran all morning and after until dinner. Visitors were restricted to certain hours and were allowed to remain only in the dormitory parlor. There was little wiggle room in the women's daily lives.

This is not to say that joining extracurricular activities was impossible. To Mrs. Poppenheim's dismay, Mary and Louisa became heavily involved with student groups, including the literary society and the choir. The girls seemed to enjoy the modicum of self-governance afforded to students, and wrote home about the activities of the government and the process of class elections. Nonetheless, their mother repeatedly cautioned that ballot boxes are "too unfair and dishonest for a lady" to be involved with.[57] Her daughters clearly struggled to balance their traditional, Southern upbringing with their new intellectual and extracurricular freedoms. Only one month after her mother urged her to beware of women's rights supporters, Mary wrote a note to Louisa about a party where she and her friends told each other's fortunes. "I would be a second Susan B. Anthony coming to [Washington] to hand a petition for women's rights to the Press," she predicted.[58]

Though we cannot know for certain, Mary's frequent mention of the *Miscellany* in her letters to her sister and mother, along with this suggestive interest in women's freedom of the press, hints that she might have written for the literary magazine. More suggestive was an 1884 essay in the *Miscellany* entitled "Why Mr. Caldwell Must Listen." The piece discusses Vassar's relationship with preparatory schools, and sharply accuses College President Samuel Caldwell of not cultivating a larger, more academically elite student body. It was signed only "MBP"—initials that could stand for Mary Bennett Poppenheim. Although an alumna could have authored this essay for the *Miscellany*, the student records indicate that Mary was the only student enrolled at Vassar in that year with those initials. Thus, there is a good chance that she eschewed the advice of her demure mother and raised a serious question about administrative actions—actions that, incidentally, made Caldwell unpopular with the Board of Trustees and hastened his resignation in 1885.[59]

It was clearly tricky for the Poppenheim sisters to honor their conservative heritage while becoming independent in an environment that encouraged women to take control. Both Mary and Louisa left

Vassar more radical than their mother might have preferred; they became co-editors of the *Keystone*, one of South Carolina's most influential women's magazines in the late 19th century.[60] Their magazine encouraged women to think and to write, two fairly radical activities in the highly conservative city of Charleston. Even if the sisters did not write for the *Miscellany* (though one could reasonable infer that both did), they were evidently inspired by the idea that women could write and publish.

Developing Structure: Writers, Readership and Ridicule

The *Vassar Miscellany*, thriving in its quarterly format, became increasingly popular for both readers and writers. The Poppenheims were not the only students writing home about the *Miscellany*. According to College Historian Elizabeth Daniels '41, students began including information from the publication in their letters home as early as the mid-1870s.[61] They listed it alongside descriptions of the Philaletheis Society and student government. The opportunity for leadership that the paper afforded these young women must have been exciting enough to merit a mention in their letters, suggesting that the *Miscellany* was of immediate importance in the life of the College.

Within its first three quarterly issues, the publication quickly grew to accommodate an Editorial Board of ten juniors and seniors; writers from all different class years served too, though they were not listed by name. The *Miscellany* began to develop a regimented style and structure. By 1873, the publication was divided into a section for current students called the "College Department" and a section for graduates called the "Alumnae Department." Both sections held poetry, short stories and essays that were usually anonymous or signed with initials. An additional branch of the paper, "De Temporibus et Moribus" (literally "Of Time and Death"), soon sprouted up as a forum for discussion for all members of the College community. The section, commonly known as De Temp, was an especially widely read feature of the *Miscellany*. "As the professedly literally part of the magazine grew heavier and more solemn," Mallon wrote, "De Temp… becomes more readable and recognizable."[62]

In addition to De Temp, the *Miscellany* of the 1880s and 1890s included the "Editor's Table" section, where readers could find editorials, personals, exchange columns for other colleges and brief items on campus news. Though this section began as only a single page, it grew over the decades as it became more popular. Tucked away behind pages of essays and poetry, the Editor's Table occasionally doled out criticisms of College policies. Editors complained about such varied topics as the campus's unkempt gardens, the boring Sunday minister, and Vassar's need for more history courses. Thus, lacking only in size and timeliness, the Editor's Table and De Temp essentially served two of the central functions of the modern newspaper—the staff editorial and letters to the editor, respectively.

However, the news, opinion and staff editorial content discussed above made up only a fraction of the total publication. The *Vassar Miscellany* was comprised almost entirely of poetry and prose; issues in the 1880s extended to 40 or 50 pages. Especially prevalent were lengthy academic essays dealing with "titanic subjects," such as poverty, nature and war.[63] The editors seemed far more concerned with proving their strength as scholars than with "attempting a variety of subject and form." In his history of Vassar, James Monroe Taylor dismissed most of these long essays as being fairly poor insights into student life.[64] A far better look into students' minds, he felt, was found in the editorial content of the Editor's Table, as well as the more humorous pieces in De Temp. "The young women who talk so seriously about women's education, culture, and harmony might seem superwomen were it not for these lighter pages," quipped Taylor.[65] On the flip side, these "lighter pages" were scrutinized by the nervous faculty conscious of media attention, and the authors of personal anecdotes would sometimes be chastised. "The worst escapade on record," Taylor recalled, "is the famous visit of a few to visit a gypsy camp to have their fortunes told, an adventure which called forth one of Dr. Raymond's [the former College President's] most scathing chapel talks." After Raymond's lecture, the humorous pieces increasingly took the form of fiction rather than nonfiction, thus hiding many of the students' indiscretions from scrutiny—and from history. Taylor admits, though, that these women's worst indiscretion was usually "fearless verbal daring."

Unfortunately, fear of national criticism seemed to put the editors on a fairly formulaic path, at least for the first decade of publication. There was a constant sense that their writing could go too far, and cause the rapid demise of their publication. Although their earlier editorials indicated the desire for a medium of free communication, the editors of the 1870s and 1880s sacrificed their own freedom of speech, or at least part of it, so that future students could "build above with polished marble," and ensure the publication's preservation as the editor's of the *Vassariana* had suggested.[66]

Moving to Monthly: Continued Growth and Struggle

Despite its initial success and popularity, the *Miscellany* was in a constant struggle to retain writers. Many students wrote only once or twice and then disappeared, making it difficult to build a reliable staff. By their third issue, the editors found themselves lobbying students to "[carry] on the good work that has been committed to their hands. Whether this help be given in lengthening the subscription list or in filling the pages of the magazine, every student is in honor bound to give it; every student must give it if she would see the *Miscellany* where she wishes it to be."[67] Sure enough, the staff grew between 1874 and 1876.[68] To reflect its larger size, the *Miscellany* was given its first official office in Main Building in Fall 1876. The paper also added the position of Business Manager to its ranks, an addition that demonstrated its growing autonomy. Subscription and advertising revenue was now the sole responsibility of the students.

Just two years after the *Miscellany* debuted, the paper increased its frequency from quarterly (four issues per school year) to monthly (ten issues per school year). The Students' Association proposed this change in September of 1874 with intense urging from the editors. The editorial announcing this change in frequency referred to monthly publication as "one of the dreams of its Editors," suggesting that the higher frequency had been planned for some time.[69] This shift not only made the paper more visible on campus, but also increased revenues significantly. Less time and money went into each monthly issue, and the increase in issues merited an increase in subscription fees. Previously, the quarterly subscription fee had barely been enough to "defray current expenses," in Mallon's words.[70] With this change, the *Vassar Miscellany* became the *Vassar Miscellany Monthly*.

The paper's ten editors also hoped that the monthly format would allow for more campus news and opinions, while maintaining a focus on literature. "We really believe that news three months old is not very entertaining," they stated plainly in their first editorial as a monthly.[71] The burgeoning interest in timeliness is significant, since it was this seed of journalistic ethos that would eventually sprout into the modern newspaper. Financial success, greater publication frequency and a focus on timely news came together to increase the publication's autonomy and influence. One example of this rising autonomy came in 1881, when the Students' Association gave up the right to select *Miscellany* editors. According to Mallon, the Association realized that "the editing of a magazine is highly specialized work," and that hiring decisions should be left to those on the inside.[72] Though the paper was still considered the "organ" of the student government, the Editorial Board would now make appointments. Each year, graduating editors would consult with three students from the same class year as an applicant. After "determining the individual's character and work ethic," the most senior editors would make a report to the Board, and the Board would cast its vote. The staff was no longer just "the arm of the Students' Association," as in the past. They had both financial and bureaucratic autonomy.

With this independence came some structural changes to the Editorial Board. According to the staff information of the first monthly issue, one senior had sole charge of literature—the most prestigious position with the most content. Another two seniors controlled De Temporibus et Moribus (which became Points of View in 1891), and another one edited Home Matters. Two juniors were given the less prominent sections of College Notes and Exchange Notes, which were smaller calendar items and announcements. The seniors on staff worked together to craft the Editor's Table section, and worked together to write the monthly editorial. Points of View and the Editor's Table were usually found toward the back of the *Miscellany*. "The back," as it was known among students, blended editorials, letters to the editor, pithy news, and humorous stories. Between 1891 and 1914, "the back" became the most popular section of the paper, though it was only a tiny fraction of the literary-dominated *Miscellany*. Modern readers might wonder, then, why this popular section was so petite, representing only about one-fifth of each monthly issue. The goals of the *Miscellany*'s editors remained decidedly literary.[73]

Academic Essays in the *Miscellany*

No amount of popularity changed the ratio of "literature" to news. Literature, the term used by the contemporary editors, applied to a wide swath of articles and items. At various times, it included essays, poetry, personal anecdotes and short stories. Though timely news pieces multiplied following the 1874 transition to monthly publication, poetry and prose continued to dominate around 80 percent of each issue. It is useful to separate our examination into the two most common genres: academic essays and poetry.

Showcasing student essays was of paramount concern to the editors. The style of the academic prose in the *Miscellany* can be divided into two rough chronological periods. The first ranges from 1872 to 1892. Long, heavy, and often tedious essays characterize this period. Even skimming through them, it is frankly difficult to imagine how students would have enjoyed reading the *Miscellany* on a casual afternoon. Headlines included "The Effect of Astronomical Discovery on the Imagination," "Does a College Education Tend to Produce Atheism?" and "The Joys of Watching Bread Rise." Essays about Plato, the Roman Empire, and the beauty of Greek sculpture were also included. Though these subjects might have been engaging, the writing was pedantic.

In this respect, the *Miscellany* was not unlike its peer institutions. Charles Thwing, President of Western Reserve University in Cleveland and a historian of higher education, penned a brief 1878 article about the phenomenon of college journalism.[74] Though he praised student journalists, he favored shorter weekly papers, "written under the pressure of college work," because they demonstrated clarity and conciseness "worthy of professional journalists." Thwing disliked college papers published monthly or quarterly because they rarely exhibited such brevity. "The subjects of the leading articles in the magazines seldom possess immediate interest, and the style is often labored and oratorical," he wrote. "In topic and treatment, they are not dissimilar to the forensics and theses that a senior writes for his professor of rhetoric." It would be hard to devise a better description for many of the essays published in the *Miscellany Monthly*. Indeed, *Miscellany* essays tended to be longer than those found in peer publications; these items often spanned more than ten pages of solid, uninterrupted text. Students seemed to pride themselves not on finding their own unique voice, but

paper · voice   32   *writing → body*

on imitating scholarly jargon and quoting classical philosophers. For a modern reader, many of these essays read sluggishly. One struggles to hear the students' unique and youthful voices.

The same might have even been true for the 19th-century reader. Letters in De Temp suggest that this overly academic tone lowered student interest in the *Miscellany* during the 1880s. Staff levels declined slightly, and the paper came to be regarded as "aloof and detached from the rest of the College community."[75] As Mallon asserts, the *Miscellany* of the 1880s is "saved from being… prosaic only by De Temp." The "light sketches" and opinions in 'the back' seemed to many students "more profound and entertaining than [items] in 'the front.'"[76] This corroborates Taylor's similar views on these heavy essays. In short, the dry *Miscellany* began to bore students.

But then came a second period. The lull of the 1880s ended in 1892, when the editors suddenly pushed for major content changes. There seemed to be a conscious decision that the *Miscellany* should not be designed for faculty and alumnae consumption, nor for the publicity and glorification of Vassar. Rather, it should be for the entertainment of students. This shift made the tone of the entire publication more like De Temp—"serious and amusing, venturesome and conservative."[77] More personal essays were now included, particularly pieces unique to Vassar life. Once the writing centered on the students' own experiences, their prose became far more readable and relatable. The *Miscellany* slowly began to lose its "old heaviness" and recognized the virtues of the content previously relegated to De Temp and the Editor's Table. Thus, 1892, the year of its 20th birthday, saw "rejuvenation" as one editorial noted. Points of View became a longer opinions forum dedicated to "expressing thoughts on all undergraduate problems."[78] Coverage of campus news, previously housed in the popular but brief Editor's Table, was dramatically expanded into its own section. Editors split the news into four regular columns—Social Events, Educational Records, Personals and Faculty Notes. Another trendy section, Reviews, was established in 1893 and included assessments of books and plays, along with lectures and artwork.

Reviews became increasingly popular, especially the biting ones. Writers for the *Miscellany* were apparently unafraid to criticize distinguished College guests and speakers. Even on May 17, 1867, back in the days of the *Vassariana*, students critically listened to a lecture by the distinguished poet and philosopher Ralph Waldo Emerson.[79] Some in the audience were thoroughly unimpressed with his speaking style, later describing him as having an "indefinable lack of fashion" and "broken sequence" manner of talking. They did, however, enjoy Emerson's poetry. *Miscellany* writers were not pleased when the renowned poet Matthew Arnold came to campus in 1894 to critique Emerson's work.[80] Arnold called Emerson "neither a great poet nor a man or letters," and accused his work of lacking "directness, completeness, [and] energy." A student reviewing Arnold's lecture in the April 1894 *Miscellany* charged that Arnold exercised only "academic narrowness," and said that Vassar students would not be "led back to medievalism, even by such cultured and classic teachers as Matthew Arnold."[81] This review was edgy, and caught the attention of no fewer than three students and two faculty members who wrote back in both support and rebuttal. The *Miscellany* was sparking conversations.

Essentially, the "essays" were becoming more like modern-day "articles"—prose closer to what we might find in the features section of a contemporary magazine. The content, sometimes provocative, was becoming more about the lives of students themselves, and less about academic pretention and abstract scholarly theories. Long-winded essays continued to exist in the *Miscellany*, but their topics slowly became less lofty and more centered around common experiences. And although this prose still approached haughtiness at times, the personal subject matter changed the general tone and made the writing more acceptable to a younger audience. This shift was crucial to maintaining interest in the *Miscellany*—for both readers and writers—as the 19th century came to a close.

In Search of Student Voice in Verse

But academic essays were only half of the "literature" in the *Miscellany*. Student poetry also comprised a significant portion. This genre sometimes provides a better window into the lives of these young women than their essays, particularly during and after the 1890s. In his 1915 history of the College, President Taylor, noted the importance of this creative writing (rather than the *Miscellany*'s academic writing) in trying to understand the "actual character of early students."[82] Indeed,

Taylor incorporated some of the opinions expressed in these poems into the social history chapters of his book. "Nothing gives so vivid an idea of student life in the early days as the [poetry in the] first magazines which students brought out," he wrote of the poems in the *Vassar Miscellany Monthly*.

In these works, like in the editorial content, we see the seeds of the independent student voice. Anonymity certainly helped to nurture these seeds; bylines were given for poems even less frequently than for essays and opinions pieces. The practice of omitting bylines or using false names was popular in early student publications. Daniel Webster, for example, wrote for the *Dartmouth Gazette* in 1802 under the pseudonym "Icarus." As for the *Miscellany*, the publication included a staff box of editor's names, but often omitted bylines from specific pieces. This was particularly true for poetry and prose that was critical of Vassar. In other words, anonymity helped these young writers express their true opinions, which they otherwise might have been afraid to commit to paper.

A look at student poetry gives us a sense of the early investigation and radicalism that would eventually grow into more conventional journalism. Twice in the publication's history—once in 1893 and again in 1916—the Editorial Board published retrospective anthologies that included "verse of the highest possible excellence of standards."[83] The first anthology covered the years from 1872 to 1893, and was edited by Edith Colby Banfield '92 and Sarah Elizabeth Woodbridge '92. Banfield and Woodbridge gathered dozens of poems from the *Miscellany*'s archives. Cambridge University Press then published the anthology.[84] These two editors had a strong sense of historical preservation, noting in their preface that "the favor that Vassar poems have won… warrant" their preservation. *Miscellany* poetry had already been reprinted in numerous college publications, including the *Harvard Register* and the *Yale Daily News*, and now they hoped to spread Vassar authors even further. Two distinct periods in *Miscellany* poetry—which roughly overlap with the ones for academic essays—coincide with the two different anthologies.

On first glance, the poetry that dominated Vassar's primary student publication between 1872 and 1893 might seem inaccessible, even boring. Out of the 70 poems in the first anthology, 47 are odes to

Covering the Campus

nature. Titles include "The March Wind," "A Late October Day," and "In a Wheat Field." By today's standards, these poems are about as energetic as their titles. They would be considered what scholars today refer to as academic poetry. Academic poetry, according to one recent critic, is "intelligent but dull."[85] Poetry of this genre usually has a strict adherence to meter and rhythm. Interesting subject matter takes a backseat to perfect style. The students who wrote for the *Vassar Miscellany Monthly* were taught in their English classes to emulate poets such as William Wordsworth, John Keats and Samuel Coleridge. Their voice as individuals is somewhat lost in their faithfulness to these styles—styles that they likely learned and mastered in the Vassar classroom. Interestingly, this adherence was out of sync with the Romantic Movement occurring beyond the ivory tower in the later 19th century. While the radical innovations of poets such as Walt Whitman, Emily Dickinson, and Ralph Waldo Emerson dominated the literary scene, Vassar students continued to emulate the poetry popular two generations earlier.

Like academic essays, poetry experienced a striking change in tone in the early 1890s. Beginning roughly in 1894, the poetry started to exude a much more recognizable student voice. Some of the students' words are playful, such as Mary Fleming's proclamation that her classmates should "Dance! Lilt! And sing!" as a means of both liberation and personal expression. Fleming used an irregular meter and original form, a break from the academic style. Other writers aimed for expression in other ways, sometimes with sexual undertones. Henriette Blanding's "The Wing Song" was published in 1912, and her metaphors are far from subtle. The speaker wishes to "toss... the taut-stretched sail" into the "treasure-laden" rocks. For the sail to enter the cave, she wrote, it must first pass the "sea-weed black" and "soft, towering waves." There will be a "thundering roar [and] rhythmic beat," and when the tossing finally finishes, someone will emit the "wild coyote's cry to the stars." Though the poem incorporates these suggestive tidbits into a larger oceanic tale, it seems evident that the speaker is hinting at sexual intercourse, ending with an orgasmic "cry to the stars." Whether these undertones originate from Blanding's experiences or fantasies is of less importance than the fact that she was able to write, conceal, and publish these imaginings.

Vassar women also used poetry in the *Miscellany* as a means of theological questioning. Though Vassar students came from predominately Protestant families, many of these young girls were evidently thinking outside of the theological box. "I am a pagan, I!" declared Beatrice Daw '10 in her 1909 poem "A Pagan." The speaker, presumably Daw herself, is captivated by nature and rejects the Christian view that humans will eventually be sent to Heaven or Hell. Instead, she prefers to forever "revel in [the earth's] joys of sight and sound." Daw was not the only student to question Judeo-Christian models. In 1913, Elizabeth Toof '14 wrote "A Prayer to Buddha," in which she describes the majesty of Buddhist temples, the enchantment of lotus flowers and the supremacy of Buddha as a spiritual leader. Clearly, poems like these call into question the long-standing notion that only "upper class WASP families of… the oldest Protestant stock" attended Vassar and schools like it.[86] The writing suggests that the girls happily parted with Protestantism, at least in some cases.

Not only did students imagine and re-imagine their place in the spiritual world, but also the gendered physical world. "Swing in the Swing" by Vivian Gurney '15 is an excellent example. The speaker sits in a tree swing, dreaming about how she would act "if I was a lady." While much of women's literature glorified the dignity of wives and mothers in the late 19th century, Gurney had a very different idea of womanhood. "If I was a Lady / I'd never stop eating candy, / [and] I'd never go up to bed," she proclaimed. "And when [adults] talked about secrets / I wouldn't be sent up ahead." The young poet conflates womanhood with physical and intellectual freedom. Significantly, though, this conflation occurs only in her daydream. And once her dream is complete, she "jump[s] to the ground in the end." The implication seems to be that the speaker jumps off the swing knowing that womanhood will not feel nearly so free.

Why is this poem—and many other *Miscellany* poems that subtly spoke to the advancement of women—historically significant? The cult of domesticity, an ideology introduced in the early 1800s, was solidly entrenched by the century's end.[87] This ideology gave women a central albeit passive role in family life, elevating the roles of wives and mothers to society's guardians of moral purity. Women's magazines and popular literature of the period are full of advice about proper housekeeping; implicit in these advice columns was the notion that by keeping a clean, pious home, women were achieving their highest calling by mothering the next generation. The movement to elevate the status of housework found an early voice in the writings of Catherine Beecher.[88] Beecher devoted much of her life to glorifying housekeeping and attempting to convince her readers that their daily duties, however tedious, were of the utmost importance. In the first three decades of Vassar's existence, some 95 percent of married women remained at home full-time. Few women attended professional schools, and by 1880, only 5 percent of doctors and 2 percent of lawyers in the United States were female.[89] Far from Gurney's playful dream of physical and intellectual freedom, women were denied both education and the opportunity for professional advancement.

Yet as the 19th century passed into the 20th, this situation began to change. With growing industrialization, jobs opened up in factories and retail establishments particularly in urban areas. These jobs often required minimal education, and for their efforts women received equally minimal pay. But at the same time, such jobs opened new possibilities, possibilities that had been promised, but not delivered en masse, as early as Lucretia Mott and Elizabeth Cady Stanton's 1848 Seneca Falls Convention on women's rights. Vivian Gurney, all of 18 years old, managed to playfully summarize the hopeful daydream that countless progressive reformers across the country were having.

Miscellany poetry clearly spoke to issues far beyond Vassar's gates. But beyond issues of sexuality, religion and gender, Vassar students did occasionally turn their critical pens onto the College itself. In "Lament," a poem signed only with the initials K.T., the speaker complains about the laziness of her classmates. The Vassar student "well displays / Her slothful disposition / She twines about the classroom chairs / In serpentine positions." The speaker bemoans that "In Sunday Evening Music too / [the girls] find it more pleasing / to lie recumbent on their seats." The theme of this commentary—that Vassar students are too idle and do not take advantage of the classes and experiences that the College has to offer—has since been repeated in staff editorials for generations. Even today, at least once each semester, the Editorial Board will fume about students' lack of interest in the affairs of the College. Perhaps because writers and editors spend their days learning about the wide variety of activities at Vassar, they have always been particularly incensed when other students do not take advantage of those activities. K.T.'s 1910 poem offers a similar critique of students' unwillingness to engage with Vassar's academics, albeit through verse rather than editorial prose.

Writers also criticized Vassar's staff and faculty. C.C.W. in 1916 penned "Spring Song," which gently admonished the janitorial staff for not "removing" the worms that covered the path between Josselyn House and Main Building after an April rain. But not all criticism of employees was so tongue and cheek. "A Psychological Delusion," written by H.B. (likely Henriette Blanding '12), gives a scathing review of her literature professor. "Three lectures a week /And nothing she'd tell you was new, / The quizzes were easy and in the whole year / There were only three topics to do." The speaker is angry that the professor designed a facile syllabus that did not challenge her students. In true Vassar spirit, H.B. entered the classroom with the hope of becoming engaged in the material. She was naturally disappointed when her professor did not facilitate that engagement.

Thus, even before the *Miscellany* became a conventional newspaper, the *Monthly* managed to perform two of a campus newspaper's most important functions. First, it used poetry and prose to discuss campus events. Second, it added its own unique, sometimes critical perspective. In this way, we can hear the voices of these early Vassar students on a variety of topics through their poetry and analytical essays, even though they do not always spell out their criticisms directly using passionate editorials and investigative articles.

Growth 1000

Miscellany Grows in Size and Scope

As we have seen, the tone of the *Miscellany* changed dramatically during the 1890s, coinciding with a more general period of expansion at Vassar. With the arrival of President James Monroe Taylor to campus in 1886, the College began its first large-scale fundraising campaign.[90] As its first generation of graduates began to give back to their alma mater, Vassar's resources swelled. The student body expanded to over 1,000 by the end of Monroe's tenure in 1914. Strong House, the first of the four quadrangle dormitories, was built in 1893 to accommodate the additional students who could no longer fit into Main Building.

Taylor enriched more than Vassar's buildings and enrollment; he led an effort to revitalize the academic curriculum, and also gave the student government more responsibility and jurisdiction than ever before. These increases in student control—and in College budgets—extended to the *Vassar Miscellany*.

The essays and poetry clearly changed in the early 1890s, becoming more student-centered and less prosaic and academic. At the same time, the monthly volumes ballooned in size; by the turn of the century, some volumes were between five and six inches thick. The larger student population seemed more than willing to contribute to Vassar's publication, submitting their literary works at a record pace. The larger staff had regular conversations about the function and purpose of the paper. Out of these conversations came the realization that the *Miscellany Monthly* had two incompatible missions.[91] While the bulk of the paper strove to be a literary magazine, "the back" of the paper strove to be a source of campus news and opinions. Students increasingly desired a timelier source of information and dialogue. Some suggested that the *Miscellany* should appear twice each month rather than once. But the progression from a quarterly to a monthly to a biweekly still would not be enough, others argued. It was not simply a question of frequency; it was a question of mission. "What should the *Miscellany* seek to accomplish?" asked a 1911 staff editorial.[92]

In Fall 1913, the Editorial Board made a historic announcement. Beginning that winter, the literary *Miscellany* would continue to be published monthly, but a "supplemental" campus-oriented *Miscellany* would be published weekly. The Students' Association enthusiastically approved the financing for this plan on October 13, 1913.[93]

Upon hearing the announcement, the College faculty protested vehemently. Just as the faculty had opposed the creation of a quarterly, and then the transition to a monthly, so too did they oppose the birth of a weekly. Mostly, they felt uncomfortable giving the Students' Association total authority over extracurricular activities. The student government, however, as part of a greater effort to enhance its own control over student life, circulated a petition overwhelmingly in favor weekly publication. After a campaign that lasted through the fall semester with "considerable agitation," the students won the day in a faculty vote.[94] Officially called the *Vassar Miscellany News Supplement*, the first issue of the *Miscellany Weekly*—known simply as "the *Weekly*" among students—was published on February 6, 1914. It would be the last time in Vassar's history that the faculty had the authority to vote on anything related to the production of the *Miscellany News*.

The *Weekly* and the *Monthly* were essentially two different organizations functioning under the same tent. The *Weekly* quickly tried to recruit a more inclusive staff than the *Monthly*, whose members were overwhelmingly English or writing students. The first few issues were full of advertisements for writers, columnists and editors—a practice that the *Monthly* had done only rarely.[95] The selection process for editorships was also radically different between the two publications. For the *Monthly*, a candidate for the Editorial Board had to have published a specific number of words in the paper. After that hurdle, candidates were selected by the sitting Editorial Board, approved by a vote of their class, and finally ratified by the Students' Association.[96] The *Weekly* strived for a more inclusive process. The required word count was dropped, and any Vassar student could nominate an editor. A committee chaired by the Editor in Chief and including the President of the Students' Association, a member of the English Department, and the presidents of the junior and senior classes reviewed these nominees. The *Weekly* and *Monthly* also differed on other policies, such as the method for editorial writing, layout, and even the local printed they employed.

Time only increased the differences between the two *Miscellany* publications. The *Weekly* robbed the *Monthly* of all campus-related coverage. The *Monthly* no longer attempted to publish much news, and published fewer letters to the editor. The Editor's Table shrank, as did Points of View—two of its most popular sections. While the *Weekly* was an instant hit, the *Monthly* struggled with its new mission as solely a literary publication. "The Alumnae Department," the sizable part of the publication devoted to the writing and opinions of alumnae, spun off into the *Vassar Quarterly* in 1916. The *Quarterly* was managed entirely by the Alumnae Association. The size of the *Monthly* shrunk dramatically after this point, and it seemed that fewer and fewer members of the College community were active readers. The *Monthly* became closer to what the *Vassariana* and *Transcript* had been—showpieces for the College, exhibited to alumnae and outsiders.[97] No longer was the

Miscellany Monthly the embodiment of student news and opinions. In the years following 1914, the two *Miscellany* publications drifted further apart. What began as a joint project devolved into two separate, autonomous organizations that shared only a business staff. By 1924, the *Monthly* editors acknowledged that their publication "was failing to achieve its aims." The *Monthly* vanished the next year, leaving behind its younger, more successful partner.

29 The legend is especially dubious since the story can only be verified orally. The tale was never recorded in Vassar's autobiography, nor in any subsequent histories of the College.

30 James Monroe Taylor and Elizabeth Hazelton Haight, *Vassar*. (New York: Oxford University Press, 1915), p. 19.

31 The *Vassariana*, June, 1866.

32 *Ibid.*

33 The *Transcript*, June, 1867.

34 "More Copies," The *Transcript*, June, 1869.

35 James Monroe Taylor and Elizabeth Hazelton Haight, *Vassar*. (New York: Oxford University Press, 1915), p. 113.

36 Mary Mallon, "The *Vassar Miscellany*," The *Vassar Miscellany Monthly*, April 1915, p. 116.

37 "*Miscellany News*iana: Its History and Editors," The *Vassar Miscellany News,* May 1, 1940.

38 The *Transcript*, June, 1867.

39 Most of the early archives of the *Yale Daily News* and the *Harvard Crimson* are available on the Web sites of the Yale and Harvard University libraries, respectively. By the 1850s, both papers are willing to take critical views of their fellow students, professors and administrators. The *Miscellany* only began to take such stances in the 1890s, and even then criticisms were often muted, apologetic, or hidden in poetic verse. The ideals and expectations surrounding Victorian femininity—which demanded that women remain generally quiet and submissive regarding public affairs—almost certainly accounts for these differences in tone. Also accounting for the difference was the relatively small space devoted to editorials and opinions in the literary *Miscellany*, compared to the space accorded to student and alumnae poetry and essays.

40 Mary Mallon, "The *Vassar Miscellany,*" The *Vassar Miscellany Monthly*, April 1915, p. 115.

41 Jan Whitt, *Women in American Journalism: A New History*. (Urbana: University of Illinois Press), 2008, p. 19.

42 *Ibid*, p. 117.

43 The *Vassar Miscellany*, April, 1872.

44 Sarah Riane Harper, The *Miscellany Monthly*, edited by Elizabeth Daniels, 2006. http://vcencyclopedia.vassar.edu/index.php/The_*Miscellany*_Monthly   (accessed April 8, 2008).

45 "Editorial," The *Vassar Miscellany*, April, 1872.

46 Mary Mallon, "The *Vassar Miscellany,*" The *Vassar Miscellany Monthly*, April 1915, p. 128.

47 "Editorial," The *Vassar Miscellany*, April, 1874.

48 "Local Students," Poughkeepsie News Press on April 16, 1896

49 "Editorial," The *Vassar Miscellany*, April, 1872.

50 William Madden, "The Victorian Sensibility" in *Victorian Studies*, (Indiana University Press: September, 1963), p. 67-97.

51 Elizabeth Sewell as quoted in Joan Perkins, *Victorian Women*, (New York: New York University Press, 1995), p. 2.

52 Alison MacKinnon, "Educated Doubt: Women, Religion and the Challenge of Higher Education, 1870-1920," *Women's History Review*, 1998, p. 247.

53 "Editorial," The *Vassar Miscellany*, April, 1873.

54 Joan Johnson, ed. *Southern Women at Vassar: The Poppenheim Family Letters*, 1882-1916 (Columbia: University of South Carolina Press, 2002), p. 11.

55 *Ibid.*, p. 13.

56 *Ibid.*, p. 14.

57 *Ibid.*, p. 15.

58 *Ibid.*, p. 14.

59 Sarah Riane Harper, *Samuel L. Caldwell*, edited by Elizabeth Daniels, 2006. http://vcencyclopedia.vassar.edu/index.php/Samuel_L._Caldwell (accessed December 1, 2008).

60 Lorine Swainston Goodwin, *The Pure Food, Drink, and Drug Crusaders, 1879-1914*. (Jefferson: McFarland Press, 1999), p. 128.

61 The Archives and Special Collections Library houses hundreds of letters from the students of this period.

62 Mary Mallon, "The *Vassar Miscellany*," The *Vassar Miscellany Monthly*, April 1915, p. 118.

63 *Ibid.*, p. 115.

64 James Monroe Taylor and Elizabeth Hazelton Haight, *Vassar*. (New York: Oxford University Press, 1915), p. 114.

65 *Ibid.*, p. 115.

66 The *Vassariana*, June, 1866.

67 The *Vassar Miscellany Monthly*, October, 1875.

68 Similar pleas for writers surface constantly over the nearly 150-year history of the paper, and 'in-house' advertisements are a regular feature of today's paper.

69 "Editorial," The *Vassar Miscellany Monthly*, April, 1874.

70 Mary Mallon, "The *Vassar Miscellany*," The *Vassar Miscellany Monthly*, April 1915, p. 119.

71 "Editorial," The *Vassar Miscellany Monthly*, September, 1875.

72 Mary Mallon, "The *Vassar Miscellany*," The *Vassar Miscellany Monthly*, April 1915, p. 121.

73 This structure for the publication and the staff continued relatively unaltered through the 1880s. Mallon noticed that "The editors seem to have divided the work of the Board much more strictly than is customary among the present [1915] editors." Work seems to have been highly specialized, given the small size of the staff. Most editors and writers worked exclusively on content, leaving issues of layout and production to the older members of the Editorial Board. This model went out of fashion for the later part of the 20th century when editors began to design their own layouts, but then returned in 2009. As for the academic essays and poetry in the *Miscellany Monthly*, those items remain somewhat foreign to modern readers, defying our definitions of news and journalism.

74 Charles Franklin Thwing, "College Journalism," *Scribners Monthly: An Illustrated Magazine for the People*, October 1878: p. 812.

75 Mary Mallon, "The *Vassar Miscellany*," The *Vassar Miscellany Monthly*, April, 1915, p. 123.

76 *Ibid.*, p. 122.

77 *Ibid.*, p. 123.

78 "Editor's Note," The *Vassar Miscellany Monthly*, October, 1892.

79 "Emerson Comes to Vassar," The *Transcript*, June, 1867.

80 "Matthew Arnold Comes to Vassar," The *Miscellany Monthly*, October, 1894.

81 *Ibid.*

82 James Monroe Taylor and Elizabeth Hazelton Haight, Vassar. (New York: Oxford University Press, 1915), p. 113.

83 Edith Colby Banfield and Sarah Elizabeth Woodbridge, *A Book of Vassar Verse: Reprints from the Vassar Miscellany Monthly, 1894-1916*, Cambridge University Press, 1916.

84 Though somewhat rare, the anthology currently circulates in a number of academic and public libraries.

85 Paul Negri, *English Victorian Poetry: An Anthology,* (New York: Dover Publications, 1999), p. 18.

86 E. Digby Baltzell, *Judgment and Sensibility: Religion and Stratification*, (New York: Transaction Publishers, 1994), p. 80.

87 Eleanor Gordon, *Public Lives: Women, Family and Society in Victorian Britain* (New Haven: Yale University Press, 2003), p. 210.

88 Willystine Goodsell, *Pioneers of women's education in the United States: Emma Willard, Catherine Beecher, Mary Lyon.* (New York: McGraw-Hill, 1831), p. 222.

89 Joan Burstyn, *Victorian Education and the Ideal of Womanhood* (London: Croom Helm, 1980), p. 48.

90 Maryann Bruno and Elizabeth Daniels, *Vassar College,* (London: Arcadia, 2001), p. 35.

91 *"Miscellany* Undefined," The *Vassar Miscellany Monthly*, February 19, 1911.

92 "Editorial," The *Vassar Miscellany Monthly*, October 1911.

93 Special Collections, Vassar College Archives, comp. "VC Government (1868-1920)." *Subject File* 23.79.

94 *"Miscellany News*iana: Its History and Editors," The *Vassar Miscellany News*, May 1, 1940.

95 "Contribute," The *Vassar Miscellany News* Supplement, February 20, 1914.

96 Special Collections, Vassar College Archives, comp. "VC Government (1868-1920)." *Subject File* 23.79.

97 "Editor's Note," The *Vassar Miscellany Monthly*, 1916.

Chapter Two:
The Dawn of Weekly Publication,
1914-1938

I n the shadows of the First World War, the newly-minted weekly paper chose a turbulent time to come into its own. Editorials and news stories struggled to cover the increasingly complicated global situation while maintaining a focus on Vassar. Covering both the College and the world was not always graceful; as the writers of a 1940 retrospective wrote, articles on bloody European battles were "side by side… with sentiments on Valentine's Day and disapproving words for the young man who smoked a cigar in Main."[98] Without a national affairs section, the staff awkwardly meshed news of minute school events with news of combat and casualty rates.

Often the War was ignored altogether. Future editors would complain that the paper's staff did not adequately investigate the international news of the day; instead, their focus was overly "parochial" and "seemingly oblivious" to events outside of campus.[99] This "myopic concentration" represented the difficulties of transitioning the *Vassar Miscellany Monthly*—a literary showcase inherently concerned with the College and its inhabitants—into the *Vassar Miscellany News*, an informational newspaper. It would take about 15 years of practice in this new genre for the *Miscellany* to more adroitly engage with the world beyond Vassar.

It is fitting that the *Miscellany* begins weekly publication in 1914, the final year of James Taylor's tenure as College President. Henry Noble MacCracken, Vassar's next leader, turned the school's inward focus decidedly outward.[100] MacCracken, only 34 years old and "immersed in the pre-war changing ideas about student culture," came to the College six months before his inauguration in October of 1915.[101] During those six months he encouraged many changes in student life, "encouraging the students who had been desirous of forming a Suffrage Club and a Socialist Club to do so, and accommodating many other pent-up student demands." Change did not stop there. During MacCracken's lengthy tenure from 1915 to 1946, Vassar became a leader in academic research. Prominent visitors, including Franklin Roosevelt, lectured and talked with students about world affairs. Politics suddenly became a legitimate student interest, and MacCracken happily encouraged the formation of the Political Association, a group that met to discuss global issues, just as members of Philalatheis met to discuss literature. The College, and the student newspaper, would take an active role in pushing for women's suffrage in New York. Before long, international issues—namely the Great Depression and World War II—forced students to engage with life beyond the ivory tower. As the 1920s turned into the 30s and 40s, editors increasingly included articles about Vassar's relation to the world beyond.

The ideological changes that unfolded during MacCracken's tenure were accompanied by major utilitarian changes. Faster-paced technology aided the growth of campus media. The early 20th century saw a sudden rise in electrical equipment at the College. By 1912, students enjoyed electric lighting and heating in Main Building, the residence halls, the Library and many academic buildings around campus. Although the campus had a telephone system as early as 1902, outside communication first became possible in 1916 when a service line connected Vassar to the New York Telephone Company.[102] The system expanded even further in 1926 when phones and wiring were installed in academic buildings and dormitories. Given the noticeable rise in quotations from outsiders in *Miscellany* articles around this time, one might assume that reporters used the technology to their advantage.[103] To select just one example, articles about the Town of Poughkeepsie after mid-1926 began to feature comments from citizens and town officials, where they previously had not. This suggests that writers now had the ability to conduct telephone interviews. Conceptually and practically, the world was quickly becoming bigger, faster and filled with more possibilities for the staff of the *Miscellany*.

Negotiating as a Weekly, Negotiating as a Newspaper

In this time of tremendous change for the world and for the College, the *Vassar Miscellany News Supplement* published its first issue as a weekly on February 6, 1914. Its first editorial explained the 'new' publication's rationale: "It comes to answer an old need of the College for a more efficient bulletin of events and for a better means of comment than the [literary] *Miscellany* could afford… College life will find itself reflected in the *Weekly* from various angles. All events of importance to the College at large, it will try to record clearly. It will endeavor to bring events of world interest into closer connection with the college."[104] The *Weekly* essentially cannibalized all the journalistic aspects of the *Monthly*.[105] The news supplement encompassed "the back" of the *Monthly*, which previously included Home Matters (campus news) and Points of View (opinions pieces). The *Vassar Miscellany News Supplement* dramatically expanded these sections, which despite their popularity were afterthoughts in the *Monthly*.

The first issue included a calendar of campus events, an article on President Taylor's retirement and various bulletins on campus happenings. It also allowed for brief letters to the editor, which appeared essentially as they did in the *Monthly*—as small initialed items, rarely more than a few paragraphs. The *Weekly* often blurred the lines between news writing and opinionated writing, with short articles that had distinct points of view. Between 1914 and 1916, the *Miscellany* developed an editorial policy very similar to the one currently in use today. The editors described the paper as a "free forum" for members of the community to debate issues.[106] They would "not refuse any contribution which is authorized by the writer's signature, [although] the editors do not hold themselves responsible for any expressions of personal opinions. If they are objectionable, the columns of the next issue are at the command of anyone who puts their objection into writing." The editors aimed to be "non-partisan in playing umpire." The *Miscellany News*'s policy on opinionated submissions is almost identical today; although the paper has faced criticism for printing certain letters and columns, the Editorial Board maintains the century-old "free forum" approach. Like the *Monthly*, the *Weekly* also included a staff editorial, an unsigned article reflecting the opinion of a two-thirds majority of the Editorial Board. Again, this feature is also found in today's paper.[107] The sequence of staff editorials in the *Weekly* and the *Monthly* suggests at least some coordination between editors to avoid overlap; the topics chosen by the two were rarely the same. Even when the subject matter was similar, it seemed that the publications made sure to include different facts and arguments.

But the synergy between the two did not last for long. Even by the end of the spring semester of 1914, there was evidence of less communication between the staffs. Essays and editorials printed in the *Monthly* began to repeat topics already covered by the *Weekly*. When the *Weekly* would adopt slight formatting changes, such as bolder title fonts, the *Monthly* would copy those alterations—but only after several weeks. The editors of the two publications apparently made decisions independently and did not share information about formatting changes. Though the *Weekly* and *Monthly* staffs might have worked together for the first few weeks or months, the *Weekly* grew increasingly autonomous, gaining control over its own unique editorial voice. By 1917, the only connection between the two was a joint business board to manage subscription sales and advertising revenue.[108] As the years progressed, they grew further and further apart, sometimes referencing one another in staff editorials as if they were entirely foreign entities. As Sarah Riane Harper noted, the tenth issue of the *Weekly* began to feature reviews of the literature in the *Monthly* publication, "a sign of the gap between the sister papers"; one review even claimed that "the poetry of the month was drier than usual, [and the] language lacked in elegance and flair."[109] Today, this would be as awkward as the *New York Times* publishing a review of the *New York Times Magazine*.

The news "supplement" quickly proved to be more than just a supplement. Students began to regard *it*, rather than the fifty-year-old *Monthly*, as the primary student voice. Responding to its popularity, the paper sometimes appeared twice each week instead of once beginning in 1916. The Students' Association records do not indicate any sort of discussion or vote on this matter, which indicates that the Editorial Board made the decision independently—a big step, considering how contentious changes in frequency had been earlier in the paper's history. By Fall 1917, the habit of biweekly publication had become permanent; the *Vassar Miscellany News* was now published on Wednesdays and Sundays. The diminutive "Supplement" in its title was dropped.

Formula and Routine in the *Weekly*[110]

For the first 30 years of weekly publication, very little changed about the look and feel of the *Vassar Miscellany News*. The paper began at four pages, but soon expanded to eight by October 1914. Apart from that initial change in length, the format remained remarkably consistent for decades. The first page began with a calendar of events on the top left column, and a small section featuring faculty news on the lower right. Page two featured the names of editors and writers in the upper left column, and the staff editorial below. The rest of the page was left for pithy letters to the editor. The next three of four pages were comprised of articles on a variety of topics. The student government, administrative decisions, and ongoing plays and recitals were some of the most common subjects. Borrowing from the literary *Miscellany Monthly*, articles often took the form of essays on such heady topics as "Social Laws" and "Intelligence and Law Breaking"—hardly typical newspaper items. They closely resembled truncated versions of the types of pieces found in the *Monthly*, a sign of the slow adjustment to a traditional newspaper. The final two pages of the paper were comprised entirely of advertisements, often repeating the same ads from local businesses for years.

The early *Miscellany* was clearly formulaic. Editors essentially filled the same mold with different content for each issue. This is not to say that there were *no* formatting shifts during the early 20th century. By 1917, advertisements were scattered across the paper's eight pages, rather than clumped into the two final pages. These graphic elements made the paper easier to read, adding some variety to the rows of text. By 1918, editors began to experiment with different fonts, typesets and stylistic elements. After 1919, text was occasionally rendered in bold with different sizes available for headlines. The growth of original photography was one of the most noticeable innovations. The first *Miscellany* photograph, published on November 12, 1915, depicted a performance of a play entitled *Italian Street*. Photography was not common, however, until the later 1920s. Until then, most issues included one or two small images at most. Cartoons also made their first appearance during the first decade of weekly publication; the first depicted Vassar girls preparing for their junior prom on April 19, 1919.

Just as the 1910s and 1920s saw gradual shifts within a fairly regularized structure, so too did article content. While the majority of articles were strictly confined to campus affairs, the *Miscellany* of the 1920s and 1930s saw articles on topics ranging from international politics to Buddhist mysticism. Coverage of national and international politics surfaced only occasionally. Clearly the publication was still searching for its scope and defining its mission. Would it be a newspaper of words and ideas, like the *Monthly*, a global news source like the *New York Times*, or a journal of news related only to Vassar? During its first two decades of publication, the paper was essentially a combination.

So although there was a fairly regular layout during the paper's first 30 years, nothing was entirely static. The gradual development of content and appearance during the 1910s and 1920s paved the way for the broader shifts in content and formatting that would occur in the 1930s and 1940s.

The Paper in Context

By the late 1920s, the *Weekly* had become an entrenched part of campus life. Its staff was, by today's standards, enormous. Although the paper came out twice each week, it averaged only about four or eight pages in length, with about 25 percent of that space occupied by advertisements. Yet in 1927, the paper had an astounding 48 staffers, including 21 reporters, two full-time art critics, two office assistants, one music critic, one head Business Manager and one Assistant Business Manager. Although the paper today has a comparable staff of about 35, we print one 20 or 24 page issue each week, and cover a much larger campus and student body than the one that existed in the 1920s. Compared to Vassar's 2,450 students today, the campus of the 1920s had only about 1,000 students. Fewer students meant fewer student organizations, which meant less news. Thus, the size of their staff is remarkable and shows that there was a great interest in journalism as an extracurricular activity.

The Vassar Miscellany

(News Supplement)

VOL. 1.   POUGHKEEPSIE, N. Y., FEBRUARY 6, 1914.   No. 1.

CALENDAR

FRIDAY, FEB. 6

8 P. M.   Lecture by Professor von der Leyen, visiting professor at Yale. "Neue Richtungen in der deutschen Erzälungskunst."

SUNDAY, FEB. 8

11 A. M.   Preacher—Dr. H. E. Cobb, West End Collegiate Church, New York.

7 P. M.   Address by Miss Margaret Matthew, a Vassar graduate, on Japan and the Japanese Woman of Today.

WEDNESDAY, FEB. 11

4:45 P. M.   First of a series of Art Lectures by Prof. Alfred V. Churchill of Smith College.

THURSDAY, FEB. 12

7:30 P. M.   Address by Dr. Zwemer, of Cairo, Africa.

FRIDAY, FEB. 13

8 P. M.   Concert by the choir.

SATURDAY, FEB. 14

4 P. M.   Junior Prom.

WEDNESDAY, FEB. 18

4:45 P. M.   Recital: Modern Russian Songs, Edward Bromberg.

THURSDAY, FEB. 19

7:30 P. M.   Address by Rev. Mr. Tertius Van Dyke, on The Spring Street Church.

PRESIDENT TAYLOR RETIRES

We have all been dreading the moment when Dr. Taylor should leave us but we did not know until Friday night just how much it meant to each one of us personally. Dr. Taylor's few parting words to us in chapel last week and Friday night after the serenade not only touched us, but made us realize how much of his life he had given to the college. And although Dr. Taylor would be the first to deny the necessity of telling of his work for the college, it seems only fitting to mention at least a little of it. Dr. Taylor came here in 1887 after study in the University of Rochester and in Europe, training in the Theological Seminary, and work in the Ministry. When he came to the college almost everything took place in the Main Building. Through Dr. Taylor's efforts we now have more than twenty buildings for college purposes. The beautiful Taylor Art Building now being erected will stand as a fitting monument to this work of his.

In 1886 Vassar consisted of the college, a preparatory school and separate Music and Art schools. Feeling that the work needed to be more concentrated, Dr. Taylor succeeded in abolishing the preparatory school and in uniting the Music and Art schools with the College proper. This gave the professors of Music and Art a place on the faculty and enabled the students to count the courses in theory and history of music and history of art toward the baccalaureate degree. These and many other changes have been the result of serious educational problems that Dr. Taylor has had to meet. In all his work he has kept to one policy—that "the single purpose of Vassar is to maintain and advance the standards of education of young women." His whole attitude is summed up in the words of President Raymond: "The Institution was not founded and is not administered in the interest of any doctrine or class of doctrines. . . . . The mission of Vassar College is not to reform society but to educate women." Dr. Taylor has unbounded faith in the institution. He says, "Its foundations are sound—its ideals clear and exalted, and its opportunities will be steadily enlarged." His faith in the college and his work for it have been constant and helpful, and it is with great regret that we see him go.

As was announced in chapel last Monday night, contrary to current rumors, no one has been chosen as yet to take Dr. Taylor's place. For the coming semester Dr. Hill is to take charge of the chapel services and the Sunday evening meetings of the Christian Association, and Professor Mills is to act as chairman of the Faculty. The executive power is vested in a committee consisting of the Dean, the Head Warden and the chairman of the Faculty. It is a time when the general responsibility of the welfare of the college falls more particularly on the student body than ever. A genuine coöperation with those who are in authority will not only lighten their burden but will show to a slight degree that we have recognized and are anxious to uphold the spirit of the service that for so many years Dr. Taylor has willingly and faithfully given to us.

K. S. O., 1915

CHANGES IN THE FACULTY

Miss Robinson has resigned to become Dean of the new Womens' Affiliated College of Newark, Delaware. She is to be congratulated on her opportunity for doing constructive work in a field of such great possibilities. Her plans include a new chapel cut system and the installment of a new department of Household Economy. Through her long association with the College, Miss

(Continued on page 4)

Reprinted here is the February 6, 1914 issue of the *Vassar Miscellany News Supplement*—the very first weekly issue of the paper. The publication was only four pages long, although the length doubled by October that year.

53

THE WEEKLY NEWS SUPPLEMENT

The Vassar Miscellany

(NEWS SUPPLEMENT)

Vassar College, Poughkeepsie, N.Y.   Feb. 6, 1914

Issued weekly during the college year.

Board of Editors.

EDITOR-IN-CHIEF
Mary Pemberton Nourse, 1914

EDITORS OF THE WEEKLY
Louise H. Seaman, 1915
Gertrude Folks, 1916

EDITORS OF THE MONTHLY
Charlotte Greenebaum, 1914   Mary Mallon, 1914
Dorothy S. Phillips, 1914   Katherine S. Oliver, 1915
Ruth T. Pickering, 1914   Mary E. Ross, 1915

Business Managers.

Katherine N. Wilson, 1914
Frances T. Marburg, 1915   Frances Sasser, 1915

AN OLD NEED ANSWERED BY A
NEW OPPORTUNITY

The WEEKLY NEWS SUPPLEMENT greets the college with every good wish for the new semester and the new régime. It comes to answer an old need of the college for a more efficient bulletin of events and for a better means of comment than the MISCELLANY could afford. During the discussion of last fall, it was decided that the length of time necessary for the publication of a literary magazine made it useless as a live medium for report and comment on college activities. In planning to issue the material contained in the back part of the MISCELLANY in a News Supplement coming every week, it was hoped not only that the work of the board of literary editors would be lightened, but also that the interest of the college would be quickened to a broader understanding of its problems, and a stronger sense of coöperation in working them out.

College life will find itself reflected in the WEEKLY from various angles. All events of importance to the college at large, it will try to record clearly. It will endeavor to bring events of world interest into closer connection with the college. It will voice any opinion in matters of interest to the college world. Through some one of these channels there is opportunity for expression for each individual.

To reflect current opinion faithfully, the WEEKLY will be a "free forum." It will not refuse any contribution which is authorized by the writer's signature. The editors do not hold themselves responsible for any expressions of personal opinions. If they are objectionable, the columns of the next issue are at the command of anyone who puts their objection into writing, and "the fight is a fair one." The editors will be non-partisan in playing umpire. They will hold themselves bound, as acting under the Students' Association, to an attitude neutral, but not therefore inactive.

The WEEKLY cordially invites the faculty and alumnae, the administrative and undergraduate bodies to work with it during the next semester toward an understanding and a sense of coöperation that will result in the widest and truest appreciation of college life.

THE STUDENTS' ASSOCIATION NEEDS
THE RENEWED INTEREST OF
EACH MEMBER

At the beginning of a college year we all pass judgment on what kind of a year it is going to be, whether the standards of the student body are going to be high or low, and whether there is going to be a sense of responsibility among the students that will show itself in loyalty to the ideals of the Students' Association and other college organizations as well as to those in authority.

At the end of the college year we all pass judgment on the year again and say what kind of a year it has been—and where we have failed and where we have succeeded. We are apt to forget that one of the best times to judge of the college year is in the middle of it. We have gone a certain distance and we can look back and judge of the successes and failures that we have made during that time. We still have a certain distance to go. We can look forward to the time ahead as offering an opportunity to improve upon what we have already done and as a chance to make up for what we have not done. It is the best time to say to yourself and also to other people, "Are you satisfied with the way that the year is going? Are you doing what you said to yourself at the beginning of the year that you would do and are other people doing what they said that they would do?"

If you are not satisfied with the way that the year is going, that is, with the spirit of the student body, and with its attitude toward the life of the community which it constitutes, now is the time to say so, and not at the end of the year. If you are not satisfied with the way in which you as an individual are doing your part, or if you are not doing your part at all, or if you are not satisfied with the way that others are doing their parts, now is the time to brace up and make other people brace up. You can do your part better, you can take a more active interest in student affairs, you can look to see whether changes or improvements are needed, and you can stir up others to do the same; or else you can settle back into your rut if you are in one and let the year go as it will. And this applies not only to the Students' Association but to all student activities. It goes beyond student activities and applies to "the larger college" which now, if ever, needs the loyal support of the student body.

It remains for us each to ask ourselves the question, "Am I satisfied?" If we are not satisfied then how can we make this year count for more in spirit, in strength of public opinion, in a sense of responsibility, in support of necessary laws, and in loyalty to the college in general?

M. M. A., 1914

FIRE PROTECTION

The general student opinion concerning the restriction of the use of alcohol burners reflects a real interest in the student body for protective measures against the dangers of fire. The executive committee considered the student attitude toward the present unrestricted use of alcohol lamps, chafing dishes and so on, and has investigated the possibilities of installing fire-proof kitchens throughout the college. Until a substitute is instituted for cooking purposes, we have been urged to be extremely cautious in our use of alcohol burners. The other colleges have sent us reports of their "rules and restrictions" in regard to chafing dishes. The majority of the colleges either do not allow alcohol to be used at all, or limit its use very decidedly.

The student ruling of this year in regard to fire drills has aimed at promoting general safety by insuring more efficient drills. We are fined for non-participation in drills because of the obvious danger if everyone does not drill in case of real fire. A girl is given a "calldown" for talking or making any unnecessary noise during a drill; this rule is an attempt to minimize disorder and confusion.

The drills have had organized fire drills this year which have not been entirely successful. Our orderliness and co-operative spirit in drilling should set a fit standard for them to follow. The executive committee has been considering plans for a new and distinctive fire call system. The speed of our drills will surely be increased by a new bell system, but even with the bells at our disposal now, the drills have been much too slow. It has taken over five minutes to empty Main. If each individual acts quickly, and in a military fashion, the speed of the drills can be vastly increased and the greater safety of all thereby insured.

R. H. 1914

THE NEW EXCUSE SYSTEM

The notices on the bulletin boards make clear what the new excuse system is, and the attention of those who lack the "bulletin board habit" will probably in the near future be forcibly directed to it. Just how the system will work is of course one of those very debatable questions concerning which one can only await a semester while the system works. But at present it seems a decided advance, in centralization and despatch, over the old system. Where before each instructor had the task of keeping track of absences and excuses and reporting them to the Warden, the absences are now reported each day to the Dean's office, and excuses sent by the students directly to her. The instructor is thus relieved of the responsibility of attending to excuses; the absences and excuses instead of going to the Warden go directly to the Dean to whose office such academic matters rightly belong, and instead of handing an excuse to each instructor, or forgetting to, the student drops all in one box in her own hall. With all excuses going directly to one office there should be no confusion or delay in straightening out records. There is one disadvantage in that the instructor does not know why a girl is absent, whether from illness or absence from college, or this, that and the other thing—as oversleeping!—but as the records will be open to the instructors, this will be minimized. And there is the additional advantage of having one office deal with all excuses not technically within the law. Excessive absences will be dealt with as before by the wardens, which links them to a certain extent with the Dean's office. The penalty for excessive classroom absences or abuse of the system is as before a social one, although to a certain extent absence from class carries its own penalty in less efficient work. We may still long for a cut system, but in unity, centralization and convenience this is an advance. Meanwhile, we hope.

K. Z. W., 1915

WHY HAVE EXAMS?

At last they are over! Everyone, even she who has emerged the worse for wear, feels a load lifted from her shoulders. The whole aspect of college has changed! No more slowly-plodding feet leaving the Library at nine-thirty; no more empty seats in chapel, in order to use "that valuable twenty minutes;" no more splitting headaches and "baked brains;" and no more endless waiting outside the mailbox for the flunk-note that isn't out yet. And yet some people say they like exam week. "Why, you can get so much exercise, and then you have a whole week, except for five periods, all to yourself. D's the best time of the whole year!" After all, this would be a sensible way to look at the week, but how many of us do it? Exam time, to most people, resembles one prolonged execution time. The executioners wander around in the background, just waiting to catch their victims with sundry pitfalls and torturing devices, before the final consummation of the punishment in the shape of a small stampless envelope, having in one corner

Return to Vassar College,
Poughkeepsie, N. Y.

Aside from all this unnecessary torture, what do we get from the examinations? At times it is hard to discover their real good, when we hear bits of conversation like the following:

"Wasn't I lucky to have learned, by heart, that list of men, just five minutes before the exam. I know I should have flunked if I hadn't."

"That exam was a perfect snap, not that I knew much, but it was the kind you could bluff anything."

"What under the sun made him give us that kind of a paper? Why I know I could have answered every question, without having gone to one lecture all semester."

"My, what a relief it will be to tear up all my notes! We somehow get the impression that if we could successfully answer six or eight questions in two hours, we have completely exhausted a certain subject. It re-

Covering the Campus

minds us of the college boy, who, immediately after receiving his diploma telegraphed his mother: "Educated, by gosh."

Of course it is impossible to sum up a whole course in a two-hour written, but the chief advantage of such an exam is the inevitable review that has gone before. However, no matter how well certain students may know their subject, it is impossible for them under nervous tension, to write a good paper. Might not a scheme of monthly writtens, in the place of semester EXAMINATIONS, give far better results to teacher and student, both in obtaining a more just and proportionate view of a subject, as well as in obviating the strain of "exam-week?"

        M. B., 1915

CLASS ELECTIONS

1917

President—Mildred Cook; Vice-president—Hester Smith; Secretary—Dorothy Copenhaver; Treasurer—Luby Smith.

1916

President—Phebe Briggs; Vice-president—Katherine VanDusen; Secretary—Mary Hendrickson; Treasurer—Marian Robbins.

1915

President—Catherine Davidson; Vice-president—Helen Strait; Secretary—Dinsmore Patrick; Treasurer—Hilda Verity.

Dance Committee

Dorothy Holt, Chairman—Ruth Lockwood, Natalie Kneeland, Elizabeth Van Brunt, Helen Ewen, Marjorie Kendig.

THE ALUMNAE PLAY

The New York Branch of the Vassar Alumnae presented *The Man of Destiny* by G. Bernard Shaw, and *Nance Oldfield* by Charles Reade, Friday evening, January twenty-third at the Aerial Theatre. The cast was as follows:

The Man of Destiny

Napoleon	E. Fatman
Guiseppe	E. James
The Lieutenant	E. Davis
The Lady	Sydney Thompson

Nance Oldfield

Nance Oldfield	Ines Milholland Boissevain
Susan	Gabrielle Elliot
Nathan Oldworthy	L. Reed
Alexander Oldworthy	I. Mills
Robert	E. Davis

Miss M. B. Townsend coached the Players.
The proceeds will be used to furnish the living room

of the new home of the Woman's University Club, No. 106 East Fifty-second Street.

The performance is to be repeated shortly in the Collingwood Opera House.

SECOND HALL PLAY

Lists to sign for parts in Second Hall Play, "The Critic," by H. B. Sheridan, are on Philaletheis Bulletin Board. The lists will be closed February seventh, and trials will be held February ninth to fourteenth. Copies of the play are in the Philaletheis alcove in the library. Trials are open to all classes. The committee is as follows: Martha Strong,'14, Chairman, Dorothy Meigs, '14, Jeannette Merrell,'14, Theodosia Jessup,'15, Theresa Lesher,'15, Katharine Jeffries, '16, Katharine Van Duzen, '16.

THIRD HALL PLAY

On May 16th, "A Midsummer Night's Dream" will be given on Sunset Hill. Trials were held before Christmas. The committee is: Elizabeth French, '14, Chairman, Marjorie Woods, '14, Mary Nourse '14, Sophie White, '15, Dorothy Holt, '15, Julia Norton, '16, Emma Downer, '16, Annie Thorp,'17, Louise Twaddell '17.

THE INTERCOLLEGIATE DEBATE

The topic for the Mt. Holyoke debate was announced Monday night. The provisional wording is as follows: "Resolved; that minimum wage legislation should be applied in workshops, factories, and sweating industries in the United States." The chairman on material will hold office hours in the Philosophy Seminar rooms every day, including Saturdays, between fourth hour and lunch. All those who wish to do work either on material or debating are asked to report to her at this time. The debate committee is as follows: Adeline DeSale,'14, Chairman, Alfreda Mosscrop, '14, Lois Treadwell,'14, Marion Wanger,'14, Elizabeth Adams, '15, Katherine Z. Wells, '15, Margaret Taylor, '15

(Continued from page 1)

Robinson was closely connected with its activities, and her loss will be felt keenly. Her classes will be taken by Miss Cutter, and Miss Patton will take her place as Warden of Strong Hall.

Professor Leach will spend the rest of the year travelling abroad. Miss K. M. Cochran, V. C. 1890, will take her place.

Miss Conrow is leaving for a period of study at Columbia and in Paris. Miss Gerr replaces her in the French Department. At Christmas Time, Miss Schindler took Miss Vignont's place.

During the next semester, Miss Emma Lance will substitute for Miss Stroebe, and Miss Ethel Brewster for Miss Peaks.

Miss Florence Cunningham has been appointed to assist Miss Landon.

In other respects, though, the *Vassar Miscellany News* was still years behind student papers at peer institutions. Many of the characteristics that Charles Thwing considered common among student newspapers by the end of the 19th century did not come into the *Miscellany* until the 1930s and 1940s.[111] For example, Thwing wrote that by 1878, college papers had become "reflective of the moral and intellectual conditions of an institution."[112] The Harvard paper, he explained, described life at Harvard not only for Harvard students, but also for outsiders, much in the same way that American newspapers represent American life to Europeans. As such, many student papers devoted a great deal of space to the news of other institutions. "To a considerable and growing extent," it had become customary for college publications to devote one or two pages exclusively to exchange columns—pieces written by students at other colleges. Thwing believed that such exchanges promoted "inter-collegiate friendship," in addition to spreading information about peer institutions. But the *Miscellany* remained fairly isolated from the community of college journalism.[113] The editors had made two half-hearted attempts to join the East Coast Collegiate Press Association in 1918 and again in 1923. On both occasions, the *Miscellany* dropped out within a single year.

The *Weekly* thus had its flaws—and Vassar students noticed. Though faithful readers of the *Miscellany*, the student body occasionally complained about the lack of professionalism in the paper. A 1920 letter to the editor, signed "O.C. and R.J. Class of 1918," spelled out of the paper's problems: "The paper on a whole is dry, and its headlines do not tempt the reader," they wrote.[114] "Its editorials and reports try harder to maintain literary high-brow [like the *Monthly*] than to secure the wandering attention of the average college girl." A satirical piece printed in the *Miscellany*, entitled "Vassar Press Upheaves," also conveys many of the criticisms leveled against the paper. Published on March 23, 1923, this article ridiculed the *Vassar Millennium News*.[115] "Their old-fashioned ways had just gotten two [*sic*] much for us," wrote *Miscellany* editor Lucy Hodgens '22, imitating her newspaper's detractors. Hodgens complained of the *Millennium*'s poor spelling, while making purposeful typographical errors of her own. She haughtily contested that Vassar should have a publication that could "give the public a chance at a paper as it ought to be." This new paper, she asserted, should have a "Misquoted Department" that would correct all of the "many errors" made by the *Millennium* and publish the "stacks of unprinted errata" hidden in the newspaper's office.

Clearly, Hodgens exaggerated and made light of the criticisms apparently leveled against the *Miscellany*. But she also seemed to offer an implicit challenge: if any student felt that they could produce a better newspaper with fewer inaccuracies, then they should try. As far as the archives tell us, no one seemed to answer Hodgens' call. Though not all members of the Vassar community felt that the paper spoke for them, there was never a successful effort to form a rival paper of a higher quality. The *Miscellany* remained unchallenged in the 1920s as Vassar's newspaper.

Parochialism and Progressivism in the *Miscellany*

And the paper was indeed *Vassar's* newspaper. The question of scope had been decided by the early 1920s; the *Miscellany* would focus almost exclusively on College life and mostly ignore the outside world. Approximately 80 to 90 percent of article content in each issue during the 1910s and 1920s related to the affairs of the College and its students.[116] Even if 'real' news did occasionally slip into the *Miscellany*'s news coverage, staff editorials rarely commented on them. When staff editorials about national politics or controversies did appear, they were fairly tame and usually supportive of government policies.

Hilda Scott Lass '36, a former editor, remembers the sensitive nature of the editorial page. "Vassar was a very socially conservative place back then, and there was certainly a time [about ten] years before my arrival when the editors really did not want to ruffle any feathers," she said. "Sitting on the Editorial Board, I always wanted to make political commentaries in our editorials, and I remember some of the older faculty thinking that such declarations were not appropriate. I think that many would have preferred for us to limit our coverage to College life, and most of the editors felt the same way. Make the paper all about cutesy Vassar girls writing about being educated debutants, that sort of thing." Lass nevertheless wanted the Board to comment on "issues that mattered," by which she meant issues beyond the campus. She encouraged her cohorts to take firm stances and publish sharp criticisms of authorities at home and abroad.

Though she was in the minority, Lass was not the only editor who wished to use the *Miscellany* to express her own opinions on world affairs. For the April 1938 issue of the *Vassar Quarterly*, Editor in Chief Vivian Liebman '38 penned some reflections of the *Miscellany's* last twenty years.[117] Her essay centered on "the old mirror question": should a college newspaper attempt to "mirror" campus opinion, or should it be shaped by the opinion of its Editorial Board? Should it limit its coverage to the Vassar campus, or should it look outward? In Liebman's words, "Should it be a follower or a leader?" In so many ways, these questions would haunt the paper throughout its history as new editors answered them in different ways. She knew her own answers: a college paper should reflect the opinions of its editors, not try to placate the opinions of the community, and should wield its staff editorial—its institutional voice—as a tool of shaping the College and society as a whole.

Through this lens, the graduating Liebman looked back on two decades of archives. She derided the first generation of *Weekly* editors who served during World War I between 1914 and 1918. Liebman believed that there was not nearly enough coverage or commenting on the War. "It may seem incredible to us today that in 1917, the College paper should not have seen fit to express its opinion on the War, on the advisability of America's entrance, or on the possibilities of peace," she wrote. Liebman did have a point. On the occasions that coverage entered the paper, it was usually kept to a column diminutively titled, "War in a Nut Shell."[118]The paper might have publicized student campaigns to raise money for the French Tuberculosis War Victims fund and the Red Cross, and wrote about Vassar women who traveled to Europe to lend a hand. But such pieces were generally short and lacking in substance. One of the few editorial comments on War policy was in answer to an alumna who had submitted a piece on the pacifists' efforts to end the conflict. The fairly conservative *Miscellany* editors dismissed this as "so typical of the collegiate tendency to stick to theory and avoid practical matters that it is amusing."[119] A 1918 editorial made the outward claim of interest in world affairs: "For a year and a half," it read, "every thought and activity has definitely been colored with the thought that we are at war." But there was a clear limit to the critical analysis that the paper gave to the War.

Liebman correctly attributed this lack of coverage to the editors' idea that the College newspaper should center only on the College and that it should have a fundamental respect for authority. Her analysis was probably accurate. Editors of the 1910s and 1920s felt that national news was beyond their scope, unless the news affected students. In terms of World War I, the *Miscellany* probably presented a fairly accurate "mirror" of campus opinion: it supported the war, but not excessively, and was generally uninterested and uninformed.

Liebman felt that her predecessors had taken the wrong approach to the "mirror problem" of the *Miscellany*. "Today, when the whole campus is speculating on European developments and [the Editorial Board] stays up far into the night working on an editorial that condemns Chamberlain's foreign policy, it may well be though amazing that during the World War a college newspaper never should have… doubted for a moment the complete validity of the Allied claims," she wrote.

Significantly, the generation of Lass and Liebman—who felt the need to extend their role as journalists but were constrained by Vassar's conservative leanings—was the first generation of *Miscellany* writers able to put their skills to professional use. Both women achieved great success as writers after college. Liebman rose through the ranks to become Editor in Chief of *Working Mother Magazine* and Vice President of the McCall Publishing Company. Lass's entry into writing was a bit more complicated. She had wanted to serve on her high school's paper, but was discouraged upon seeing that all of the editors were male. A feeling of terror filled her when she "tried out" for the *Miscellany* in September 1933, her freshman year. Lass and the other freshmen were assigned stories, and the older editors judged applicants' work without sympathy. She was thrilled with the high level of professionalism and immediately planned to make her career in journalism. Though women "were still not considered suitable for public writing," Lass was offered a prestigious job at *TIME Magazine* after her graduation. Women could not become reporters, but they could still function as researchers—"which meant that we did everything except get the byline," quipped Lass. She spent ten years at *TIME*, after which she traveled through Europe. There, she became fascinated with women's rights and published several books on the state of women in Sweden and Eastern Europe. She also wrote about the effects of poverty and

chapel

socialism on women. After receiving notoriety as women's advocate, the *Boston Globe* asked her to write a weekly column, a job that she happily accepted. "I really credit the *Miscellany* with my career," she said. "Working with those women who just took the job so seriously, even though their editorial voice was restricted… I saw that it was absolutely possible for female writers and editors to do work that was comparable to their male counterparts. Even if we were told something different when we went to look for jobs, it really helped me to know in the back of my mind that, you know what, I can do this job. I knew that because I *did it* already at Vassar."

The changing journalistic ideologies of editors like Lass and Liebman pushed the *Miscellany* in bolder and broader directions. Over time, the paper expanded its focus to comment on local, national and international events, and took increasingly liberal positions on political issues. This budding progressivism also affected the editors' stances on campus issues. Beginning in 1915, for example, the *Miscellany* complained about Vassar's policy of mandatory chapel attendance.[120] The editors "wistfully noted the abandonment" of such policies at other colleges, like Dartmouth and Yale. The paper offered many suggestions, including mandatory chapel attendance only every other week, or making attendance optional for juniors and seniors. But in addition to these practical solutions, the editors also made strong ideological appeals for greater religious freedom:

> Compulsory chapel is dogmatic, and narrow to a degree. In regard to the feeling of solidarity that is to be got from daily chapel service, we think solidarity is a valuable experience, but not one to be confused with the devotional idea of the services… Deep prayer does not always take place in public group setting. Worship is, and should be, the private business of students.[121]

When the Board of Trustees finally voted to make attendance optional in 1926, the *Miscellany* happily endorsed the decision, "which the majority of the College community welcomes as a broad-minded step."[122] A decade later, the editors of the *Miscellany* were among the first on campus to petition the faculty for an "opening of the curriculum"— that is, fewer requirements and more academic freedom for students to experiment with classes.[123] The *New York Times* picked up on the conflict between Vassar students and its faculty, and seemed to side with the newspaper, reporting that many of the College's curricular policies and requirements had remained unchanged since the school's founding in 1861.[124] As Liebman desired, the paper aspired to be a leader rather than a follower.

Progressivism or Radicalism?

Even as early as the 1920s, the paper's slow march toward progressivism worried some beyond Vassar's gates. Somewhat surprisingly, it aroused the concerns of the conservative Republican Vice President of the United States—and later the 30th President—John Calvin Coolidge. During the Red Scare that followed World War I, social tensions increased across the country. Americans feared that radicalism abroad, namely the Bolshevik Revolution of 1917, could sow the seeds for social disruption at home. The fear was manifested both inwardly and outwardly. In New York, for example, the state legislature expelled five of its elected members because they were members of the Socialist Party.[125] The legislature also passed a number of anti-sedition bills, restricting civil liberties in order to curtail "radical politics."

Coolidge penned a series of articles to the *Delineator* explaining the vulnerability of America's colleges to radicalism. *The Forbes Library (left) and the Mount Holyoke Libraries (right).*

Calvin Coolidge worried that Vassar students were spending their most formative years soaking their minds in radicalism. The progressivism of College President Henry Noble MacCracken—who supported such controversial practices as overseas cultural exchanges, religious pluralism and even experimental theater—was well known.[126] Coolidge feared that schools across the country were susceptible to intellectual deviants; Women's schools were of particular concern. Beginning in June 1921, he published a three-part series of articles on radicalism in women's colleges in the *Delineator*—one of America's most popular women's magazines for lifestyle, fashion and art.[127] His articles were aimed at the "mothers and mothers-to-be of America," with the hope of quelling the spread of "leftist" education. Coolidge used sentiments expressed in the *Miscellany* as a definitive proof of radicalism:

> *The spirit of this radical element is all too clearly expressed by a student in the* Miscellany News. *"I know what I am. I'm not an optimist. I'm not a pessimist. I'm just antagonistic." There one has it. That is not a sporadic incident of a sophomore conclusion… An examination of recent publications shows a friendly familiarity with that antagonistic attitude toward our institutions, and not without support by some faculty members, who permit its exercise under a cloak or claim of academic freedom.*

The very idea of "antagonism" annoyed the conservative Coolidge, who feared that liberal faculty members were helping to spread such rebellious ideas. In particular, he singled out an incident recorded in the *Miscellany* about faculty member Winifred Smith. An article in the paper recorded Smith's visit to Washington D.C. during the spring vacation in 1920. In Washington, she attended various Senate hearings and met with a Soviet ambassador. Smith was quoted in the paper to have been "quite favorably impressed" by the ambassador, and was "struck by his moderation and intelligence compared to the narrowness of some of the committee."[128] This sentiment enraged Coolidge, who concluded that Vassar's faculty was not only advocating "antagonistic" attitudes toward the United States government and its established policies, but was also inculcating students with these radical beliefs. The conservative Republican wrote harshly against this academic indoctrination:

> *Adherence to radical doctrines [like socialism] means the ultimate breaking down of the old sturdy virtues of manhood and womanhood, the insidious destruction of character, the weakening of the moral*

> *fiber of the individual, [and] the destruction of the foundations of civilization.*

In later articles in the *Delineator,* Coolidge explained his vision for women in fighting radicalism.[129] Women, he argued, are in the unique position as the nation's homemakers to champion "true" patriotism. Though his articles annoyed and frightened the liberal factions of many colleges and universities, including Vassar, they succeeded in inspiring the Daughters of the American Revolution to take a strong stance against radicalism in classrooms.[130] Whether contemporary Americans agree with his philosophies or not, Coolidge correctly identified the growing independence expressed in the pages of the *Miscellany.*

Politics Turn Further Outward

To Liebman's pleasure and Coolidge's misery, the *Miscellany's* gentle approach toward questioning authority and commenting on international issues began to change in the late 1920s. Students learned that they could not divorce themselves from world events. The paper became dedicated to pressing students to learn about current events, even assuring its readers that the Editorial Board would prefer that they devote their time to reading the *New York Times* rather than the *Miscellany.*[131] In 1922, the paper pushed students to form a political organization to generate interest and activism. Sure enough, the Political Association was formed. But even with this editorial nudging, the paper's content changed only slightly. Only one or two stories each week would mention affairs beyond the College's gates. Despite the latent liberalism on the Editorial Board and at the College during the 1920s, Vassar as a whole was fairly conservative and parochial. Students remained generally uninformed about world events, a condition fairly unchanged since World War I.[132] The students on the newspaper, as well as those in the Political Association, seemed to be the most interested and informed on campus. While letters to the editor focused almost exclusively on affairs of the College, editorials increasingly focused on national politics by the end of the decade. The Editorial Board clearly made a decided effort to foster global consciousness, even if the majority of students were interested mostly in local matters.

The factor that would shatter this Vassar bubble in the interwar period was the Great Depression of October 1929. At first, the paper did not even recognize the Depression in its editorial columns until December 1930. "It was only after we began to see that it was affecting people that we knew, our College, our families even, that we started inquiring and trying to find out what it really meant," read the staff editorial.[133] Beginning the next semester, the *Miscellany* began to interview faculty and students who were affected by the Depression. They investigated numerous angles to the Depression, including its effect on Poughkeepsie and on the finances of the College. When they found unnecessary expenditures at Vassar, the Editorial Board skillfully pointed fingers.

Vivian Liebman '38, an economics major, wrote a reflection of the student newspaper's scope and mission for the alumnae magazine. The *Vassar Quarterly*.

Vassar proms provide one such example. The proms were an "old and expensive" tradition at the College, costing thousands of dollars for the "luxurious hall rental, the band, taxis, flowers, [and] gowns."[134] The tradition began in 1915. Students and their male companions began the evening with a "grand march" into an extravagant dance hall led by Henry Noble MacCracken himself. But when it came time for the 1932 Junior Prom, the *Miscellany* editors railed against the ostentatious event. In a passionate editorial that angered many students, they argued that there was no justification for Vassar "to flaunt its extravagance in the face of a community which has learned the meaning of starvation."[135] The editorial continued:

> It is manifestly unessential to our well-being that we expose ourselves annually to the delights of Prom… Have we any right to go on fulfilling Hollywood's picture of the Vassar girl when it involves a greater expense than we have been willing to devote to organizations which are striving to alleviate the misery of every Main Street?

The editors argued that students and College officials should cancel the self-indulgent prom, partly to save money and partly out of respect for the surrounding Poughkeepsie community that had been hit hard by the Depression. Vassar, they asserted, had fallen behind other schools in eliminating "frivolity" from their routines. "Yale realized the necessity and eliminated its Derby Day celebrations; Williams has given up its fall house parties," they noted. "If we dispense with our proms [now], we shall not have the glory of the innovators, but if we do not we shall deserve the ultimate criticism of blindness and egotism."[136]

Criticism of the prom grew stronger over the course of the semester. The *Miscellany* ran four editorials attacking the insensitivity of those planning the party. In the face of these attacks, the prom organizers aimed for compromise: they would cut the price of the prom tickets by one-third and donate 50 cents from each ticket to aid the unemployed in the Poughkeepsie community. The *Miscellany* had effectively shifted College policy, though the paper continued to push for the cancelation of the prom entirely. Editors understood that their criticism reflected "a school of thought flourishing in this world debacle" that promoted a level of social responsibility that would have been alien to their predecessors in the 1920s.[137] As they wrote in November of 1932:

> The theme song of the school [should be] "make the younger generation aware of the unhappy world, the community of which they are a part," shatter the prejudices they inherit from their upper middle class relatives, shatter the eat-drink-and-be-merry-ness with which they pursue pleasure at proms and on weekends; make them see that they are dancing on the edge of a volcano; make them feel the next war, the 12 million unemployed, the race conflicts, the undernourished children... destroy their complacency, make them challenge the status quo.[138]

The prom of 1932 went on as scheduled, despite the objections of the *Miscellany*. But the severe criticism harkened a defiant shift away from apolitical student culture. In the wake of the Depression, the Board freely editorialized not just on local matters, but also on national economic plans. These editorials, unlike many earlier attempts at writing on national issues, seem to have been thoroughly researched. Many were written with just as much passion as editorials concerning relatively trivial Vassar matters.

According to Liebman, who served between 1934 and 1938, the

staff was often inspired by the investigative work their paper had done in the years before they arrived. "Ever since 1930, the *Misc* has been… trying to interpret things to the best of its abilities, and to point to what it considers solutions for some of the problems which the Great Depression brought," Liebman wrote. In other words, the Depression sparked the desire to think critically about local and global problems. No longer would the *Miscellany* hold back on analyzing a situation, offering its own opinions, and taking a blatantly antagonistic attitude toward the status quo.

In many ways, the situation was Coolidge's worst nightmare. Not only did the newspaper begin to think critically, but it also advocated fairly radical left-wing politics. As the Great Depression worsened, students grew increasingly interested in socialism. To many, it seemed like a natural response. For a short time, a number of students discussed "a new social order" as being the nation's only hope.[139] The Student League for Industrial Democracy was formed in 1932, and the *Miscellany News* gave this group its full support.[140] Socialism was certainly a presence at the College, as evidenced by the *Miscellany*'s 1932 polling of students about their preferred candidate in the general election. Socialist candidate Norman Thomas won 208 votes out of the 1,000-person student body. By the mid-1930s, barely an issue of the paper passed without an editorial attempting to solve some sort of national problem. "The *Misc* was definitely crusading—and crusading to the left," Liebman recalled. The student body as a whole, however, was not nearly so radical. The 1932 poll results also showed that the traditionally Republican Vassar students gave the conservative Herbert Hoover 563 votes, almost twice as many as they gave to the liberal Franklin Roosevelt. So while socialism and leftist politics might have been a presence on campus, the majority of students remained conservative. Regardless, the *Miscellany News* had abandoned the "mirror" approach to college journalism that sought to mimic the attitudes of the majority; instead, it declared that it would "not be a tool of propaganda, but a crusading newspaper."[141]

At least in its staff editorials, the Editorial Board was willing to write against the majority of student opinion. The paper certainly received letters arguing with their liberalism, but on the whole, these letters were surprisingly respectful. Students and faculty who wrote

example for today

opinionated submissions were willing to debate the *Miscellany* editors in a calm and sophisticated manner. Nowhere did administrators seem eager to shut the paper down, or to remove its left-leaning editors. Although the liberal paper must have raised eyebrows among more conservative alumnae and faculty, freedom of speech was maintained.

Perhaps this was because most of the paper, apart from the staff editorial, was fair and non-partisan. The majority of the coverage focused on affairs of the College. When they emphasized international and national news, editors ensured that the articles adroitly balanced liberal and conservative stances. Their efforts at political balance were noted in a 1936 *New York Times* article, which complimented the paper for keeping the student body abreast of world affairs. "The *Miscellany News* often devotes an entire page of each issue to political discussion," the *Times* lauded.[142] "Representation is accorded [equally] to Republican and Democratic [student] clubs, as well as to a left wing club that argues the merits of the Socialist and Communist platforms." With this "open discussion of politics," the *Miscellany* tried to "stimulate interest in... national elections." In that spirit, the paper partnered with the newspaper of Princeton University, the *Daily Princetonian*, to conduct a poll of American undergraduates prior to the 1936 presidential election. Under the direction of Editor in Chief Anna de Cormis '37, the *Miscellany* staff surveyed some 92 institutions—more than 80,000 students—and turned the results over to the *Times*.[143]

Without any question, the *Miscellany* was making a conscious effort to look outward. Although the socialist craze of the early 1930s had died down by the end of the decade, the paper did continue to crusade in other ways. According to Liebman, the 1938 staff fully realized that "students cannot escape the problems of war and economic security." The result was a fundamentally different newspaper—rather than simply listing calendar events and heralding the accomplishments of the faculty, the *Miscellany* began to challenge the student body to think critically about the world around them.

good balance. Today

98 "*Misc* Then," The *Vassar Miscellany News*, October 9, 1940.

99 "Looking Back," The *Vassar Miscellany News*, October 9, 1940.

100 Elizabeth Daniels, Bridges to the World: Henry Noble MacCracken and Vassar College, (Clifton Corners: College Avenue Press, 1994), p. 12.

101 Elizabeth Daniels, Vassar Proms, Elizabeth Daniels, 2004. http://vcencyclopedia. vassar.edu/index.php/Vassar_Proms (accessed December 29, 2008).

102 Maya Peraza-Baker, The Telephone, edited by Elizabeth Daniels, 2006. http:// vcencyclopedia.vassar.edu/index.php/The_Telephone (accessed April 12, 2008).

103 I surmise this by comparing *Miscellany* articles about similar subject areas written before and after the proliferation of the telephone. For example, consider "A New Council Takes Office" from April 7, 1914 and "The Fairgrounds Are Up" from May 1, 1917. Both articles deal with public events in the Poughkeepsie community, yet the 1917 article includes quotes from three local residents. The 1914 article merely summarizes an article that had been printed in a local paper several days earlier, and does not include any original quotations. This general pattern of quoting more sources from outside of Vassar seems to be correlated with the expanded availability of telephones at the College.

104 An Old Need Answered By a New Opportunity," The *Vassar Miscellany News* Supplement," February 6, 1914.

105 Sarah Riane Harper, The *Miscellany Monthly*, edited by Elizabeth A. Daniels, 2006. http://vcencyclopedia.vassar.edu/index.php/The_*Miscellany*_Monthly (accessed April 8, 2008).

106 "An Old Need Answered By a New Opportunity," The *Vassar Miscellany News* Supplement, February 6, 1914.

107 "Bylaws," The *Miscellany News*, 2008.

108 When the Weekly first began in February 1914, the staff was unable to accomplish one of their objectives—to send the paper out to all of Vassar's alumnae each week. The venture was too expensive, according to Business Manager Frances Skinner '16, who wrote a small apology note in a March 1914 issue. However, by the subsequent autumn, the Business Board had applied for a second class mailing permit for the Weekly allowing the editors to send the paper out through inexpensive mass mailings. They were able to mail the paper to hundreds of graduates during the 1914-15 academic year. They soon began charging for the paper, just like the Monthly had done for decades. The next fall, Skinner proudly declared that more alumnae subscribed to the Weekly than to the Monthly.

109 Harper's use of the phrase "sister papers" is interesting. After 1914, it seems as if the Editorial Boards of the Weekly and Monthly were sisters more in theory than in practice. Since all alumnae from this period are now deceased, it is impossible to know exactly how much the editors of the literary magazine and the newspaper held discussions or worked together on long-term projects. Even if they did meet regularly, it is not entirely clear how the two Boards could productively work together on much of anything, given the radically different natures of their publications.

110 To reiterate, the official title at this point was The *Vassar Miscellany News*. Yet editors, students, faculty, and alumnae in the *Vassar Quarterly* referred to it as the Weekly until the mid-1920s. Most likely, the community was simply accustomed to thinking of the *Miscellany* as a monthly literary publication. As a result, the "new" weekly publication was labeled differently in the minds of most Vassarions.

111 Charles Franklin Thwing, "College Journalism," *Scribners Monthly: An Illustrated Magazine for the People*, October 1878: p. 809.

112 Charles Franklin Thwing, "College Journalism," *Scribners Monthly: An Illustrated Magazine for the People*, October 1878: p. 811.

113 Mary Mallon, "The *Vassar Miscellany*." The *Vassar Miscellany Monthly*, April, 1915, p. 130.

114 "Where the Weekly Fails," The *Vassar Miscellany* Weekly, May 14, 1920.

115 "Vassar Press Upheaves," The *Vassar Miscellany News*, March 23, 1923.

116 Based on counting articles contained in the first three issues of the 1920-1921 academic year. I found no cases where articles took a Vassar angle on a national or international event; in all cases, the story was either about the College or about the world at large, with very relatively few fitting into the second category.

117 Vivian Liebman, "The *Miscellany News*, 1918-1938," The *Vassar Quarterly*, April, 1938.

118 "War in a Nut Shell," The *Vassar Miscellany News*, February 17, 1917.

119 "Editorial," The *Vassar Miscellany News*, February 17, 1917.

120 The College had never professed to be a religiously affiliated institution, but Vassar, like most American colleges of the nineteenth century, included strong elements of Christianity from the start. The first three presidents were ministers, giving regular services to the student body. Diaries and letters from the earliest Vassar students show that many found the services increasingly tedious by the 1910s. The 1920s brought with them a liberalization of social life; students and faculty alike began to recognize that compulsory attendance in religious services was more likely to turn off individuals from religion than convert them. There was also growing recognition that not all Vassar students worshipped in the same way. Of course, much of this early dialogue focused on Catholicism and Judaism, though there were also small numbers of Buddhist and Muslim students.

121 "Compulsory Chapel Again," The *Vassar Miscellany* Weekly, November 5, 1915.

122 "Editorial," The *Vassar Miscellany* Weekly, December 10, 1926.

123 "Editorial," The *Vassar Miscellany News*, May 4, 1936.

124 "Curricular differences in New York women's college," The *New York Times*, March 9, 1936.

125 David Colburn, "Govenor Alfred E. Smith and the Red Scare, 1919-20," *Political Science Quarterly*, September 1973.

126 Elizabeth Daniels, *Bridges to the World: Henry Noble MacCracken and Vassar College*, (Clifton Corners: College Avenue Press, 1994), p. 162-63.

127 Calvin Coolidge, "Enemies of the Republic: Are the 'Reds' Stalking Our College Women?" The Delineator, June 1921: p. 4-5, 66-67.

128 "Smith Heads to Capital," The *Vassar Miscellany News*, March 29, 1920.

129 Coolidge famously had trouble communicating with both women and liberals, and was known for his conservative family values that ignored the social currents of the Progressive Era and Roaring Twenties. He was also known for his poor conversational abilities and quiet demeanor. According to one popular legend, Coolidge once sat next to the left-wing writer Dorothy Parker at a dinner party. "Mr. Coolidge, I've made a bet against a fellow who said it was impossible to get more than two words out of you," nudged Parker. Coolidge momentarily looked up from his dinner plate and gently replied, "You lose."

130 Kim Nielsen, *Un-American Womanhood: Antiradicalism, Antifeminism and the First Red Scare,* (Cleveland: Ohio State University Press, 2001), p. 34.

131 "Editorial," The *Vassar Miscellany News*, May 11, 1922.

132 Based on interviews with alumnae from the 1930s and early 1940s, who universally recall hearing that Vassar in the 1920s was socially conservative and inwardly focused. From its founding, Vassar has developed a fascinating political history. Its first students came from largely conservative families, yet they participated in one of the 19th century's most progressive causes—women's education. Between the founding of the College and coeducation, the student body was at once progressive and conservative, depending on the year and the issue. After coeducation, Vassar students became overwhelmingly liberal or moderate.

133 "Editorial," The *Vassar Miscellany News*, December 2, 1930.

134 Robert Cohen, *When the Old Left was Young: Student Radicals and America's First Mass Student Movement, 1929-1941*, (New York: Oxford University Press, 1993), p. 20.

135 "Editorial," The *Vassar Miscellany News*, November 2, 1932.

136 *Ibid.*

137 Robert Cohen, *When the Old Left was Young: Student Radicals and America's First Mass Student Movement, 1929-1941*, (New York: Oxford University Press, 1993), p. 21.

138 "Editorial," The *Vassar Miscellany News*, November 2, 1932.

Covering the Campus

139   "Students Engage with Economy," The *Vassar Miscellany News*, March 3, 1931.

140   "Editorial," The *Vassar Miscellany News*, November 21, 1932.

141   Vivian Liebman, "The *Miscellany News*, 1918-1938," The *Vassar Quarterly*, April, 1938.

142   "Vassar Interest Lags in Politics," The *New York Times*, October 18, 1936.

143   "Princeton Closes Poll of Colleges," The *New York Times*, October 30, 1936.

Chapter Three:
The Campus Voice, 1938-1968

Evidently, Vassar students enjoyed the challenge. It is no exaggeration to say that the *Miscellany News* was more admired and more widely read in the 30 years between 1938 and 1968 than at any time before. Although the length held fairly steady at 12 pages each week, it garnered increasing amounts of attention from students, administrators and outsiders.

This interest can be measured by the number of opinionated submissions to the paper. Since the 1870s, the *Miscellany* printed letters to the editor. In the earlier days, these "letters" were usually short paragraphs praising a particular campus event or conveying a humorous anecdote about student life. With the advent of weekly publication, the 1910s and 1920s saw longer, more pointed letters—letters that were often critical of the College or *Miscellany* coverage. But beginning in the late 1930s, students put pen to paper at a record rate, sending in more letters than ever before.

Letters to the editor are a useful historical indicator. Objectively, they indicate that students are reading and responding to events covered in the newspaper—a sign that the paper is read and respected as a forum. Subjectively, a high number of letters tends to correlate with the overall quality of the *Miscellany*. Obviously, 'quality' cannot be quantified numerically, but it *can* be described. Issues of the *Miscellany* from the 1930s through the 1960s, from the 1990s, and since 2004 are the most professional in appearance. The writing is more engaging, the formatting is cleaner and there are fewer typographical errors. Issues from the early 1970s, by contrast—a period with a marked decline in letters to the editor—saw numerous spelling and grammar errors, sloppy formatting and shoddy reporting.

The following chart and table show the average number of letters printed per moth since February 1914.

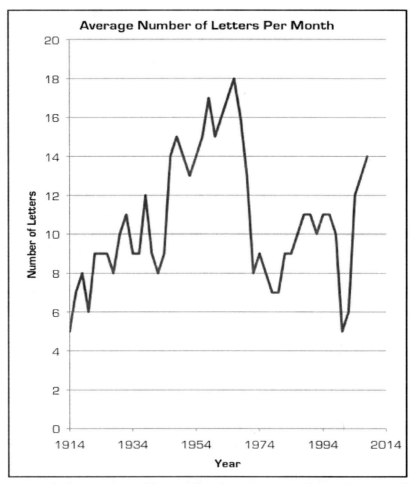

Between the late 1930s and late 1960s, the paper printed more letters to the editor than it ever had before or since. On the whole, these letters were longer, sharper and more substantive than those from earlier periods.

Year	Average Number of Letters Per Month
1914	5
1916	7
1918	8
1920	6
1922	9
1924	9
1926	9
1928	8
1930	10
1932	11
1934	9
1936	9
1938	12
1940	9
1942	8
1944	9
1946	14
1948	15
1950	14
1952	13
1954	14
1956	15
1958	17
1960	15
1962	16
1964	17
1966	18
1968	16
1970	10
1972	6
1974	8
1976	8
1978	7
1980	7
1982	9
1984	9
1986	10
1988	11
1990	11
1992	10
1994	11
1996	11
1998	10
2000	5
2002	6
2004	12
2006	13
2008	14

The year 1930 saw a record average of 10 letters per month.[144] By 1938, that number jumped to 12, and by 1968 it stood at 16. In the 50 years since, no monthly average has been that high.

Boosted Quality, Popularity and Legacy

Contributing to the paper's improvements in spelling, writing and layout was the shift back to a weekly from biweekly. The paper had been biweekly since 1917, distributed on Wednesdays and Saturdays. This changed in 1942. "In the strains of the three-year plan, it has thankfully become a weekly again," wrote the *Vassarion*, Vassar's yearbook.[145] The three-year plan, an accelerated graduation schedule during World War II, allowed students to graduate in only three years, so that they could enter the work force and aid Allied efforts. Though this plan meant frequent changes in editors, it also allowed editors to concentrate on longer issues with more in-depth coverage, rather than having to split their time and energy between two issues each week. This increase in quality likely drew more readers to the *Miscellany*.

On many fronts, the *Miscellany* was growing—in pages, in popularity, and even in office space. In 1940, the paper expanded its cramped corner office in the Students' Building to include a large storage room. Previously, the office has been cluttered and "paper-strewn," as one editor described it. The extra space was used to organize and hold the paper's archives. For the first time since Mary Mallon, there was a renewed attention among editors to the paper's legacy. In April 1940, the *Miscellany* published a lengthy article entitled "Miscellany Newsiana," which gave readers a brief sketch of the paper's past and future.[146] Although several facts seem distorted (including their characterization of the *Transcript* and their perception of the growing size of the Editorial Board over time), the article proves that these editors had an eye toward legacy. This went beyond a rudimentary history of the paper; editors claimed to be "surrounded by the ghosts of the past." They kept shelves of old issues from the "dirty thirties," and engraved the names of former editors into the newsroom's oak conference table. The table could not have held many names, since the Students' Building was only completed in 1913—almost fifty years after the paper's founding. Nevertheless, editors from the 1940s describe their deep sense of "writing Vassar's history." Continuous leadership was also important. Editors in Chief during this period tended to serve two, sometimes three semesters. This continuity ensured institutional memory and imbued the staff of the *Miscellany* with acute awareness of the past, and of their own role in recording history.

Miscellany Goes to War: Increasing Liberalism and Globalism

Beyond Vassar's history, editors during this period wrote about the *nation's* history. As Vivian Liebman had seen, students became increasingly cognizant of the world around them in the 1930s, a feeling that intensified in the 1940s. Socio-political issues began to overtake the paper following the Great Depression, but the beginning of World War II brought politics to center stage. Barbara Muhs Walker '48, who wrote occasional news articles for the paper between 1945 and 1948, drew editorial cartoons to print along side staff editorials. "I drew all sorts of political images," she said. "One cartoon showed the destruction that occurred in South Africa under Apartheid, and another showed a man and woman doing the same job for different salaries." The *Miscellany's* somewhat liberal and progressive perspective became radically more pronounced. Walker also helped to write an editorial supporting the Progressive Party candidate Henry Wallace in his 1948 presidential bid. Wallace had very left-wing leanings, supporting unprecedented legislation to give African Americans new opportunities for education and employment. Though the Editorial Board eventually endorsed the Republican Thomas Dewey, several conflicting editorials over the course of the fall semester suggested that a number of editors had strong leftist leanings.

As a freshman, Jeannette Hopkins '44 remembers being labeled by the seniors as a "writer to watch," and soon found herself "drawn into various bull sessions with some very radical editors."[147] Many of them, she recalls, were members of the Activist Students Union. Some sought to defy the College administration, Hopkins recalled, because of their anti-authoritarian ideology. Hopkins herself would soon adopt this attitude. For example, President Henry Noble MacCracken had a deep fear of student suicide during the war. "He admonished me as Editor to submit any poem or story about suicide to the College Physician," she remembered, noting that such a poem had recently been published in the *Vassar Brew*, and the author took her own life the next summer. "MacCracken feared a contagion of such events as he told me there had been on the campus in World War I," said Hopkins. "I regarded it as censorship and planned to disobey, but was rather disappointed when no similar writing by a student was submitted." Nevertheless, the fact that Hopkins entertained the thought of disobeying a direct request from MacCracken demonstrates the growing radicalism on the newspaper.

The War created much agitation at the College. Much was in flux, from the accelerated graduation schedule of two commencements each year, to the constant news of violence. The fighting in Europe resulted in the deaths of many Vassar parents, as well as the fiancés of numerous students. Hopkins recalls having her birthday party in Main Building on December 7 when news of the Pearl Harbor attack came over the radio and interrupted the music. One of the women at the party later discovered that she had lost her boyfriend, who was stationed in Hawaii. Life after Vassar was also in flux during the War. While many women had previously started families soon following graduation, the College instead encouraged graduates to serve their country. Before attending the Columbia School of Journalism, Hopkins was encouraged to take a job at a military technology facility in Camden, New Jersey guarding the radar instruction manuals.

The *Miscellany* reported and editorialized vigorously on developments in Europe. Between 1943 and 1945, the front pages were replete with accounts of battles, military strategies and Vassar students volunteering to lend a hand. In its editorials, the paper followed a traditionally liberal course in virtually every area. It encouraged wartime economic spending by the Federal government, which dramatically increased employment; in 1940, there were eight million Americans unemployed. By 1941, the *Miscellany* pointed out that unemployment was almost eradicated. Though some conservatives continued to attack New Deal policies, job growth during the War helped to assuage these concerns. As a result of the increased demand for labor, more women entered the workforce, taking industrial jobs that had once been reserved for men. "Rosie the Riveter," reprinted beside one staff editorial, became a popular American icon. By 1945, women made up 36 percent of the nation's total workforce, and the *Miscellany* continually pushed Vassar women to "ensure that this happy trend remains upward."[148] The paper also encouraged the creation of the United Nations as a forum for international dialogue. A 1943 editorial asserted that the "common meeting of nations is the best, maybe the only, sure method of keeping a permanent peace."[149] Peace was certainly a paramount concern of the paper, as the editors put forth countless editorials advocating different models and methods of settling the global conflict.

When students returned to campus in Fall 1945, the War had been brought to a close. The Senate had ratified the United Nations Charter, and the world seemed to have returned to normalcy. The Editorial Board's highly regarded September 6, 1945 editorial "Ruins and Visions" provided a pensive and provocative take on the relationship between the recent international violence and the "shielded peace" of academia.[150] "The world did not stop for [our] two months vacation," the editors wrote in an editorial that was republished in the *Poughkeepsie Journal* and quoted in the *Harvard Crimson* and the *New York Times*. "In our eight weeks away, the earth underwent changes at atomic speed. We return to a world at peace. Education is a weapon for good and for action. The events of summer '45 affect our lives at Vassar and increase the responsibility we have as members of an enlightened community to participate in shaping the future." In an eloquent editorial that bridged Vassar to the world at large, the editors described the importance of education in ensuring a peaceful global future. With the end of the War, women should not stop participating in democracy. Vassar should continue to produce "active citizens," just as the administration had encouraged for the past five years.

Further, the editors weaved the *Miscellany* itself into the process of building sustainable peace. "We hope to stimulate thought and constructive action in the student body through the pages of the *Miscellany* by considering vital current problems," they wrote in their first issue of the school year. "We welcome the class of '48 and invite them to make use of our Public Opinion columns to air their views on any world or Vassar topic. We hope they will find Vassar an able training ground for world citizenship." The *Miscellany* proudly proclaimed its role as a forum for dialogue on any topic, national or local. "Whereas previous letters to the editor and editorials had argued one position or another, there was never any sort of reasoning behind it all," said Hopkins. "I think the War made us realize the importance of conversation. It made student editors realize the value of writing... and using words to make arguments. Did we believe that we could end violence through writing? No. But I think we did *want* to believe that, and just that belief made our jobs as moderators of the written dialogue all the more significant."

Editorial

"Let us go on record . . ."

Anne Cleveland, Vassar: A Second Glance

Indeed, the *Miscellany* strived to facilitate conversation on a variety of thorny issues during the 1940s. Race was one such topic. Race was a hotly contested facet of American society after the War, particularly in secondary and higher education. At Vassar, this was the first decade that black students were permitted to enroll. Anita Hemmings, the school's first black student, earned her degree in 1897 only because administrators believed that she was white.[151] In the early 1940s, Vassar became the last of the Seven Sister colleges to admit African Americans. Even then, only a token number were taken, and there are few records on how well these students were integrated into social activities.

Obviously, racial tension was not limited to blacks and whites in the United States. Because of the ongoing War, Japanese Americans were subjected to incredible prejudice. In February 1942, President

Franklin Roosevelt ordered Japanese Americans and immigrants of Japanese descent to be exiled to "relocation centers." At the time, the *Miscellany* did not take a stand on the issue, although the majority of the patriotic student body likely never considered the policy from a human rights perspective. This would change later that year.

In April, famed civil rights activist W.E.B. Du Bois came to Vassar to deliver a passionate lecture on "the global color line and internal and external imperialist racial oppression."[152] Though he was known mostly for his ideas on Pan-Africanism, his speech touched on oppression and segregation more broadly. He also sat for an extensive interview with the *Miscellany*. In this interview, Du Bois noted that Vassar was "very fortunate" to have a handful black students, but he challenged the College to admit 100 black students, about 10 percent of its student body.[153]

Pinar Batur, an Associate Professor of Sociology at Vassar, found that Du Bois had a remarkable influence on the paper's editors. While he was on campus, the College was celebrating its annual Founder's Day—"a day of community celebration, sports, and leisure activities."[154] One of the activities was a booth in which students could "heave darts at a caricature of a presumed Japanese head," a game that the organizing committee had called "Slap a Jap." The committee hoped that this game would foster patriotism and encourage students to purchase of War Savings Stamps.

The Editorial Board sharply condemned this activity the very next day, though some students had simply rationalized that "this kind of advertising was taking place all over the country and the Japs probably did worse things."[155] Acknowledging Du Bois's speech and his "position regarding American democracy," the editorial asserted that "the vast majority of people follow their leader in their thinking, and the leader in this case is race prejudice and hatred." They challenged Vassar students to consider the words of Du Bois, posing the question that, "Perhaps it is impossible really to practice democracy, or isn't this a test case?"

From that point on, the *Miscellany News* continually pushed the College to commit to quantitative racial diversity and qualitative tolerance. In 1947, the paper urged the Admissions Office to redesign its publications to "discourage the stereotype of Vassar as a rich girls' college or finishing school."[156] Editors noted that because of these images, "potential students who are graduated from public schools, or… require scholarship assistance, are often reluctant to apply to Vassar. Members of minority groups—particularly Negroes—may shy away from the College for the same reasons." The next year, the editors blasted the apathetic attitude of students toward racism, and further encouraged the College to admit black students and set up "exchange programs with Southern Negro schools such that we can promote a fuller and more inclusive community."[157] They seemed to take Du Bois' message of inclusion to heart.

As Hopkins said, the editors truly realized the importance of their newspaper as a means of beginning difficult conversations. Although many editorials of this period were concerned purely with international affairs, others drew analytical, intricate connections between Vassar and the world at large.

The Battle for the Hearts and Minds

In the 150-year history of the *Miscellany*, the paper has rarely faced serious competition. Occasionally, other student publications have popped up, generally with significantly smaller staffs, budgets and circulations. Most have aimed at specific demographics or interests; a monthly music magazine appeared in the 1950s, for example, and several feminist publications went in and out of circulation between the 1970s and 1990s. All of these were generally short-lived and rarely attempted to replace the *Miscellany* as the campus's primary source of news and opinion writing—except for one.

The *Vassar Chronicle* first appeared on March 1, 1944. It would enter into a decade-long competition with the *Miscellany* that divided the College between the two rivals. Founded by Mariajane Clarke, Phyllis Safarik and Audrey Talmage, all former editors of the *Miscellany* and members of the Class of 1945, the *Chronicle* considered Vassar's student newspaper too liberal. Although the editors would outwardly deny any conservative bias, *Miscellany* alumnae/i from the 1940s and 1950s remember their competitor as being politically reactionary and generally more loyal to the College administration. The student body at the time was ideologically split, divided between liberals and conservatives. Many liberal students were offended by the *Chronicle*'s presentation of news. The paper responded to these concerns in an defensive editorial. "Endless rumors have come to our ears… that we are reactionary, anti-Semitic, backed financially by the administration, and… commissioned by the officers of the Students' Association."[158] Yet the editors could "only laugh" at these suggestions, and continued writing with the "highest journalistic standards."

The *Miscellany*, known for its generally progressive politics, was a natural opponent to the *Chronicle*. The two papers often printed opposing editorials within a given week.[159] The *Miscellany* came out on Wednesdays and the *Chronicle* on Saturdays, giving their respective editorial boards a chance to respond to one another. Often, they took dramatically different views of College policies. Generally, the *Miscellany* was far more critical of the Vassar administration and the student government, while the *Chronicle* tended to agree with their decisions. These loyal and radical leanings played out on an international scale.

A clear example of this conflict came at the beginning of the Cold War in a debate between the two papers over the Truman Doctrine. In May 1947, the *Chronicle* strongly backed the Doctrine, which stated that the United States would economically and militarily support Greece and Turkey in order to prevent their falling under Soviet control.[160] This strategy would epitomize American foreign policy during the Cold War. The *Chronicle* drew a hard ideological distinction between "Russian Communism" and "American Capitalism"; the *Miscellany* argued for a more nuanced understanding of the situation, asserting that it was imperative to separate "theoretical political systems and the contemporary situations existing in states." Indeed, the *Miscellany* took a hard stand against the Truman Doctrine, prophetically identifying it as the beginning of a slippery slope of conflict:

> The Truman Doctrine, as it was passed by the nation's legislatures, is a direct violation of the highest political and ethical principles that the American people and their government hold. Instead of promoting one world at peace with itself, this policy would create two worlds in a vacuum, each suspicious and fearful of the other disregarding the rights of smaller nations and using them as tools against each other.[161]

While the *Chronicle* happily argued that the Doctrine would "spread our influence" and instill American values abroad, the *Miscellany* condemned that it would "only further America's capitalist agenda… and do nothing to heal the wounds of the world." Instead of the Truman Doctrine and the Marshall Plan, the editors argued that European recovery should be sponsored by the United Nations rather than the United States.[162]

On international issues, the ideological divide was clear. The same distinction was true on the national level: the *Miscellany* tended to endorse Democratic candidates whereas the *Chronicle* tended to endorse Republican candidates.

The rivalry between the two papers seemed to play out more between the two editorial boards than anyone else. College Historian Elizabeth Daniels '41 recalls that most students looked at both papers each week, not paying much attention to the brand. If there was a competition, the *Miscellany* certainly had a significant advantage in budget and reputation. Yet the *Chronicle* had the advantage of newness. Given the conservative leanings of the student body, the paper also gained popularity by its political ideologies. "We certainly were the liberal paper and the *Chronicle* was the conservative paper," recalled Nancy Alderman Ransom '50. "The positions the papers took on politics and social issues reflected the differences, but I don't think the student body thought too much about that."

The relationship between the two papers was thus rather strange. Although ostensible rivals, both papers seemed to be read equally by students—a fact that annoyed *Miscellany* editors to no end. For years, the two editorial boards began an odd love-hate relationship. Right after publishing directly opposing editorials, the two papers would collaborate on stories, share reporters and even publish joint issues to investigate a particular topic. The first of these joint issues occurred on April 8, 1948. The *Chronicle* and *Miscellany* worked together to examine the proposal for the so-called five-day scheduling plan. This controversial plan would have changed the scheduling of classes and disrupted many student internships. The editorial boards jointly critiqued the idea as "ill-founded" and "detrimental to our education."[163]

The two papers worked together on several more issues during the early 1950s, and over time the *Chronicle*'s conservative bias had disappeared. This was likely because of an increasingly liberal student body; as editors graduated, they were replaced with younger students who, according to school-wide *Miscellany* polls, increasingly identified with the Democratic Party.[164] The rivalry between the papers, which began "during the War when every local and national problem was crucial and highly debatable," now seemed unnecessary.[165] Vassar's two newspapers looked increasingly alike. An examination of the two papers reveals similar headlines, top stories and editorial topics.

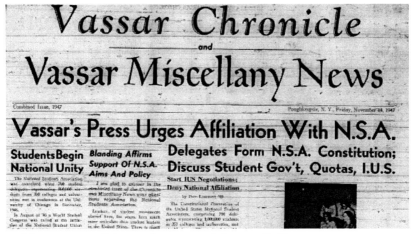

The papers collaborated on several issues, finding a common cause to champion or examine. In this case from November 14, 1947, both the *Chronicle* and *Miscellany* advocated that Vassar join the National Students' Association, a confederation of American college students.

These growing similarities raised questions about duplication from students and administrators alike. In 1959, College President Sarah Gibson Blanding's Coordinating Committee on Educational Policy recommended that the two papers be consolidated to save money and resources. The Committee suggested that the large number of students interested in journalism might benefit from working together on a single, well-edited publication. And so the merger debate began.

On February 7, 1959, a *Chronicle* editorial entitled "As We View the *Misc*" and another the following week called "The *Misc* and We" took the bold step of advocating a full merger. "The dissemination of good news and superb journalism should be our ideal," the editors wrote.[166] "We could [accomplish] this in a more mature way if we could put aside our differences and combine our two journalistic efforts." The *Chronicle*'s goals seemed earnest—to join forces to create a longer and more incisive weekly paper. The *Chronicle* then extended its invitation to meet with *Miscellany* editors and hash out their differences.

The *Miscellany News* wanted no part of it. Still bitter about having a competitor publication, the editors bristled at the idea of abandoning their legacy and acknowledging the equality of their rival. Occasionally writing alongside the competing editors was one thing; merging was quite another. The *Miscellany* editors publicly denied the request for a meeting and claimed that the *Chronicle* only wanted a merger to save face, alleging that their revenue was shrinking and their debt was climbing. They had to either merge or fold, the *Miscellany* argued. They also pointed out that the *Chronicle* abided by fundamentally different journalistic practices—their staff editorial, for example, was based on the unanimous opinion of its Editorial Board rather than on a two-thirds majority opinion. "The *Miscellany News* does not believe that a paper is read strictly for its news coverage," the *Miscellany* wrote on February 11.[167] "We have always believed that a paper... owes to its readers a definite personality, an editorial identity. We believe that we have such an identity." For another carefully crafted 800 words, the *Miscellany* defended its editorial policy and the value of its individual identity. Although their arguments about different editorial policies were passionately presented, they seem to be only rationalizations for avoiding the merger. More likely, the *Miscellany* editors simply did not want to abandon their paper's century-long legacy and prized place as Vassar's newspaper of record, especially to a relative newcomer.

But the *Miscellany*'s early refusal did not stop the vigorous deliberation. Arguments for and against the merger sparked a fierce campus debate for months. Letters flowed into both publications; some claimed that the *Chronicle* should fold, others claimed that the *Miscellany* should fold, and others pushed for a merger under a new name. Few, however, maintained that the two papers should continue side by side. It seemed as if the College community desired a single, high quality paper. Since the *Miscellany* had much deeper roots than the 15 year-old *Chronicle*, most letters expressed a hope that the more traditional newspaper would win the day.

After the brutal semester-long debate was complete, the *Chronicle* finally agreed to heed the majority opinion of the campus and cease publication. Its final issue was published on May 19, 1959, and included a letter from College Warden Elizabeth Drouilhet vouching that their publication was actually in fine financial health, "putting an end to rumors of financial insecurity" that seem to have been falsely propagated by the *Miscellany*.

Nevertheless, *Miscellany* editors rejoiced. Certainly other student publications popped up now and again over the 20th century—but none were as worthy competitors as the *Chronicle* had been. After a half-hearted publication called *Verbatim* debuted in 1964, one student wrote to the

Miscellany, "Congratulations! You've never looked so good as when you came out the day after *Verbatim*."[168] In the battle against the greatest threat to its supremacy, the Editorial Board emerged victorious.

Divided Politics of the 1948 Presidential Election

The *Miscellany* editors might have been more liberal than their counterparts on the *Chronicle* in the late 1940s, but like all of Vassar, the Board's politics were decidedly mixed. A case in point was the vigorous debate surrounding the 1948 national election. Since 1916, the paper had endorsed presidential candidates in the primary and general elections (see Chapter 7, "Change and Continuity Over Time"). When there were multiple compelling candidates for a particular party, the Board often gave its advice—despite the fact that the voting age at the time was 21, meaning that almost all Vassar students were unable to vote. Although many editors supported the candidacy of the independent progressive Henry Wallace, there were large dissenting factions who argued for Democrat Harry Truman. "Although in general the *Misc* Editorial Board is in accord on basic progressive principles," the editors wrote, "we have not reached a unanimous decision."[169] The group was unable to come to a vote by a two-thirds majority—the minimum requirement for a staff editorial topic to be selected. "The divergence of opinion is enough to publish [two] editorials," they determined.

Thus, in a two-page special feature, the editors penned two separate editorials, one supporting Wallace and the other supporting Truman. Each editorial picked apart the arguments of the other, analyzing national issues from either a liberal or a moderate position. Those who supported Wallace asserted that the Democrats had failed to devise an "adequately liberal" platform.[170] As such, "the only way for a liberal vote to express itself was through an independent candidate." Condemning the Democratic Party for being overly moderate, this group did not "think that Truman's domestic or foreign policy is sufficiently different from that of the Republican Party to warrant supporting him as the lesser of two evils." Wallace, they argued, understood the housing needs of the poor, and would stand behind workers. They also condemned Truman's foreign policy, "supported by both parties," of reacting against Russian communism through pawn countries like Greece and Korea.

Wallace, these editors believed, would "unify the world rather than divide it."

The group who supported Truman's bid for the presidency argued that Wallace was too leftist to be taken seriously. "Wallace's [only accomplishment] will be succeeding in getting the liberals laughed at and not listened to," they wrote.[171] "The *Miscellany News* has always stood for liberal ideas… [and has come] out against discrimination and subjugation… but Wallace is simply too antagonistic and radical." There was a clear divide among the editors—and a divide between the Editorial Board and the rest of the College.

The week after the two editorials ran, the *Miscellany* published a lengthy poll of students' political opinions. The student body rejected both Truman and Wallace. Of the 862 who responded, only 16 said that they might consider an independent progressive candidate. 375 said that they would prefer a Democrat, while 467 hoped for a Republican. A majority of the student body said that, if the election were held that day, they would vote for the conservative Thomas Dewey. Many wrote letters published in that same issue, complaining that some of the "leftist" editors would support a "nutty and dangerous" candidate like Wallace. "Frankly, I am shocked to find that educated people would even consider supporting a man as incompetent as Wallace for the presidency," wrote an unnamed student living in Main Building. A student from Cushing House concurred: "I can't understand why there is such emphasis being placed on Wallace. It seems to me that he… is being supported only by a handful of irresponsible radicals." Some even claimed that the newspaper's poll was unfair, since it asked more questions about students' attitudes toward Truman and Wallace than toward the possible Republican candidates. "It is quite evident from the superfluity of questions about [leftist candidates] that the *Miscellany News* is dominated by a large faction of liberals who are trying desperately to dominate Vassar's political status," accused a student living in Davison House. "Is this action to be considered fair?" In a note directly below this comment, the editors declared "Liberal? Yes! Dominating? No!" But although they denied biased coverage, it is significant that the editors so boldly declared their liberalism.

This liberalism caught the attention of the man who would become the most highly regarded conservative thinker of the 20th century—

William F. Buckley Jr. At the time, Buckley was an undergraduate student at Yale University and Editor in Chief of the *Yale Daily News*. After his sister, a Vassar student, told him of the *Miscellany*'s advocacy of Truman and Wallace, Buckley and his roommate Brent Bozell wrote tersely to the editor:

TO THE EDITOR IN CHIEF:

RESPECTFULLY REQUEST OPPORTUNITY TO DEBATE WITH YOU AND ASSOCIATE ON WALLACE AS A CANDIDATE FOR PRESIDENT. FEEL YOUR BLURB IN *MISC* WAS NAÏVE IF INTENDED SERIOUSLY. IF IT WAS ALL A BIG JOKE, APOLOGIES AND CONGRATULATIONS ON SUBTLE HUMOR.

The shorthanded style and biting tone would become Buckley's hallmark throughout his career as a conservative author and commentator. On March 18, 1948, *Miscellany* editors Marilyn Lammert '49 and Constance Mann '50 took the Yale boys up on their challenge, travelling to New Haven for a well-publicized debate with Buckley and Bozell. Vassar's famed English professor Winifred Smith tagged along to watch. The next week, after returning to Vassar, Smith wrote a letter to the *Miscellany* congratulating the editors on their performance. "Your editors had assembled a number of pertinent facts about Mr. Wallace and his platform and presented them directly, honestly and most sincerely," lauded Smith.[172] "The Yale boys had not bothered to go behind the accusations of communism hurled at Mr. Wallace... by the Un-American Activities Committee and other anti-New Deal organs." Smith argued that Buckley and Bozell had only succeeded on "propaganda techniques of speech and manner," noting that their voices were clear and passionate, and their rhetoric included the occasional joke to "assure" the audience. Considering Buckley's astounding talents for debate, these conclusions are hardly surprising; the *Miscellany* editors likely lost the debate by a wide margin in the eyes of most audience members. Nevertheless, Smith condemned the rhetoric of the Yale students: "It is high time that we all learned to distinguish sound from unsound thinking and to beware of the kind of oratory that dictators and their minions use to hypnotize the masses," she concluded.

The next week, Buckley's sister Patricia Lee Buckley '50 (who would eventually marry Bozell) wrote a letter to the editor criticizing Smith's pro-Wallace stance.[173] She accused the professor of "inconsistent thinking" and "unsubstantiated accusations" against her brother. The *Miscellany* editors, she argued, debated in "low and un-emphatic tones" compared to their Yale opponents. Further, she accused "Wallace enthusiasts" like Smith of being intolerant to conservative ideologies, regardless of the merits of their arguments or effective debate presentation.

Buckley wrote back to the paper himself on April 17, 1948. He scorned Smith for misunderstanding that Wallace's campaign was "inspired by communism."[174] The fact that she disagreed with their characterizations of several of his policies was as insignificant as "the concerns of a patient afflicted with incurable cancer with a case of acne." He ruthlessly asserted that "Miss Smith has resorted to intellectually dishonest, evasive and unsupported accusations shameful to the teaching profession."

For Buckley, Wallace's bid in the 1948 election represented a clear split between communism and capitalism. Most Americans—indeed, most Vassar students—agreed with him. As the editors of the *Miscellany* quickly discovered, the post-War period was a difficult time to wholeheartedly embrace liberalism.

Censorship and Fear: The McCarthy Era

The period following World War II was a frightening era for journalists across the United States. Like the Red Scare after World War I, the Second Red Scare was defined by perpetual fear of communist and radical influence on American society. Senator Joseph McCarthy drove the efforts to find and prosecute individuals with suspected communist ties, producing countless lists of alleged Soviet sympathizers. "Today we are engaged in a final, all-out battle between communistic atheism and Christianity," McCarthy shouted in a February 1950 speech in Wheeling, West Virginia.[175] "The great difference between our western Christian world and the atheistic Communist world is not political [but]… moral." Xenophobia and intolerance were hallmarks of what became known as the "communist witch hunt" of the late 1940s and 1950s. Those who attempted to criticize the government's authority to persecute deviants were themselves accused and targeted.

Not surprisingly, many of the individuals accused of being Soviet sympathizers were journalists, writers and intellectuals. College professors across the country were being fired or "suspended" for their political beliefs.

Student newspapers across the country had to navigate this hostile climate, especially those that hoped to comment on national or international affairs. As we have seen, the *Miscellany News* had grown accustomed to covering and editorializing on global politics since the 1930s. Suddenly, however, the editors became aware that their writings could have grave consequences if their opinions angered the wrong people. Unlike the written assault of Calvin Coolidge three decades earlier, the government suddenly empowered itself to do more than simply *complain* about radicals; the government could now persecute them. Emily Weston Frankovich '52 remembers that the Editorial Board tried its best to "discourage the swing to the right" that plagued many other student papers. "We were crusaders for the liberal cause," she bragged. Frankovich especially remembers the visit of renowned MIT mathematician Dirk Struik to campus. McCarthy had famously accused the bookish Struik of being a Soviet spy. Although he denied this charge, he invoked the First and Fifth Amendments of the Constitution to refuse to answer the badgering questions of Federal authorities. For this refusal, he was suspended from teaching for five years. According to Frankovich, Struik was nevertheless greeted as a hero by the *Miscellany* editors, who viewed him as a martyr to the cause of liberalism and due process. The paper wrote a favorable piece about his lecture and his accomplishments in mathematics. In the following weeks, the paper received no fewer than three furious letters about publishing the article—one from a student, one from a professor and one from a resident of Pougheepsie.

Still, some editors were concerned about the cost of their liberalism. "Young liberals like *Miscellany News* editors felt very threatened," recalled Nancy Ransom '50. "I knew a number of students who were eager to go to work in Washington after graduation, and they were afraid to join campus organizations that might taint their reputations." Ransom remembers that, as a whole, the editors were an ambitious group, and the thought of ruining their chances of professional success was more of a risk than many were willing to take.

In addition to fearing reprisal from the government, the paper also had to worry about the College administration. In 1950, there was a small scandal involving the plagiarism of a story in a student publication. "All the editors of all publications were called to a meeting with President Blanding, who spoke to us with deadly seriousness about the offense, which we certainly considered appalling," recalled Ransom. The offending writer did not work for the *Miscellany*, but Blanding's involvement in the incident concerned some editors, including Ransom, about the level of control that the administration could exercise over the student press. Some felt that administrative reprimands were a slippery slope. Tailoring coverage to the whims non-students contradicted editors' liberalism.

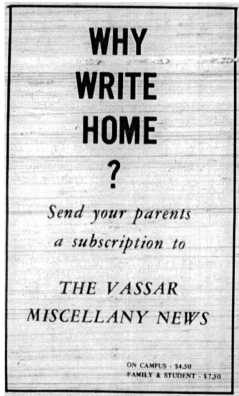

WHY WRITE HOME ?

Send your parents a subscription to

THE VASSAR MISCELLANY NEWS

ON CAMPUS - $4.50
FAMILY & STUDENT - $7.50

To raise money, the *Miscellany* often pushed parents and loved ones to subscribe. This successful advertisement first ran on October 4, 1958.

For a very brief period, several alumnae/i accounts suggest that the paper did succumb to a conservative swing to the right during the early and mid 1950s. Joan Gunn '51 served as Distribution Manager for two years, gathering and folding each new edition of the paper. Gunn, who described herself as fairly conservative, recalled feeling at home on the *Miscellany* staff because of the paper's political leanings. "[Some on] the *Misc* were definitely conservative," she recalled, "I think the *Misc* appealed to the minority." Gunn grew up in a small, Republican town surrounded by small business owners. She recalled a liberal English professor making fun of her political background, forcing her to stand in front of the class while ridiculing her conservatism. "So the *Misc* was my haven of comfortableness," she said, noting that she forged lasting relationships with like-minded individuals on the paper. Still, though, she always felt that "most of my classmates saw eye-to-eye with the English teacher."

At the same time, many editors continued to resist authority and carried on the *Miscellany*'s established tradition of progressivism. According to a report in the *New York Times*, seven college newspapers including the *Miscellany* petitioned the Soviet Embassy to grant them journalist visas to Moscow.[176] Editor in Chief Natalie Becker '55 and the other college editors wrote in a statement that they hoped that an overseas trip would "further international understanding." The Soviet Embassy granted the editors the right to travel "anywhere," a pronouncement that the *Times* considered a mere public relations maneuver. Nonetheless, the fact that the editor of the *Miscellany* and her colleagues wrote the petition is significant in and of itself. Although voyages to Moscow were hardly encouraged by the United States government—any trip behind the Iron Curtain had to be approved by the State Department's passport division—the *Miscellany* was daring enough to make an attempt in the pursuit of knowledge and tolerance.

The Fifties from the Eyes of an Average Reporter

The ideological concerns of the McCarthy Era did not ruin the *Miscellany* experience for its loyal staffers. To the contrary, many average writers from the period barely remember feeling any administrative or governmental influence. The paper continued to instill its reporters with enormous pride just as it had throughout its history, and many graduated Vassar ready and able to join the journalistic workforce. To understand the lives of average reporters during the 1950s, the experiences of Karin Chapman Bond '53 offer a useful case study.

Bond first volunteered to work on the *Miscellany* during her sophomore year. Shy and naïve, she found herself "thoroughly in awe" of the intelligent and worldly women who worked on the paper's staff. Her father was a newspaperman himself, and encouraged his timid daughter to put her byline in the spotlight. Her knack for news writing quickly landed her a spot as a full-time reporter, covering campus happenings from lectures and announcements to

"O God, five minutes and three centuries to go . . ."

Jean Anderson, Vassar: A Second Glance

student government meetings. She also recruited faculty members to write about "the truly important stuff," submitting contributions whenever there was a particularly significant event or administrative policy that needed explanation.[177] For Bond, it was fortunate that she had these faculty contributors, since she quickly found herself at a loss for reporters. Most of her friends worked for the more conservative *Vassar Chronicle*. "Rather than go to the editors and confess my problem, I started attending almost everything myself, writing up each event in a different style in an attempt to disguise my inadequacies," she recalled. Thus, Bond learned about a wide variety of topics, including underwater archeology (thanks to an archaeologist she interviewed who inspired her to take SCUBA lessons), how to ski (thanks to an on-stage demonstration by skiing pioneer Hannes Schneider), and about the South Sea islanders.

This last topic was courtesy of a lecture by the groundbreaking anthropologist Margaret Mead.[178] During her time on the paper, Bond was able to interview Mead, as well as the famous pianist Vladimir Horowitz. Her article about Horowitz's concert, originally scheduled for Skinner Hall, created such fervor among students that the venue had to be changed to accommodate hundreds of students, rather than just the two-dozen music students and faculty who were originally invited.

The hard-working editor climbed the paper's hierarchy, joining the Editorial Board during her junior year. Bond and her fellow editors gathered each week in their Students' Building office to layout the paper. The Editorial Board's structure in the 1940s and 1950s was perhaps more egalitarian than today's structure; rather than having stringently defined sections (like News or Sports), members of the Editorial Board had much broader responsibilities. All editors had input into every story in the paper, and there was a high level of collective decision making about which articles should be prioritized and what edits were required. It was a closely-knit group, maybe by necessity.

Those on the paper often considered themselves to be more progressive, better informed and frankly smarter than many of their non-*Miscellany* classmates. The newspaper's staff enjoyed many privileges that gave the young women a sense of importance. Because of the late hours the newspaper required, staffers were also allowed to stay out past the strict 10:30 p.m. curfew.[179] On production nights, they could come and go as they pleased. According to Business Manager Anne Susswein '61, the "biggest perk" was being allowed to have telephones their private dorm rooms. "It made one very popular with the people rooming in the vicinity," she gloated. "The phones really were a necessity as I would have to contact advertisers and the printer." At that time, private telephones were still uncommon, thus adding an extra allure to the *Miscellany*.

Interviewing academic celebrities and holding so many responsibilities endowed the timid Karin Chapman Bond with a feeling of personal significance. The entire job—the weekly meetings, the pace of the production cycle, the ability to have a phone in her room at a time when other students could not—all made her feel pride and importance for her contribution to the community.

The *Miscellany* taught valuable lessons to its staffers, and wanted to publicize this fact to freshmen students in the hope that they might join the paper. To avoid seeming aloof, the paper would often include a personal essay about a staff member's experiences. These essays would usually be printed in the Freshman Issue of the *Miscellany*, distributed during orientation. Below is an anonymous letter published in September 1962 that sums up many of the emotions and experiences that Bond herself felt a decade earlier:

> As I approached the office of the *Miscellany News* for the first time one September evening, my knees weren't exactly clattering together, but they were not, on the other hand, relaxed to any great degree either. Strange visions of a cigar-in-mouthed monster screaming unintelligible directions overwhelmed me as I came to the door. I took a breath, didn't smell any cigar smoke, and walked in.
>
> I'm rather blind at distances of more than eight inches, and an abhorrence of glasses complicates and lessens the picture, but even so, I could find no evil monster. As a matter of fact, there seemed to be a large group of witty and pleasant conversationalists seated around a large table. This opinion was confirmed as I came nearer.
>
> Smiling introductions were transacted as I sat down at the wide oak table, which was engraved with such journalistic ponderings as "Yale," "Tom," "12 x 2 x 24," and "Princeton." I soon discovered that some of the girls around me were freshmen too, and this was conducive to a feeling of happy identity. After some introductory remarks by the editors, we were put on a trial period for two weeks, during which we were to hand in two articles.
>
> Two weeks later, I received a little note in the unstamped mail, which began, "The *Miscellany News* is pleased to welcome you…" From then on, my weeks became patterned around Tuesday assignment meetings and Monday deadines. I soon began attending the Monday night sessions of "putting the paper to bed." My assignments were always interesting and often exciting, ranging from an interview with Pete Seeger to an account of a freedom ride that I had been on. But the *Misc*'s real significance soon came to mean Monday bedtimes.
>
> These Mondays began around 7 or 8 p.m. and reached a feverish intensity by midnight, although we average reporters could leave earlier if necessary. But the editors stayed, and I did too. I was curious I suppose, or sleepless, or looking for something exciting and important enough to require late bedtimes. To the tune of "Where's my head-sheet!" and "How many counts in a line?" and "She didn't type it 10-72!" and "Call her up and find out where the Hell that article is, we have to lead it!"—the *Misc* assumed its final form. Sometimes, hunger provided the biggest crisis: "What do you mean they don't deliver pizza after midnight?" shouted one of the editors into an old telephone lying on a paper-strewn desk. "This is the *Misc*!" Often, other problems were encountered: "I know it's 12:30, but you'll just have to take it all apart and put the front page back together again with that story first."

> There was a great sense of satisfaction in seeing the finished product, black and white and shiny and wonderful because of the headline I was so proud of on the bottom of the third page or the story with my very first byline. And also because of every little black letter that had, in one way or another, been contributed by every other member of the staff. We had combined our collective genius to create a being, and even while we bewailed each week's mistakes, we thought the *Misc* was wonderful.[180]

Although anonymous, this piece is incredibly personal. It would have been the ideal recruiting tool targeted at nervous freshmen looking for a sense of purpose and comradery. But this was more than a marketing gimmick; this *was* the lived experience of staff members like Karin Chapman Bond, who found their passion and their friends with their knees "clattering together" in the office of the *Miscellany News*.

Transitioning to the Sixties Mentality

By the mid-1950s, the *Miscellany*'s liberal slant was already established. But the relatively calm liberalism of the past two decades would take a radical turn to the left during the 1960s. In hindsight, the proto-sixties mentally can be easily identified. As a freshman, Elsa Marston Harik '54 was aware of the paper's "progressive" reputation, which attracted her to join during her first few weeks on campus. She was among the next generation of more liberal Vassar students, slowly infiltrating the historically conservative College. However, as Harik put it, the 1950s were "not a time of challenge, upsetting of apple carts, rebelliousness." That stronger sense of rebellion would not come to the country or the paper for another decade. "I think most students were hoping for stability and security at that time," Harik reflected, "which mirrored the mood of the country." The student body of the early 1950s had grown up with the emptiness of Great Depression and the horrors of World War II. No sooner did the happy victory over these two challenges die down than it became clear that the world remained a dangerous place. Bloody division in India and Israel, the hoards of refugees around the world, and the proliferation of the atomic bomb all made for a fearful global climate. The Korean War and the onset of the Cold War made for a rapidly changing global frontier. The added domestic threat of McCarthyism created unease within Vassar's atmosphere of academic freedom. Though many students wanted to respond to the actions of McCarthy and the House Un-American Activities Committee, the vehicles for protest used so commonly in the 1960s were not yet popular. "We thought that global problems were going to be solved by victory in the War, but instead, the world immediately became far more complex, baffling, and threatening," Harik explained. "It was an interesting time—too interesting—to come of age and try to figure out your role in a rapidly changing world."

Though freshman Harik saw the *Miscellany* as progressive, the adult Harik now understands that it was "still pretty tame and parochial." While the paper was sprinkled with news articles and editorials on global affairs, Vassar College remained the editors' primary mission, Harik never recalls hearing discussions among staff about "what we should be doing to make the world a better place"; instead, most discussions about global news were academic and abstract. Neither does she recall hearing the paper frequently criticized by students, which suggests that the paper did a fairly good job of reflecting students' equally parochial interests. "I don't think that most of us in the 1950s connected our role as journalists with the ability to make global change. There were some exceptions, but by and large, our focus was the College."

As the sixties drew closer, student life became a priority in the paper's coverage. Though the *Miscellany* was already at a height of popularity, the late 1950s and early 1960s elevated the paper even higher. A spike in letters suggests greater community attention. One explanation for the increased recognition might have been the emphasis on student-centered articles. While the *Miscellany* of the 1940s and 1950s almost always began with stories about the nation or the College, front-page headlines from the 1960s tended to focus on realistic looks into the lives of Vassar women—including previously downplayed topics like drinking, partying and dating.

As Harper found, the *Miscellany News* began to create "guides" to the men at other colleges, particularly the Ivy League schools.[181] Such features debuted in the first issue of the 1956-1957 school year, and continued until coeducation. "Of particular interest to new Vassar girls is Yale," the paper wrote.[182] "Yalies are much in evidence on the Poughkeepsie campus. Your first contact with a Yalie will probably be at a mixer, where his blue blazer and matching striped Eli Yale tie can identify him. If he tells you he's a junior, he's probably a sophomore: if he tells you he's a sophomore, he's probably a freshman. It is a good idea to indicate that in your opinion, Yale is even better than Harvard."

The humor and wit exhibited here is emblematic of the changing tone of the *Miscellany* in the late 1950s and early 1960s. Beyond their coverage and editorializing on global affairs, the paper included more down-to-earth features and cartoons to reflect the realities of student life. As Harper wrote, "their public acknowledgment [of dating and male companions] points to the loosening of moral structures on campus." The fact that the campus newspaper began to acknowledge casual relationships and coed parties demonstrates the burgeoning social shifting. American youth across the nation began to rebel against the conservative norms that were so prevalent in previous decades. Far from being trivial, the inclusion of these male dating guides in the *Miscellany*—which predated the inclusion of men themselves into the College—was a manifestation of the sixties culture. Harper incisively observed that "Alongside these tongue-in-cheek dating rules ran stories openly discussing sex, race, and campus regulation of the private lives of its students." Even when coverage centered on the campus, the editors examined social life through an increasingly progressive lens.

This social progressivism soon turned political. Judith Stein '60 sat on the Editorial Board for four years. Now a historian at the City University of New York (CUNY), she remembers her *Miscellany* experiences well. As a historian, Stein also put her experiences in the context of the past. Her class—the last Vassar class to attend the school in the 1950s—saw the beginnings of the dramatic change that the next decade would bring. "We really had no idea what was coming, but looking back, I can see that we represented the final strain of 1950s mentality," she said. "In the sixties, students across the country assumed that they were smarter than adults, and usually assumed that they could and should say whatever they wanted. We on the *Misc* in the late fifties did not exactly feel that way, at least not completely."

In particular, she remembers the Editorial Board's existential crisis about its role in commenting on affairs beyond Vassar's gates—a strange conversation, given the move in this direction over the past decades. The archives between the 1930s and 1950s are teeming with news and editorial coverage of issues from the local Poughkeepsie government to national tax policies. Nonetheless, the Editorial Board suddenly questioned their scope—"an existential crisis of mission," as Stein described it. Stein now sees those heated discussions as a conflict between fifties and sixties mentalities. "Some people thought we should comment on whatever was important to us, whether on campus or in the world at large," she remembered. "But others said that we shouldn't comment on 'issues beyond us,' like world affairs. These women were hardly conservative or prude, but they just did not think that a group of students could possibly have anything independent or worthwhile to say about those big issues."

Stein recalls the Woolworth Protests, a national movement of protests pressuring the Woolworth department stores to end segregation. When the protests hit the Poughkeepsie branch of Woolworth in Spring 1960, some Vassar students including Stein picketed; others (including several *Miscellany* editors) felt it was "not their place" to protest publicly. For Stein, that protest would be a defining moment in her understanding of the national ideological struggle. "Poughkeepsie was a bastion of McCarthyism, and I was suddenly very aware of the ideological divide." One local resident shouted at the Vassar protesters, "You're nothing but a group of communists!" For Stein, that clash over American values was a pivotal point in her education at Vassar—and a telling example of the decidedly mixed politics on the Editorial Board.

For her own part in the paper, Stein's revolution was not quite so radical. "The spirit of the sixties certainly hadn't hit, but there was definitely some rebellion in the air, at least for some of us," she said. Stein recalled writing an article about the visit of a renowned scholar of French literature from Yale. "I criticized him," she said bluntly. "I disagreed with his interpretations, and I said so in print. So there I was—this teenager with one freshman course on French, criticizing one of the nation's most venerated scholars. There was a caged spirit of rebelliousness that was about to burst free."

That incipient rebelliousness would end the notion that the *Miscellany* should paint Vassar as perfect. During the early 1960s, there was in increased emphasis on colleges and universities beyond Vassar. In news articles, editors freely drew comparisons between their College and peer schools, pulling no punches in showing areas where Vassar lagged behind. Reporting on the news of peer institutions was nothing new. This began as early as 1914 with a column entitled, "What Other Colleges Do," which included tidbits about events at peer institutions, primarily as they related to affairs at Vassar.[183] Between the 1920s and 1950s, though, this column disappeared and was replaced with only occasional news stories about other schools.[184] The late 1950s saw a shift away from this institutional parochialism. Regular exchange columns began with the *Harvard Crimson* and the *Daily Princetonian*. Students could now read directly about the affairs of their peer colleges in lengthy columns written by Harvard and Princeton students. *Miscellany* columns were also published in these Ivy League newspapers. But while these sorts of exchange columns once glorified Vassar and presented only positive images of the College and its students, the articles found in the *Harvard Crimson* and *Daily Princetonian* archives from this period are far more self-critical. One article reprinted in the *Crimson* tells of frequent burglaries at Vassar; another reprinted in the *Princetonian* complains of the lethargy of Vassar students; a third from the *Princetonian* protests President Alan Simpson's Convocation address as being "so far beneath the intellectual capacities of his audience."[185] *Miscellany* writers no longer felt compelled to show Vassar as ideal. Instead, they were willing, even anxious, to point out the flaws in the established order, even if those flaws involved the College president himself.

The Sixties in Full Force: Outward and Upward

Distaste for authority was clearly brewing. And once the fears of the McCarthy Era were finally exhausted, the *Miscellany* was able to further hone its own political and editorial voice without hesitation. This happened most noticeably under the leadership of Sherry Corlan Chayat '65, who began work on the paper during her freshman year and served as Editor in Chief between 1963 and 1964. Perhaps more than any other individual, Sherry Chayat brought the spirit of the sixties to the paper. Under her influence, the *Miscellany* went from being "somewhat tame" to being decidedly and defiantly left-of-center. Looking back, Chayat described herself as a fairly unconventional Vassar student. "Vassar was quite socially conservative when I got there," she recalled. "So many of the girls I knew were involved in coming out parties and being debutants. I wasn't like that at all." Her family was lower-middle class, mostly artists and educators. Chayat was "by no means rich" and was raised with very different values than many of her classmates. Though some students labeled her as "unconventional and artsy," she soon found her niche. Chayat had worked for a local newspaper writing obituaries during her high school years, and when she got to Vassar, she immediately signed up to write for the *Miscellany*.

But the student newspaper was not her only extracurricular activity; she was an active member of the Organization for Political Awareness and Students for a Democratic Society (SDS).[186] During her tenure on the *Miscellany*, she brought her concern for social issues to the paper. "Even though the students were socially on the conservative side, they were mostly just politically uninformed," recalled Chayat. "Many of the students were simply not interested in politics, and really could care less about anything but their social lives. They would just play bridge in the parlor, and pour over the society pages to see who had just gotten married. It was really quite amazing compared to the women who would enter the school just a decade later," she said. "But in my own time, I really tried to be something of an incendiary voice, using the paper to push students beyond their own trivial pursuits. I wanted the *Misc* to really become a mouthpiece for liberalism and a haven for counter-cultural types like myself."

Chayat was heavily involved in the Civil Rights Movement, attending several freedom rides. With several other Vassar students, she attended a massive ride organized by Yale's famously liberal Dean of the Chapel, Sloan Coffin. Coffin led the group of students to the highly segregated eastern shore of Maryland. When they tried to integrate a lunch counter by sitting blacks and whites next to one another, passersby were outraged and hurled rocks at the counter. "That experience was earthshaking for me, just as the sixties were earthshaking for the country," Chayat said. "Though I was already very liberal, that experience really pushed my politics even further." When they returned to Vassar on Easter Sunday, she immediately went to work ensuring that the events were covered in the *Miscellany*. During her tenure as Editor in Chief, she continued to push civil rights debates into the center of the paper.

Not surprisingly, her political views occasionally stirred anger. The most difficult moment of her tenure, which seems relatively innocuous compared to her Maryland experience, involved a short wedding announcement. In Fall 1964, the *Miscellany* printed a brief notice about the marriage of a white Vassar student and an African American man. Chayat received dozens of angry letters and phone calls from students and alumnae alike, infuriated that the student newspaper would implicitly support an interracial union. Such attacks did not faze Chayat, however; her uncle had fought and won the country's first anti-miscegenation case, so her family was very much accustomed to public anger. She was able to survive the controversy, and in doing so set an example for younger editors on standing by one's editorial decisions.

Sex, Sensibility and Social Progressivism

Increasing attention to civil rights was just one aspect of the *Miscellany News*'s mounting liberalism. As we have already seen in the paper's "dating guides," interest in sexuality was also rising. The sixties, the decade most heavily associated with free love and open sexuality, engaged Vassar's imagination. Dating and intercourse were discussed in the *Miscellany* more than ever before, suggesting that the issues weighed on the minds of many students— much to the chagrin of the College's more conservative alumnae. On April 4, 1962, Vassar President Sarah Gibson Blanding delivered a now-infamous speech about premarital sex. The manda-

College President Sarah Gibson Blanding at her desk. *Vassar College Archives and Special Collections.*

tory Chapel speech shocked the largely liberal student body. "It was huge at the time, and just very weird," Chayat recalled.

"She basically told us that anyone who stayed the night at her boyfriend's house should withdraw from the College." At the time, women's colleges were said to be *in locus parentis*—existing in place of parents as ethical guides. Blanding was likely responding to the concerns of older alumnae and parents, and her speech was designed to assure these important constituencies that the administration encouraged Vassar girls to remain pure and virginal. "Of course, there weren't really many virgins," quipped Chayat.

For the progressive *Miscellany* editors, the speech was a call to action. They immediately went to publishing a two-page supplemental issue solely on Blanding's speech. This supplement included opinion pieces from students and alumnae/i, along with information about the policies of peer colleges. The editors contacted Inez Nelbach, Dean of Students at Barnard College, to explain Barnard's "unwritten code of ethical conduct" for students.[187] The editors also published a scathing staff editorial. Not mincing any words, they blasted Blanding's words as "a radical shift in policy [toward]… moral dictatorship."[188] Such an attitude toward sexuality would bring Vassar backward generations, they argued, forcing students to adhere to old-world Victorian standards for women. "Girls who experiment sexually prior to marriage are not necessarily corrupt or immoral," the editorial proclaimed indignantly, noting that a campus that was honest with itself would be far better than a group of "promiscuous girls who pretend to virtue." The staff editorial, the news coverage of the speech and all of the letters were very much one-sided; all of them decried Blanding's words and implied that her vision for Vassar was out of sync with reality. Indeed, a *Miscellany* poll taken after the speech confirmed that a clear majority of students were offended and did not plan to change their sexual mores because of the Chapel talk.[189]

To layout the paper during this period, editors followed a rigorous process of "pinning" a dummy copy. That copy would then be given to the printer (as seen above in the 1962 yearbook) to feed through the mimeograph press. *Vassarion.*

After the *Miscellany*'s supplemental issue hit the stands, *Newsweek* and *TIME Magazine* picked up the story. "The whole thing really opened up an enormous dialogue on sex in society, particularly for women of the sixties," Chayat said of the media attention. "It was just so unique that we, a bunch of college newspaper editors, were able to start that sort of discussion." Indeed, the *Miscellany* was the spark that lit the flames of the media, who began questioning the ideals of the College and the alleged chastity of Vassar girls.

Soon after these events, Blanding called Chayat to her office. Terrified that she would be punished for writing about the speech, Chayat slowly made her way to the President's inner sanctum. "I remember thinking, 'This is it, she's going to kick me out. She's going to shut down the paper.' As I stood there in her office, she just looked penetratingly at me. 'You know,' she said in her slow, deep voice, 'every spring, the girls walk on the grass. I wonder could you please write an editorial to have them stay on the path.' And with that, she let me go, still looking at me as if she were looking through me." Although the *Miscellany* wrote a brief editorial asking students to refrain from crushing the fresh spring grass, the student newspaper faced no repercussions for igniting a storm of negative media attenton.[190]

Indeed, the College administration on the whole had very little control of the *Miscellany*. Writers and editors from the 1960s recall no instances of administrative censorship, in part because of the great tradition of free speech at Vassar. In the 1950s, Vassar was one of a handful of private institutions that refused to allow Senator Joseph McCarthy to investigate the campus. The College went to great lengths to protect the privacy and autonomy of its professors—"a group much more radical than their students," according to one reporter—from any sort of government interference. In this way, the College community was already prepared for the explosion of free speech that would define the paper's mission for the coming decades.

Chayat exemplified the sixties mentality for the *Miscellany*. In addition keeping the Civil Rights Movement in the public discourse and publicizing Blanding's speech, she tried to expand Vassar's cultural parochialism. For example, she wrote about the visit of Ravi Shanker, one of the most famous Indian musicians of the 20th century. She also tried to include articles about the ongoing Cold War. "The Bay of Pigs occurred during my freshman year, and suddenly all of these girls who were socially conservative and politically unaware became very afraid," she said. "There was this sense that the sky could fall at any moment." That feeling swelled in 1963 with the assassination of President John F. Kennedy. "Everyone was so shaken, so frightened," recalled Chayat. "But I remember thinking to myself that this could be a turning point in how students thought about politics. This could be a turning point for the paper, not just in occasionally covering national events, but also in connecting those events to the lives of Vassar students. It wasn't abstract any more; it was very real." In other words, Chayat hoped to combine student life coverage and global coverage, to show how national events impacted Vassar. This sense of hopeful hopelessness was conveyed in the *Miscellany's* December 4, 1963 editorial entitled "A Man for All Nations":

> It is over a week now since the President of the United States was assassinated. Banner headlines and continuous programs of sacred music, memorial services and documentary news reports have given way to a resumption of normal routine. But one does not forget... one can never forget this man who was more than a man. To a nation and to a world of nations he was a symbol—of courage and positive leadership, of freedom and human dignity, of creativity and artistic endeavor, of spiritual, mental and spiritual vitality, and above all, of hope.
>
> The name of John Fitzgerald Kennedy will soon mark bridges, rocket launching sites, ski slopes, and waterfalls everywhere in memory of the man. These various gestures of dedication are commendable. But no honor could better suit this man than that of endeavoring the carry forth the principles for which he sacrificed. *Izvestya*, the Moscow newspaper, said that the best memorial the world could give Kennedy would be peace. We must construct our memorials not as dead tombstones, but as living, soaring monuments upon the foundations that have been laid. Such a man cannot have lived and died in vain:
>
>> "Read history: so learn your place in time;
>> And go to sleep: all this was done before;
>> We do it better, fouling every shore;
>> We disinfect, we do not probe the crime.
>> Our engines plunge into the seas, they climb
>> Above our atmosphere; we grow not more
>> Profound as we approach the ocean's floor;
>> Our flight is lofty, it is not sublime.
>> Yet long ago this Earth by struggling men
>> Was scuffed, was scraped by mouths, that
>>   bubbled mud:
>> And will be so again, and yet again:
>> Until we trace our poison to its bud
>> And root, and there uproot it: until then,

Earth will be warmer each winter by man's
blood."
—Edna St. Vincent Millay '17

"A Man for All Nations" won much critical acclaim within the Vassar community for its eloquent prose and calming message. The editors ended their piece by quoting *Miscellany* alumna Edna St. Vincent Millay's *Mine the Harvest*, a lengthy poem about overcoming tragedy. The newspaper's coverage of the assassination, as well as its powerful editorial predicting both action and renewal, stirred the College community. Students' overwhelming political lethargy was replaced with curiosity, activism and liberalism.

Such feeling intensified in 1968 with the assassination of Martin Luther King Jr. "I can still vividly picture the issue we put out reporting his death," said Wendy Knickerbocker '70. "The front page had a thick black border, and it was as somber as our typographic and layout skills could make it." The liberal-minded, pro-civil rights editors were heartbroken at King's assassination. "There was a constant push-pull between social progress and hatred, between tolerance and destruction," she said. "We on the Editorial Board certainly felt those social swings in the 1960s. And we always used the paper to push as hard as we could toward tolerance." After King's assassination, the editors made an even greater commitment to furthering the civil rights agenda. They wrote and published a series of lengthy investigative stories that examined race relations at Vassar and within the surrounding community. "Summer Program Benefits White, Not Blacks," for example, examined the costs of a Vassar summer program designed to help integrate the largely white student body with local minority groups.[191]

Liberal editors like Chayat and Knickerbocker did not, however, throw out the paper's history for the sake of this new political agenda. The beginning of Chayat's tenure, in fact, displayed renewed interest in the paper's history. On February 5, 1964, the entire front page was devoted to the 50th anniversary of weekly publication. The lead article noted that "the *Miscellany*'s supplement has far outlived its parent publication," the *Miscellany Monthly*.[192] With the aid of Vassar Bibliographer Dorothy Plum (the precursor to the College Historian), the staff wrote several short articles on different aspects of the paper's history. Oddly enough, legacy remained important to the editors, even with the changing times of the sixties.

Still, Knickerbocker continued to push the *Miscellany* to question authority. Knickerbocker did not graduate from Vassar, but instead graduated from Colby College as a member of their Class of 1973. However, she was Editor in Chief of the *Miscellany* for a short time during the 1967-68 school year. One of her greatest memories of working on the paper was an exclusive interview she had with the famed American author Timothy Leary. Leary, the poster-child for 1960s counterculture, was a major advocate of psychedelic drug use, and had gotten arrested for possession of drugs in March 1968. A resident of Poughkeepsie, he was being held in a local prison and Knickerbocker was able to interview him. "He was just as wacko as you'd think, and he gave a really drifty interview. I have this vague memory of him trying to flirt with me, too," she recalled. Leary asked if he could speak at Vassar after his release; to her shock, Dean of the College Elizabeth Drouilhet allowed him to speak, so long as the event was entirely sponsored by the *Miscellany*.

As Knickerbocker discovered after his lecture, Leary was something of a local staple. Whenever the Duchess County sheriff felt that he needed to please his constituents, and particularly around election times, he would conduct a drug bust, often at Leary's home. Another time, though, the sheriff staged a raid at Bard College and rounded up over 40 students, holding them all overnight even though only two were charged. One of the arrested students was a friend of Knickerbocker's roommate, which gave her an exclusive on the bust. "What I remember now is that several of the students, including him, had been hit by the sheriff's crew, and most of them, again including our friend, had been drinking but nothing more," she said. "I printed a story about the bust and I criticized the sheriff for harassing the students for no better reason than to burnish his re-election image." But the controversy intensified when the *New York Times* printed a small item about the sheriff's tactics and her story. When the sheriff denied the accusations, the *Poughkeepsie Journal* soon called Knickerbocker asking for a comment. "Well, like the 1960s righteous activist that I thought I was, I said that the sheriff was a big liar. As you can imagine, the *Journal* just loved that." A few days later, a strange man—a police officer—was following her around campus menacingly. When Drouilhet found out, she had him immediately thrown off campus, though she warned Knickerbocker to speak less radically in the future.

In a variety of ways, the 1960s created a gutsier and worldlier paper than ever before. Reporters were taking risks and questioning authority in new, bold ways. While the period between the Great Depression and the War saw an intense focus on national and world affairs, the news lacked a personal connection for much of the student body. The *Miscellany* had strong opinions about political and economic situations, but their discussions were often academic and detached. And though editors sometimes critiqued College administrators' policies, certain topics—sex, drugs and alcohol—still remained largely off the table. But the antiauthoritarianism of the 1960s turned the paper into a much more honest record of student experiences, and a much more active journalistic enterprise. Far from being academic, reporters would participate in freedom rides and go knocking on the doors of local prisons. The *Miscellany* did not just write about liberal ideas; it actively pushed the student body to embrace them.

Intensifying Ideology: "Old *Misc*" and "New *Misc*"

Beyond these increasingly frank political and social commentaries, the late 1960s also saw important shifts in behind-the-scenes policies and procedures. Inspired by the changing world around them, the editors hoped that these "new managerial solutions to old problems" would "secure the health of the *Misc* for the next generations." First, alterations were made to the structure of the Editorial Board. "The *Misc* Editorial Board always had organizational problems," wrote Editor in Chief Sara Linnie Slocum '67.[193] "After decades of the same orders and responsibly, the time had come for a structural change." Formerly, students on the newspaper staff were either writers or editors. There was no intermediate level. As a result, some writers became discouraged when they were passed over for editorships, and newly minted editors were fully unprepared for their new responsibilities. "An intermediary level was required," wrote Slocum. In 1967, the role of Associate Editor was established to fill this need.[194] Associate Editors would learn the procedures and practices of the *Miscellany* by switching their jobs each week to serve the News Editor, Copy Editor, Managing Editor or Headline Editor. Thus, the associate position provided training for future editors and gave staff members a sense upward mobility. Other structural changes were made too, streamlining the copyediting process and defining the specific responsibilities of editors.

Covering the Campus

Vissar Mascellany News

Published Briefly

Vol. 14 oz.   Poughkeepsie, N. Y., Whensday 24 Februdry 1965   Ultimate Number

H-BOMBS HIT

President Puzzled on Air Strike Responsibility

Newest Vietnam Rulers Now to Battle Chinese

Later reports from Saigon indicate that, contrary to first reports, South Vietnam is not only still there, but is actively pursuing its struggle against the Communists.

In a surprise assault last night at Ping-Pong the Viet Cong attacked a government column killing three South Vietnamese and slightly wounding 88 American advisers. The Communists compelled the government forces to retreat 200 yards, but in a counterattack U.S. soldiers supported by tanks, rocket fire, air-to-air missiles, ground-to-ground missiles, and straight-into-the-ground missiles advanced 300 yards and killed three rabbis.

In answer to the engagement of yesterday where the Viet Cong attacked an American barracks, capturing two translator radios, three pairs of underpants and six Hershey bars, American bombers today crossed the border and destroyed the North Vietnamese privy complex at Dung Ho.

On the political front at Saigon the situation was stable between two a.m. and six a.m. following last night's coup d'etat by army officers led by Colonel Ha Cha Cha and preceding this morning's abortive coup d'etat by Catholic civilians said to be resentful of Ha Cha Cha's cabinet which includes 23 Buddhists and only 24 Catholics.

An embassy spokesman, interviewed while repairing broken windows in the Ambassador's

Bomb to Increase Job Opportunities, Aid Slum Clearance

Sergent Shriver, former Director of the Peace Corps, commented optimistically on bombing's effect on urban areas. The problems of slum clearance seem to have been solved, and we expect a wide margin of success in eliminating all problem areas regardless of their problems. Moreover, for the first time in American history full employment can be categorically promised to everyone of our—at last count—thirty-one million citizens." He based this on the government's new, um, um, um, its improvement projects.

FEATURES INSIDE

▶ 13 Keep up to date; "New Styles in Home Barbecue"

▶ 81 An exciting travel article, "You Don't Have To Go To Philadelphia, It Will Come To You"

Various information sources, and the lack of them, indicate that a number of cities are missing around the whole world. Speculation has centered on the likelihood that hydrogen weapons may be involved. Seismographs shattered early this morning, but a quick finger count by SIC (Strategic Information Command) indicated either a number of explosions in the hundred megaton level.

(Continued on page 2, col. 2)

World-wide Reaction Varies; Red Leaders Hurl Threats

Moscow. Tass, Official Soviet News Agency, reported Herbert demanded that the U.S.S.R. step demanding that the U.S. step demanding that the U.S.S.R. get out of South Vietnam. Premier Kosygin, recovering from bad-line bunch, said last night that the Soviet Union wants only peace and is willing to go to war to get it. Angry crowds in Red Square last night called for help.

Monaco. Prince Rainier predicted here this morning that Monaco will be the only major power surviving the present confrontation, and declared that his country "will be prepared for this great eventuality." Rumor had it the casinos would open an hour early.

Phoenix. Like a bird from its ashes, Barry Goldwater, busily pursuing the truth on his ranch, would say only that he couldn't agree with Mr. Johnson's decisions more—"After all, Mr. Johnson is only repeating what I said last spring and summer. But," he added, "all this is no excuse for immorality."

Satellite Snug. Orbiting three hundred miles above the Pacific, Astronaut Phineas ("Happy") Humphrey reported: "It's a beaut-

ifut day up here. There seem to be interesting cloud patterns below; here and there Perth was very brightly lit this morning despite punkish clouds—they must ve improved their public lighting system."

Vatican City. James Bond, interviewed here in the wee hours this morning, said that he was "shaken, but not stirred" by international developments.

London. Prime Minister Harold Wilson stated in Parliament that apparent elimination of industrial areas would not interfere with the program for re-nationalizing the steel industry.

Cannes. "Good grief!" said Madame Nhu.

Harmon, New York. "Whether not ——, ——," said Herman Kahn, "cannot now be established. The Viet guerrillas may or may not have entered the third, or mobile, phase, but we are in some sense still phasing out stage 2.5 of the reprisal-oriented holding action, while the initiative of novel heartland operations has put our diplomacy in stage Beagle-7. Unfortunately this game is still mathematically unsolved."

(Continued on page 5, col. 1)

Civil Defense Head Presents Suggestions On Shelter Survival

It is pointed out by National Civil Defense Director Mabel Grapes that, though these may be trying times for some of our neighbors, the Public Accommodation Act does not apply to fallout shelters, and that unauthorized personnel may be ejected, without regard to creed, color, or ethnic origin. Willfully littered or trespassing signs, she noted, may be helpful, citing the booklet which will be published next month on shelter etiquette, "The Correct Thing."

Other tips: Do not look directly at outbreaks; devices for watching —— —— —— —— the purpose Keep a transistor radio turned on for news bulletins which will be interspersed with patriotic and upbeat thematic material. Plenty of canned water and Metrecal should be kept on hand, and weapons and shovels will be useful in the event of neighbors dropping by.

(Continued on page 2, col. 2)

TODAY'S WEATHER

More than partly cloudy, with occasional rain mixed with fallout. Radioactivity index stands at 911. The rain in Spain. Continued unseasonably hot weather is forecast.

President Johnson stated to reporters in Presidential Bunker No. 2 (nicknamed by newsmen Last Blast Junction, rumored to be near Gopher Holes, Miss.), "Probably this is a time for greatness. Our peaceful, nuclear air strikes against Hanoi, Peking, and Vladivostok seem to have been misunderstood; I said clearly at that time that we seek no wider war, that this escalation was not an escalation.

"Nonetheless," he continued, "even a few cities of our own is a small but where so much is to be gained in effectuating our destiny. On-going U.S. policy seems now, in fact, to be achieving the needed leverage for the Vietnam Peace Negotiations which are continuing—if Geneva is still there."

He added that he is sending what is left of McGeorge Bundy for a personal report. He also dismissed Russian claims that conventional American air-strikes in North Vietnam and Albania were unjustified since the war in South Vietnam is civil. "But they shot at us," he said gravely, and noted that some Albanian papers matches.

(Continued on page 6, col. 3)

FLASHES

Wall Street, New York. The Dow-Jones Industrial Average lost ground today through Johnson & Johnson and Upjohn were up; but trading was heavy, especially in pails and pans, day-old loaves, and sewing kits.

Saigon. In a new flood of militancy, the people of this valiant, city have begun a program of deep air-strike shelters.

Moscow. Between ultimatums this morning the Soviet government affirmed that the Bolshoi Ballet will visit New York as scheduled next month in the Mingling for Peace Program. Some observers in Western capitals were uncertain whether this was or was not another ultimatum. Senator George Murphy warned: "The Commies are on their toes; this may be an effort to infiltrate guerrillas."

Berlin. Flash ——

Geneva. The International Bomb Control Congress is reported to have adjourned indefinitely. No reasons were given.

Lexington, Massachusetts. Minute men here were arriving; it was felt locally that something was heard around the world last night.

Brush Fur, Vietnam. Although no details have been reported, alert U.S. and South Vietnamese

(Continued on page 8, col. 2)

The Beverly Hillbillies will appear one-half-hour late tonight

---

In publishing this February 24, 1965 "Joke Issue," the editors satirized the pervasive fear of nuclear disaster during the Cold War. The front page is riddled with purposeful errors and shows a fictional atomic bomb hitting Vietnam. The bottom of the page includes a note about the popular sitcom, *The Beverly Hillbillies.* The message satirizes the culture of unyielding fear of global annihilation.

The second major set of changes involved a redesign the relatively stationary layout of the past half-century. The revamp of the paper, led by Editor in Chief Beth Dunlop '69, was meant to "reflect the progressive spirit of a changing newspaper that hopes to inspire action from an often static community."[195] The "*Vassar Miscellany News*" masthead on the front page was redesigned for the first time since 1939, thanks to Parker Kent James, a graphics designer and father of editor Shirley James '67.[196] Occasionally, the editors gave the front page a rather unusual layout, placing a leading story *above* the masthead and three or more pictures on the sides of the page. A new, less expensive printing company allowed the *Miscellany*'s pages to grow wider and longer without affecting the budget. Although some columns shifted position and photographs appeared more frequently, the larger pages mostly resulted in greater amounts of blank space around the articles, helping to guide readers' eyes on the pages. Nevertheless, besides an awkwardly altered front page, the layout of the paper remained fairly regimented, though the "new" style probably resulted in the most comprehensive redesign to date.

Vassar Miscellany News

Third, along with the paper's "new look" came "bold new objectives." The editors hoped to enhance the paper's role as a vehicle for change, strengthening editorial voice and opinions. "Our ambitions are both lofty and pragmatic," they wrote. "We hope to transcend the mere reportorial role that many college newspapers choose to assume… [and become] a mouthpiece for community action."[197] For example, the paper constantly pushed against Vassar's many "antiquated and foolish" social restrictions, right up until coeducation. The editors railed against parietal hours—strict visiting hours concerning male companions.[198] Residential life officials also asked for women to keep their doors open and leave "three feet on the floor." The 'new' *Miscellany* demanded that "students rise up to… ensure that visiting hours be extended on Friday and Saturday nights. This is a personal privilege and a personal responsibility." They added that, if administrators were concerned about sexual promiscuity, they were simply forcing Vassar girls into the "motel rooms of Poughkeepsie." The newspaper was willing to be bolder and blunter than ever before.

The editors also wanted to make their mission clear by allowing students to discuss their visions for the paper. A regular column called "Symposium" featured weekly comments by members of the community about not only the *Miscellany*, but about the philosophical role of a student newspaper:

> It seems to me that a campus newspaper, like the *Miscellany*, should look around the College community, reflect on its responsibilities to all elements of the community, and do the best job that it can to convey an objective and disinterested view of campus life. It is, of course, entitled to its own opinions… but it seems to me particularly important that when it is the one newspaper for the whole community, it ought to approach its job in the spirit of good feeling and concern for the cohesiveness of the community. —Elizabeth Daniels '41, Dean of Students (now College Historian).

> The campus press [here]… seems almost to conceive its role as an editorial role *only*. The *Misc* should criticize as an adjunct to its main function as an informer. —Colton Johnson, Professor of English (now Dean of the College Emeritus).

> All of us accept the usual clichés about the responsibilities of a campus newspaper. But last year, the *Misc* took on the additional role of providing the only impetus for student action heard in a long while in Poughkeepsie. This place needs the constant kick in the pants that the *Misc* gave it. Responsible students expect the paper to continue in this role. —Patricia Turner '67, Student.[199]

While Daniels and Johnson hoped for a newspaper that was objective, unbiased and a conveyer of fact, Turner wanted a paper that would instigate and give a "constant kick in the pants." It was no secret that the Editorial Board of the 1960s sided with this final vision for the paper. Indeed, the editor's inclusion of the two faculty members' comments in the "Symposium" just demonstrates how radical they hoped to be, directly defying the wishes of administrators. Perhaps the clearest proof was a "*Misc* News Analysis" by Dunlop printed right beside this "Symposium." Dunlop's piece discussed a study of campus newspapers across the country by University of Wisconsin researcher Jeff Greenfield.[200] Greenfield had described "two distinct schools of thought" in the American collegiate press. The first is passive, "an adjunct of the university's own publications," and the second is "active, critical and skeptical." Not surprisingly, he believed that the "active" approach was far more incisive and professional.

Greenfield's discovery was not far from Vivian Liebman's old distinction between the *Miscellany* before and after the Great Depression. But this seemed to be an intensification of Liebman's philosophy. Not only should the Editorial Board declare its own opinions, but it should also use the newspaper as an instrument of social change. While the editors of 1942 academically critiqued the "Slap a Jap" booth at Founder's Day, the editors of 1966 likely would have advocated mass protests and demonstrations. The paper's goals were higher.

Clearly, the juxtaposition between the Greenfield article and the statements of Daniels and Johnson was nothing short of purposeful. The editors *wanted* to show the outmoded way of conceptualizing a student newspaper that they felt existed in the College administration. In 1965, the editors declared outright that "this year… we will take a less tolerant view of the powers-that-be on the Vassar campus."[201] In the anti-authoritarian spirit of the sixties, they sought to assert the supremacy of student voice to a greater degree than ever before. The editors reiterated their concern for student experience two years later: "We have a commitment to Vassar," they wrote in September 1967, "but not the Vassar of 1920 or of 1950, but the Vassar of 1967."[202] The editors truly believed that the arrangement of the "new *Misc*"—the restructured Editorial Board, the revised formatting and the strengthened editorial voice—would be sturdy enough to thrive for generations. Indeed, the late 1960s saw unprecedented increases in community interest and involvement in the newspaper. Readership soared.

But little did these editors know, their "newly perfected structure" was about to come suddenly and irreparably unhinged.

144   The data presented and graphed here represents weeks of counting the number of opinionated items printed in each issue of the paper, averaged together by month. Obviously, the chronology is not entirely contiguous, since no issues are printed during the summer months, or during the winter break. Also, it should be noted that there is no way to determine the number of letters that were *submitted* in a given week versus the number that were *printed*. In other words, the paper sometimes declines to print certain letters, either because there is not enough space or because the author's facts or presentation do not meet certain standards. So while this data might not be a perfect measure, it is still a useful (though broad) indicator of tracking student participation and engagement in the *Miscellany*.

145   "Misc. News," The *Vassarion*, 1944.

146   "*Miscellany News*iana," The *Vassar Miscellany News*, April 14, 1940.

147   Hopkins continued her interest in writing after Vassar, graduating from the Columbia School of Journalism in 1945. She then worked for local newspapers in New Haven, Providence and Oklahoma City before moving to Boston in 1951 to direct the American Unitarian Association (AUA) News Office. From there, she shifted into book publishing to become Senior Editor of the AUA's Beacon Press, and from there was hired by major New York publisher Harcourt, Brace, Harper & Row. Her next career move was to Wesleyan University in 1989, where she became the Director of the Wesleyan University Press and Adjunct Professor of English. Even after her "retirement" in 1992 to New Hampshire, she continues—at the age of 86— to be an active editorial consultant to writers and reporters.

148   "Changing Society," The *Vassar Miscellany*, May 2, 1944.

149   "United Nations as New Way Forward," The *Vassar Miscellany*, March 29, 1943.

150   "Ruins and Visions," The *Vassar Miscellany*, September 6, 1945.

151   Olivia Mancini, "Vassar's First Black Graduate: She Passed for White," The Journal of Blacks in Higher Education, No. 34 (Winter, 2001-2002), pp. 108-109. Mancini, a Class of 2000 graduate of Vassar, wrote an article on Hemmings for the *Vassar Quarterly*, which was reprinted in The Journal of Blacks in Higher Education. Anita Florence Hemmings is an amazing figure in Vassar's history, a figure who complicates understandings of racial identity today just as she did for students in the 1890s. When Hemmings applied to Vassar in 1893, there was nothing in her record to suggest that she would be any different from the 103 other girls entering the Class of 1897. At Vassar, she was as accomplished student, mastering Latin, ancient Greek, and French. She was also a highly regarded soprano in the College choir. Her race was never an issue, until her white roommate "voiced suspicions about Hemmings' background to her father only a few weeks before the class was due to graduate." Concerned, the roommate's father hired an investigator to travel to Hemmings' hometown of Boston. There it was "discovered that homemaker Dora Logan and janitor Robert Williamson Hemmings had conspired with their daughter" to keep Anita's race a secret. "We know our daughter went to Vassar as a white girl and stayed there as such," said her father to a Boston newspaper when the story became public in August. "As long as she conducted herself as a lady, she never thought it necessary to proclaim the fact that her parents were mulattoes." It would be 40 years before Vassar would knowingly open its doors to another African American student. By that time, many of Vassar's peer schools, even the conservative Radcliffe and Smith, had already been admitting black students for several decades. According to June Jackson Christmas, herself one of Vassar's first African American graduates, "the move to formally admit black students [to the College] was brought about by a young Presbyterian minister from Harlem, James Robinson." Robinson was invited to speak at a religious conference sponsored by the YWCA and Vassar in the late 1930s. He offered to find "a black student of Vassar caliber" for the College to enroll. "In his congregation at the Church of the Master he found Beatrix McCleary '44, a gifted student at her high school in New York," wrote Christmas in a 1988 Vassar Quarterly article. "She applied, was accepted, and in the fall of 1940 entered Vassar as the first openly acknowledged Negro student in Vassar's history."

152 Born in 1868, William Edward Burghardt Du Bois was a noted scholar, author and African American activist. He was a founding member of the National Association for the Advancement of Colored People (NAACP), which is the largest and oldest civil rights organization in America. Throughout his career, Du Bois fought discrimination and racism, writing 17 books and delivering numerous speeches across the United States.

153 Pinar Batur, "Heart of Violence: Global Racism, War and Genocide," in Handbooks of Sociology and Social Research, ed. Hernán Vera and Joe R. Feagin. (Springer, 2007), p. 451.

154 *Ibid.*

155 *Ibid.*

156 "The Whole Truth," The *Vassar Miscellany News*, June 11, 1947.

157 "Editorial," The *Vassar Miscellany News*, March 10, 1948.

158 "Reply to Rumor," The *Vassar Chronicle*, March 17, 1944.

159 Sarah Riane Harper, "The *Chronicle*," edited by Elizabeth Daniels. 2007. http://vcencyclopedia.vassar.edu/index.php/The_Chronicle (accessed June 17, 2008).

160 Ironically, the Greek communists were defeated, but not because of Truman's support. Tito, the communist leader of Yugoslavia, had been allowing the Greek communists to cross into his nation. But Tito, who became fearful that Stalin would use the Greek Communists against him, shut the border. Thus, many of the Greek communists could be captured.

161 "Same Old Doctrine," The *Vassar Miscellany News*, May 28, 1947.

162 "Error—ECA," The *Vassar Miscellany News*, May 21, 1947.

163 "Against the Proposal," The *Vassar Miscellany News* and The *Vassar Chronicle*, April 8, 1948.

164 "A Look at Politics," The *Vassar Miscellany*, October 11, 1951.

165 "The *Misc* and We," The *Vassar Chronicle*, February 14, 1959.

166 "The *Misc* and We," The *Vassar Chronicle*, February 14, 1959.

167 "Editorial I," The *Vassar Miscellany News*, February 11, 1959.

168 Arvalea Nelson, "Letter to the Editor," The *Vassar Miscellany News*, March 4, 1966.

169 "Board Declares Stand on Wallace Issue," The *Vassar Miscellany News*, October 19, 1948.

170 "Wallace for '48," The *Vassar Miscellany News*, October 19, 1948.

171 "Unwise Move," The *Vassar Miscellany News*, October 19, 1948.

172 "Letter to the Editor," The *Vassar Miscellany News*, March 25, 1948.

173 The connection between Buckley, Bozell and Vassar was a complex one. His girlfriend Patricia left Vassar in 1948 to marry Buckley, who was still at Yale. Patricia's roommate at Vassar was actually William F. Buckley's younger sister, also named Patricia. His sister would eventually marry *William's* roommate and Yale buddy Brent Bozell (with whom Buckley had debated the *Miscellany* editors)—a highly unusual coincidence. Buckley's connection to Vassar would become even stranger in 1980, when he was invited to speak at the College's graduation. Many students protested the invitation, complaining that Buckley supported the Vietnam War and was too conservative to speak for the graduating class. Buckley was sent copies of the *Miscellany News* to keep apprised of the controversy, and after reading the many letters to the editor on the subject, he decided not to speak. In a note to Vassar President Virginia Smith, Buckley wrote that "a numerical majority of the senior class recorded their opposition to my speaking at Commencement." He continued, "The majority of the senior class at Vassar does not desire my company, and I must confess, having read specimens of their thoughts and sentiments, that I do not desire the company of the majority of the senior class." Buckley's letter to Smith was obtained by the *New York Times* and quoted in an article on May 20, 1980. He referred to Vassar students as "fearfully ill-instructed" and "ferociously illiterate." On May 20, *Miscellany* editor Laura Wimmer '81 published a special, two-page 8.5 x 11 newspaper with an article about the Commencement debacle.

174 "Letter to the Editor," The *Vassar Miscellany News*, April 9, 1948.

175 Speech of Joseph McCarthy, Wheeling, West Virginia, February 9, 1950

176 "7 College Editors May Visit Moscow," The *New York Times*, September 3, 1953.

177 Actually, this was a very unusual practice after the mid-1930s, as faculty members no longer wrote extensive articles for the paper. Bond was returning to a model that had been used in the early days of the *Weekly*, whereby faculty would author their own column, "Faculty Notes," about themselves and important College policies.

178 Mead, arguably the most famous anthropologist of the 20th century, was a visiting lecturer at Vassar between 1939 and 1941. She eventually took a position at Columbia University in New York City, and still returned to Poughkeepsie occasionally to lecture.

179 In the 1950s, the *Miscellany* would fight a hard battle against the necessity of this curfew. "The regulatory power of the social system should be placed in student hands where it belongs," read a September 20, 1950 staff editorial. "Students should exercise their responsibility, as well as their freedom, by taking the initiative to prevent excessive noise."

180 "Frosh Reporter Gives Vivid Account of *Misc* from Bylines to Monday Night Sessions," The *Vassar Miscellany News*, September 1, 1962.

181 Sarah Riane Harper, "Vassar Newspapers Tackle Pressing Concern: Which College Men are Best for the "Vassar Girl?", edited by Elizabeth Daniels. 2007. http://vcencyclopedia.vassar.edu/index.php/Vassar_Newspapers_Tackle_Pressing_Concern:_Which_College_Men_are_Best_for_the_%22Vassar_Girl%3F%22 (accessed May 19, 2008).

182 "Yale," The *Vassar Miscellany*, September 1, 1968.

183 This column constantly referenced other school's newspapers, which seemed to be the editors' primary source of information. For example, the *Miscellany* often included news tidbits quoted directly from the *Johns Hopkins News-Letter*, the *Barnard Bulletin* and the *Wesleyan Argus*. This suggests that there might have been some sort of newspaper exchange between editors of the different undergraduate newspapers. Such a system exists today between the *Miscellany News*, the *Bi-College News*, the *Wesleyan Argus* and the *Smith Sophian*.

184   Yale was a notable exception to this general rule; Yale University seemed to be a fairly significant point of interest for Vassar students even decades before the proposed merger.

185   "Letdown," The *Vassar Miscellany News*, September 21, 1966. Reprinted in the *Daily Princetonian* on September 28, 1966.

186   Vassar's chapter of Students for a Democratic Society (SDS) would be a particularly active one during the 1960s. The FBI even monitored one massive 1968 rally in the Chapel.

187   "Dean Nelbach Discusses Standards, Regulations," The *Vassar Miscellany News*, April 11, 1962.

188   "Editorial," The *Vassar Miscellany News*, April 11, 1962.

189   "Vassar's Hall of Presidents," The *Vassar Quarterly*, Spring 2006.

190   Blanding's highly controversial speech might have satisfied some conservative alumnae, but it also angered many others in the Vassar community. She was cast as being behind the times, and resigned two years later in 1964 after 18 years. Interestingly, despite her conflicts with the *Miscellany News* and with Chayat, she wrote a cordial departing letter to the newspaper, printed on May 6, 1964: "My association with the *Miscellany News* has been one of long standing. In the late 20s and early 30s when I was engaged in trying to improve the student press of the university at which I was then working, I used the *Miscellany* as an example of an excellent college paper. Since coming to Vassar, my association has been much closer as I have known your editors and your reporters. While we may not have always been in agreement, I have enjoyed my encounters with the staff. A good student press is a great asset to any institution of higher education. A sound, forward-looking editorial policy can do much to influence the policies of a college; wide coverage of campus events both past and future, accurate reporting, and writing articles that use the English language with style are the qualities that make for a first-rate college paper. With the numerous pressures under which students now seem to work, these qualities are not easy of achievement, but it is my believe that Vassar students are capable of overcoming any difficulty and so I shall look forward to receiving the *Misc,* reading its editorials keeping abreast of campus events, and taking pride in its long and honorable existence. Cordially, Sarah Gibson Blanding."

191   "Summer Program Benefits White, Not Blacks," The *Vassar Miscellany News*, October 4, 1968.

192   "*Misc* Celebrates Golden Anniversary," The *Vassar Miscellany News*, February 5, 1964.

193 "*Misc* Announces Spring Promotions," The *Vassar Miscellany News*, April 13, 1966.

194 Between the 1970s and 1980s, the title of "Associate Editor" went in and out of use. Eventually, it morphed into "Assistant Editor," a position that still exists today. Assistant Editors typically serve under a section editor, and are trained by that editor in various technical and journalistic skills.

195 "New Look, Old *Misc*," The *Vassar Miscellany News*, December 9, 1966.

196 "No. 3196 Gives *Misc* New Flag," The *Vassar Miscellany News*, October 26, 1966.

197 "New Look, Old *Misc*," The *Vassar Miscellany News*, December 9, 1966.

198 "Social Regulations: Editorial," The *Vassar Miscellany News*, October 18, 1967.

199 "Symposium," The *Vassar Miscellany News*, September 26, 1966.

200 "*Misc* News Analysis: Greenfield Article Lauds Outspoken College Press," The *Vassar Miscellany News*, September 26, 1966.

201 "The New *Misc*," The *Vassar Miscellany*, September 24, 1965.

202 *Ibid.*

Chapter Four:
The Struggle for Modernity,
1968-2004

From this zenith popularity and purpose, it would seem that the *Miscellany* had nowhere to go but down. Sure enough, the next chapter in the newspaper's history was rife with more upheaval, more policy shifts and more staff turnover than ever before. The seemingly linear climb from a literary magazine to a professional, progressive, globally aware newspaper was suddenly interrupted. This tumultuous period for the paper coincided with an equally tumultuous period for the College: the dawn of coeducation in 1969. Coeducation for Vassar meant much more than simply admitting male students; it meant a tearing of the administrative and social fabric of the institution.[203] Founded as the first endowed college for women, Vassar was suddenly forced to renegotiate its identity.

The seeds of coeducation had been planted as early as the late 1950s. Declining applications led administrators to see that Vassar's single-sex environment made it an increasingly unattractive choice for progressive young women. Each weekend saw what Elizabeth Daniels '41 called a "mass exodus" from the Poughkeepsie campus to coed social functions across New York. Social life at Vassar was diminishing. The *Miscellany News*, for example, conducted several inquiries about why Vassar was "sick." "That's the word they used," said Daniels, who was Dean of Studies during the period. "Why was Vassar 'sick'? It was getting to be too parochial. Students packed their suitcases on Thursday afternoon and unpacked them Monday afternoon. There was nothing to do here on weekends." Indeed, the all-female atmosphere that had once made Vassar cutting edge now made it too insular for its students. In 1961, President Sarah Gibson Blanding famously predicted that, "Of the hundred or more women's colleges now in existence, no more than ten will be functioning in the year 2061."[204] Even early into the 21st century, her prediction is coming true. In 2007, the United States had about 60 women's colleges in only 24 states.[205] Of these, two prominent institutions, Wells College and Randolph-Macon College, went coed in 2005 and 2006, respectively. The forces currently impacting the remaining women's colleges were similar to those affecting Vassar by the late 1960s.

In short, many students and faculty members began to feel that the College's approach to women's education was outmoded. According to a poll by the committee investigating the situation, a clear majority of students felt that "the absence of men in Vassar classes involve[d]... an important loss of perspective." Perhaps more pressingly, competing coeducational schools were able to attract a larger donor base than Vassar. At a time when women's salaries lagged significantly behind men's, the College was having difficulty keeping up. A 1962 faculty vote authorized the College to consider various methods of incorporating men into the life of the institution.

With all of this swirling in the background, Vassar underwent a significant administrative change in 1964. From the long-serving James Monroe Taylor, to the liberal Henry Noble MacCracken, to the feminist Sarah Gibson Blanding, the English-born Alan Simpson assumed the presidency that summer. Simpson mixed old-world morals with a highly progressive attitude toward education. While he championed an overhauled modern curriculum, he demanded that students act with "style and grace" and once condemned the "lack of decency" found in the *Vassarion*.[206] Nevertheless, Simpson arrived at Vassar "in the decade when there were a lot of unsettled people: the Civil Rights Movement, the Vietnam War, and the fact that students all over the country and even all over the world were beginning to rise up and demand their part in colleges' governance and seemed to demand a new kind of education," said Daniels. Change was certainly in the air, and Simpson led the way.

After extensive research and discussion by the faculty working group, the first step toward coeducation came with meetings of Simpson and Yale President Kingman Brewster. Yale, which only admitted men, was itself grappling with the idea of coeducation. In 1966, the two institutions began a yearlong study on the possibility of merging. The Vassar community was thoroughly divided on the issue. While the majority of students seemed to advocate coeducation—one *Miscellany* headline following Simpson and Brewster's first meeting read, "For God, for Country, for Yale and Vassar"—some alumnae voiced extreme opposition. Even among administrators, many questions were raised: would the entire faculty move? Would Vassar's identity simply be absorbed into Yale? Would Vassar students and faculty have any level of autonomy, or would they merely be subservient to the large university?[207] While many alumnae objected to the very principle of coeducation, current students seemed to object to coeducation only if it meant losing Vassar's unique identity.

In 1967, after much internal and external debate, Vassar officially declined the merger. But at the same time, it made the historic announcement that it would open its doors to men. By Spring 1969, Vassar had become fully coeducational.

The *Miscellany News*, always progressive, supported the integration of men in numerous editorials. Far ahead of most students and faculty members, the Editorial Board first advocated coeducation in 1950.[208] The editors had interviewed numerous campus officials, ranging from the Students' Association President to the President of the College, and recorded their opinions; nearly everyone opposed coeducation at that time, except for the "dissenting voice" of the defiant Editorial Board. "Our student body should consist of 50 percent men and 50 percent women, drawn from as wide a geographical area as possible, by identical standards of admission," declared the staff. "There is a strong element of inevitability in our feeling. We not only *advocate*, we *predict*." Their words proved prophetic.

Editors for the next two decades would reiterate the arguments of that famed 1950 editorial. Indeed, the 1968 editorial following the coeducation decision reused many of the arguments nearly verbatim.[209]

"The *Misc* believes that the [Trustees'] decision to pursue coeducation was in the tradition of innovation at Vassar," they wrote, adding that they "agree with the proposal of a 1:1 relationship between men and women," just as the paper had proposed 18 years earlier. Even privately, the editors pushed for coeducation. "Men in classes and on campus is the only way to prevent stagnancy," said Managing Editor Susan Casteras '69 in an October 1968 interview with the *New York Times*.[210] "The Ivy walls have tumbled down. Mother Vassar has foresworn numerous suitors, and now she just has to relinquish her spinster bed for the sake of educating her students."

But even after the difficult decision was made, the process of integrating men was more difficult than many anticipated. An article in *Esquire* turned an uncomfortable spotlight onto the first men at Vassar, using the flamboyant character of "Jackie St. James." In one of the tamer passages, Janie Gaynor wrote, "The 'Vassar Male' has not had time to develop completely, but the preliminary model seems to be skinny with a sallow complexion." The implication was clear: *Esquire* was painting Vassar men as effeminate and weak—ironically, the exact opposite image of the stereotypically strong-willed Vassar women.[211]

The College was also bursting at the seams. In 1968, Vassar's student body numbered 1,633. By 1972, that number was 2,331—a 43 percent increase in just four years. Virtually everything had to change in order to accommodate the growth. The Town Houses and Terrace Apartments were built to accommodate the extra students. The system of dining rooms in individual dormitories was replaced with a centralized building, the renovated Students' Building. Athletics expanded. Bureaucracy increased. Vassar was in flux.

Vassar Miscellany News

Volume LIII   Poughkeepsie, N.Y.   October 4, 1968   Number 2

Vassar to Pursue Complete Coeducation ; Method and Cost Under Consideration

by Laura Jones
Editor-in-Chief

The Vassar College Board of Trustees voted July 11, 1968 to accept the Forward Planning Committee resolution "that it adopt a policy of admission of male undergraduate students on a wholly coeducational basis.

Last November in announcing the decision not to merge with Yale, the Trustees committed Vassar to educating men. The faculty voted 102-3 in favor of coeducation over coeducation last May.

At the direction of the trustees Dean Nell Eurich's office drew up a report on how Vassar could go coeducational, "Issues Involved in the Implementation of Men's Education at Vassar

College." The report discusses coeducation at Vassar in terms of timing, scheduling, recruitment, requisite construction and provision of funds.

The report was compiled from reports made last year by various committees to the Faculty Steering Committee. One major study was the Langdon-Griffen report on a coordinate men's college. The original draft was studied and revised by about forty teachers and some students in the class of '68.

A high administrative source revealed that the trustees will meet October 18 and 19. At that time they will review and probably vote on this report.

The report begins with a working hypothesis

of 2400 students in a 1:1 ratio of men and women as the goal. Forty more teachers would be added.

The report provides a possible schedule for coeducation which has Vassar admitting 215 men in the fall of 1970. Each year the school would increase the male enrollment by 250 while decreasing the female by about 40. The goal of 2400 in a 1:1 ratio would be reached in 1975.

The delay until 1975 was suggested by the report to give Vassar time to develop a strong attractive recruitment program. Vassar has long studied the needs, aptitudes and goals of women "... we must demonstrate an equal concern for men."

The relatively large number of men to be admitted is considered necessary. "It is important to the success of coeducation at Vassar College that a strong initial thrust be made away from the exclusively female image of Vassar College."

The report also includes a suggested list of physical plant changes. Some of these are needed regardless of the increased student body. Basic proposals include the rehabilitation of existing dorms and classrooms, a new food service system, construction of a new biological science building, of a new experimental theater, of a student center, of a science library or expansion of the present library, and an addition to Baldwin, the infirmary.

The present classroom space is considered sufficient for 2400 students if schedules are carefully planned. The new science building and experimental theater would provide additional classrooms and faculty office space.

The report suggests the construction of apartments and/or dorms on the east bank of Sunset Lake in the area between the golf course and the main campus. Used service would be supplied by four dining halls serving 800 each. One hall could go in the area west of the present campus on Raymond Avenue and all other could be combined with the new student center east of Raymond Avenue in some relationship to the circle, future dorms, apartment and present Main.

The report assumes that the remaining 800 would not be on a required food contract. They would either get their meals on a non-contract basis or prepare food in their apartments.

The report estimates the cost of this construction at $33,660,000. $13,900,000 is involved in construction most directly related to the increase in students and the presence of male students. These estimates are at 1968 prices. A final price for the work scheduled for completion in 1975 is inflated to the 44 to 45 million dollar range.

An article in the Wednesday issue of the New York Times quoted Lewis A. Bartlett, secretary of the college, on the college decision to go coeducational. Mr. Bartlett said that coeducation would enable Vassar to achieve a sizable male enrollment more quickly than a coordinate arrangement.

Mr. Bartlett continued: "The efficient and simple thing to do is to start new and think coeducation."

According to the Vassar College Charter, Vassar may only grant degrees to women. Legislation is now being prepared to modify this situation.

Coeducation is not the only change being contemplated at Vassar. Other proposals currently being studied include curriculum and exchanges with mens schools. Vassar considers the proposed exchanges with men's schools a good opportunity to put male reaction to Vassar classes and to work out possible residential and administrative problems.

V.C. Study Proposes Curric Reform, Offers Flexible, Individual Program

by Susan Casteras
Managing Editor

Vassar, Men's Colleges Plan Residential Exchange

by Merle Powell
News Editor

Continued on 12

NO MORE FAKE MEN!!

This front page from October 4, 1968—particularly the bottom right image—demonstrates the excitement among the editors for coeducation.

Changes and Troubles

To respond to an entirely new student body, and in the face of steep financial constrictions on its student government budget, the newspaper tried to overhaul its image. In Fall 1969, the *Vassar Miscellany News* renamed itself the *Misc*, the paper's longstanding nickname, in order to appear fresher for a modern environment. The paper's layout, which held relatively constant since the 1930s with only the slight touch-up of 1968, suddenly changed dramatically—and not for the better. Ads were placed haphazardly on the pages. Thick boxes were used (and overused) to highlight articles. Gaudy, modern fonts were used for headlines.

Although the student body had grown larger, the staff shrunk slightly in 1970 and 1971. The paper saw an all-time low in submissions of letters to the editor, suggesting that fewer students considered the *Miscellany* to be the conduit of student voice. "It didn't seem to impact anyone's day very much," recalled former Staff Writer Andrea Disario Marcusa '76. "We all had subscriptions to the *New York Times* and there wasn't much to agitate on campus about." Marcusa did not feel that the paper was taken seriously, and believed that her greatest privilege of being on the staff were free theater tickets to shows in New York City in exchange for writing short reviews.

Not everyone was quite so pessimistic. Some editors maintained the sense of mission inspired by editors like Chayat and Knickerbocker. "We were infused with the excitement of investigative journalism, and in particular the success of Woodward and Bernstein who had broken the Watergate story for the *Washington Post*," said Peter Cohen '78. "I recall working on a story about the fees paid to off-duty policemen who were required at on-campus parties." It was no Watergate, but Cohen still felt exhilarated writing for the public good.

But despite such earnest efforts, there can be no doubt that students in Fall 1970 were greeted with a very different paper than the one they left the previous spring. Indeed, many reacted against the redesigned, often sloppy paper. "Students around campus are now talking about getting together and publishing another newspaper besides the *Misc*," whined a December editorial.[212] "Last Wednesday, a meeting was held in Cushing to discuss the possibility and determine the interest among the community." The editors' response to these potential competitors can only be described as indignant. "We of the *Misc* wish them all the luck in the world. They will need it," read the editorial. "The *Misc* gets only one thing from the students—criticism." They continued:

> We are as aware as anyone, if not more so, of the failings of the paper. There ought to be more features, reviews of books and current movies, in-depth reporting of ongoing campus issues, such as Vassar's role as a landlord in Poughkeepsie and Vassar's role as an employer in Poughkeepsie. The lack of such articles is not due to a dearth of ideas on the part of the editors, but to a dearth of competent writers who will agree to do them and get them done.

The editorial essentially challenged students to create a newspaper better than the *Miscellany*. After all, the editors contested, only four editors put together the entire paper, often working "40 or 50 hours each week with little sleep."

But their appeal for sympathy fell on deaf ears. For the first time in its history, the *Miscellany* was struggling to attract readership. Thanks to a larger student body and several new local printers, publishing had become easier, allowing rival publications to sprout up on campus.[213] Although these new publications quickly folded under similar pressures, the oldest campus publication had a difficult time attracting new and energetic readers and writers. Staff came and went from the paper, making weekly production thorny. "The Editorial Board changes every week [and]... there are maybe three people who can be relied on to turn in well-written articles on time," the editors wrote in an effort to draw new recruits.[214]

On November 20, 1970, the *Miscellany* made the historic announcement that it would suspend publication for the remainder of the fall semester:

> The *Misc* is suspending publication for the rest of the semester due to lack of funds and student interest. Since the remaining financial resources could possibly run out before the end of the school year, the Editorial Board has decided to stop publishing now instead of risking having to stop in the spring so that it can use the intervening time for reorganization and possible reorientation.[215]

The four 'missing' issues represent the longest publication break in the paper's 150-year history.[216] The situation got even worse. In the last issue before the hiatus, Editor in Chief Judith Williams '70 announced her resignation—the first time that such a resignation was publically recorded. Her resignation, printed on the first page, is telling example of the problems that afflicted the century-old newspaper, as well as the College overall:

To the Students,

I'm tired and I'm depressed. I'm depressed by a college whose newspaper is barely functioning because students don't wish to write for it. I'm depressed by the fact that Main Building, which should have ten senators, has only five because only five applied for the position. I'm depressed by the fact that the newly-opened Coffee House is already having trouble getting students to help with operations and may be forced to close. But most important, the situation at Vassar seems to me to be representative of the terrible quiet crisis in America, which seems so prevalent on the nation's campuses. The apathy, the tendency to ignore important issues, the fact that although the Kent State indictments raised serious questions regarding the legal system of this country, few students have expressed concern about the situation and fewer have tried to do anything about it, are tragic.

Two years ago, I believed that our generation was in some way different. This is not true. In the early '50s, when the civil rights movement was young, optimism prevailed. The peace movement experienced a similar phase in the early '60s. The situation is no longer optimistic. Demonstrations and activities planned to end the war generally result in confrontations with the police. The Panthers have now become an entrenched political party subject to harassment and perhaps systematic elimination by the police and other elements in our society—and still we remain unaware and inactive.

I feel compelled to resign from the *Misc* because I am convinced that this is the only way to make people aware of the issues both on this campus and nationally. I can no longer participate in the farcical illusion that Vassar has a legitimate newspaper that is both for and by the students. A campus newspaper cannot function without a campus. In closing, I would like to quote Pastor Niemoller, a prominent West German religious leader who was placed in a concentration camp during the Hitler regime: "when the Nazi's came for the communists in 1933, I did not speak up because I was not a communist. Then they came for the Jews, and I did not speak up because I was not a Jew. Then they came for the trade unionists and I did not speak up because I was not a trade unionist. Then they came for the Catholics and I was a Protestant, so I did not speak up. Then they

128

came for me, and by that time there was no one to speak for anyone." The Vassar students have a choice: Will you speak or remain silent?

Sincerely,
Judith Williams[217]

The picture that Williams painted was a deeply troubling one. Problems clearly extended far beyond the publishing dilemmas *Miscellany*. It seemed that the whole College community was struggling to involve its students. The newspaper was not the only organization suffering; almost no one ran for the student government in 1970, threatening the government's very existence. "People complain ceaselessly about the student government's structure, calling it ineffective and even worthless," wrote the editors, "but it is the same old story; those who criticize do not try to involve themselves to improve what they think is wrong."[218] In short, students appeared emotionally removed from Vassar's internal affairs after coeducation.[219]

By depriving the campus of its primary newspaper, Williams and the *Miscellany* editors clearly hoped to jump start appreciation and support.[220] "The Board believes this College needs a jolt of discovering that there is not even enough interest here to sustain a decent student newspaper," the editors wrote.[221] They also knew that cutting those four issues would stave off their budget deficit and allow time for another physical redesign.

But the paper returned the following January with only small formatting alterations. The most enduring change that they made was to the name: the *Misc* shifted to the *Miscellany News*. Additionally, significantly more men had joined; by February 1971, five of the nine members of the Editorial Board were male. But the sloppy layout and writing continued with only mild improvements. The editors' hope that the production break would eliminate criticism proved false. Just a few months later, the *Miscellany* was once again facing disapproval. "A common criticism is that the paper is dull, as it contains little that is not already known, and is more oriented toward... matters such as building renovations," admitted a September 1971 editorial:

> Many have urged the radicalization of the *Misc* into a forum for left-wing politics, and anti-administration viewpoints. To be fair, it should be remembered that the ultimate purpose of the paper's existence is to inform the College community. The editorial staff has long ago given up

> the once popular image of themselves as molders of opinion. They have
> perceived a greater challenge in keeping their own biases out of articles on
> controversial issues, feeling that therein lies their service to the students.
> Believing that the Vassar student body is not a proletariat in search of a
> vanguard, articles are presented in a style that allows the individual to
> form an opinion.[222]

It seems rather strange that the editors declare that they had
"long ago given up the once popular image of themselves as molders
of public opinion"—only two years earlier, the Board asserted that
it would "take it upon itself to push the campus away from lethargy
and toward correct actions."[223] How quickly they forgot. Once again,
Vivian Liebman's "old mirror question" was coming to the forefront:
should the paper mirror the views of the campus, or mirror the views
of its editors? While the popular and progressive *Miscellany* of the
1960s allowed editors to influence coverage in the paper, often slanting
coverage against the administration or toward liberal causes, the 1971
Editorial Board adopted the more conventional, unbiased approach.
Also, note that this staff editorial mentions that "the ultimate purpose
of the paper's existence is to inform the College community." This
stands in contrast to the views of earlier editors, who asserted that the
Miscellany News should be wholly for students, both in its coverage and
in its perspectives. The times had evidently changed. The muckraking,
opinion-shaping style of journalism had been replaced by "an insistence
on objectivity."[224] Less gutsiness and zest, unfortunately, meant fewer
readers.

Although students might have been turned off by this objectivity,
the College administration rather enjoyed it. College President Alan
Simpson was quoted frequently, almost weekly, showing the strength
of his relationship with the paper. Even today, reporters only bother
the College president for comments when absolutely necessary. The
fact that the *Miscellany* was able to speak so frequently with Simpson
suggests that he viewed the paper as an important and loyal form
of student media; even if people were sometimes misquoted (as the
lengthy corrections box each week suggests) and the paper lacked some
of its former professionalism, at least it was not as critical or probing as
the *Miscellany* of the 1960s.

Similarly, the paper of the 1970s also maintained a better relationship
with the student government, giving the Student Government

Association a weekly column to discuss their work. This would have been unheard of in the 1960s, when the paper tried to remain distant from and critical of any authority. But now, the *Miscellany* merely reported the words of leaders, from the College president and student body president. This lack of critical or investigative reporting angered the increasingly liberal student body and turned many away from the paper.

Men in Charge: Coeducation Comes to the *Miscellany*

The College's character was understandably shaky during the early 1970s. The student body, once defined by its gender, suddenly lacked identity. Similarly, the *Miscellany* had a long history of female empowerment. Some of the nation's most significant female writers and publishers had gotten their start running Vassar's student newspaper. The question of men suddenly joining student organizations extended far beyond the *Miscellany News*; it was a pervasive concern among the faculty, trustees and student body. Between 1969 and 1973, men began to lead numerous groups, raising fears that the self-empowered Vassar woman was a dying breed. "Women of Vassar College, where are you?" asked an October 1971 staff editorial.[225] The candidates for the recent Student Government Association (SGA) election—just the second since coeducation—were disproportionately male. Though Vassar had 550 men out of its 2,000 students, there were 48 men running against only 41 women. "The *Misc* does not suggest that the male members of the Vassar community disassociate themselves completely from campus politics," wrote the editors, "[but] women should take a greater interest in campus issues, not for the sake of politics alone, but for the sake of remembering their roles as women at Vassar."

But the Editorial Board's criticisms of the SGA elections were a bit disingenuous considering its own makeup at the time of that editorial. After only two years of coeducation, men accounted for 46 percent of the paper's staff and only 28 percent of the student body. Throughout the 1970s, men invaded the paper quickly and disproportionately. Peter Cohen '78 recalls an increasing number of men on the staff between his freshmen and sophomore years. This also corresponds to the quick rise of men at Vassar in general; there were only 690 in 1974, and 924 by 1978. Suddenly, men were joining the staff and taking control.

"Resentment is not exactly the right word," said Andrew Getzfeld '81, who served as a photographer. "But there was definitely some unease about men working on the paper." Though Getzfeld recalls getting along very well with his female coworkers, he also felt slightly unwelcome. "There was no direct exclusion. It was just a feeling that I had," he said. "There was this feeling that I was in a space that I shouldn't be in, even into the late 1970s after men had already been at the school for multiple years."

This was not the first time that men had tried with difficultly to join the *Miscellany*. After World War II, Vassar admitted male veterans under the G.I. Bill. More than 90 men studied at Vassar during those post-War years. They were able to socialize and participate in extracurricular activities, including the campus newspaper. Pete Berg and Jack Schwarschild, listed as contributing editors in 1947, co-wrote a weekly column entitled "Male Call." Featured regularly on the top of page two, the column was popular—but it was also resented. The paper received regular letters to the editor and community responses about the "off-putting nature of seeing these men in our *Misc*."[226] Their very presence on the pages of the newspaper created unease. Needless to say, Berg and Schwarschild never rose to the upper levels of the *Miscellany*'s management. Even with male writers, women would continue to run the paper.

But this was about to change. For the first time, 1974 saw the first male Editor in Chief of the *Miscellany News*: Jason Isaacson '74. Isaacson first joined the paper during his sophomore year in 1972 designing weekly crossword puzzles. These popular puzzles grew larger and more intricate with each issue, and he soon moved to writing articles about arts and entertainment, and then onto topics like student government and College policies. Isaacson noticed the ways in which Vassar was changing over his four years. "One of the major aspects of Vassar that I saw, and that really informed my experience on the paper, was the very conscious push toward becoming male-friendly," he recalled. "There was a serious, even bizarre attempt to attract men and promote the notion of male acceptance. The Admissions Office printed these brochures that showed beefy guys playing lacrosse on the cover, and many of the frills, ranging from feminine, decorative ornamentation to the White Angels who guarded the residence halls, began to disappear."

The College was "twisting itself into knots" in order to dramatically overhaul its image and attract male students. "It seemed that for a few years in the early 1970s, the school was changing in such a way that it was losing some of the uniqueness of Vassar. I remember feeling this way even though my friends and I were obviously beneficiaries to the change to coeducation."

As Isaacson wrote articles and crossword puzzles, he quickly developed strong friendships with many of the editors. At the time, the female Editor in Chief was dating the male Managing Editor. The couple broke up, causing the Managing Editor to resign. Isaacson was asked to take over the post, and he happily assumed the role of greater power, overseeing week-to-week production of the newspaper. Only a month or so later, the Editor in Chief resigned too. Isaacson was left at the helm. "There was really

Jason Isaacson '74, the *Miscellany*'s first male Editor in Chief, works alongside Managing Editor Liz Cameron '74. The *Vassar Quarterly*.

turmoil in the ranks among this small group of editors, and not just at the top," said Isaacson, who remembered frequent staff turnover.

The young man faced other problems as well. A loud group of seniors on campus remained angry and resentful of coeducation. "They thought that admitting men was just an awful idea, that it was stifling Vassar's tradition of female empowerment," Isaacson said. Such attitudes grew as men began to lead some of the most significant student organizations. To make matters worse, Isaacson's close friend Steve Hueglin '74 was elected the first male President of the SGA in Fall 1973. "There was definitely a handful of vocal women who were really perturbed by Steve's election and by my election," Isaacson recalled. "It wasn't that they threatened us directly, or anything like that. The tension just made our jobs more difficult and focused the public eye on us, as two important student leaders. They really felt that Vassar should come to terms with its absurd mistake and reverse coeducation. There were definitely some who suddenly felt that the *Misc* was part of this new, dark era where men were taking control. So as the school was encouraging the image of Vassar as a place where men could succeed, some students certainly felt that my election was just one more harbinger of the total spoiling of the College."

Though this resentment tainted Isaacson's experiences on the paper, he also shared many of the joys and rewards of other *Miscellany* alumnae/i. A political science major at Vasssar, Isaacson went on to a prominent career in politics. After graduation, he reported for a Kansas newspaper, and then became a regular contributor to the *New York Times* and *Military Logistics Forum*, a defense industry magazine. Combining his administrative skills with his writing abilities, he then served as press secretary and chief of staff to Senator Christopher Dodd of Connecticut. Isaacson managed Dodd's legislative and political agendas, focusing on foreign policy. In particular, he concentrated on the Middle East. This prepared him for his current job: Director of the American Jewish Community's Office of Government and International Affairs in Washington, D.C. As a liaison to the White House, Congress and Federal agencies, he writes policy briefs to members of the Federal government. Isaacson believes that a direct trajectory can be drawn between his experiences on the management of the newspaper and his later work in politics. "Journalism really brought me to it," he recalled. "The experience of management and leadership especially—that has been essential to my work as an administrator."

Thus, with awkwardness and tension, coeducation came to the *Miscellany*. Despite initial unease inside and outside of the newsroom, men seemed to have integrated into the Editorial Board fairly quickly. Moreover, as Isaacson shows, *Miscellany* men got as much from their journalistic and managerial experiences on the newspaper as the countless women who came before them.

the misc

Volume LVI — Poughkeepsie, N.Y. October 1, 1971 — Number 2

Campus Shoplifting: A Reality?

by ROCHELLE PLUMENBAUM

Alums See VC on TV Monday

Dorms Vote To Decide Pets Status

Libe Gets Lounge From Class of '71

Frosh Find Campus Jobs Scarce

Women's Lib Meets; Slates Fall Activities

This uncomfortable new design, exemplified by the October 1, 1971 issue, included an amateurish title font, tiny photographs and poor article spacing. The issue also included seven typos within the first three pages, as well as frequent grammar errors and stylistic inconsistencies.

Sloppiness, Slack and Declining Respect

In 1972, the *Miscellany News* was able to move out of its crowded, aging office in the Students' Building into a larger office in the recently constructed College Center. There, the paper also had access to its own darkroom directly across from the office complex, which led to a dramatic increase in the quality and quantity of photographs by the mid-1970s. Unfortunately, the new office space and imaging capabilities still did not translate into more professional content or style. "In general, the *Misc* wasn't taken very seriously," said Jane Calem Rosen '76, who wrote for the paper. "Nor did the writers and editors take themselves too seriously. I think it was a reflection of the times—sort of the freewheeling '70s."

And freewheeling it was. In the fall semester of 1972, the layout had grown worse than ever: headlines used distracting fonts, articles were frequently cut off, and pictures were awkwardly oversized. The once-crucial staff editorial was moved from the first column of the second page, a position it had occupied since 1914, to a less central location deep inside the paper. Pages two and three became a large entertainment section; hard news coverage decreased, and sports dominated the final few pages. Rather than recruiting student cartoonists the way that the paper had done since the 1940s, the students of the 1970s paid to print the nationally syndicated Doonesbury comic strips. The *Miscellany* rarely wrote about its own policies or history during the 1970s and 1980s, a sign that institutional memory and identity had slipped out of range. As Harper wrote, "the entire paper took on a casual, haphazard personality."[227]

Among the publications that arose to challenge the *Miscellany* was the second coming of the *Vassar Chronicle*, which ran from 1974 through 1978. Unlike the first version of the *Chronicle*, which competed vigorously with the *Miscellany* in the 1940s by adopting a more conservative perspective, this *Chronicle* instead tried to be more *liberal* than the *Miscellany*. Bill Hearon '75 and Michael Solow '75 published the first issue on September 23, 1974. The *Chronicle* was printed twice each week, and contained a much wider range of topics than the *Miscellany*. It also made a point of including more controversial topics such as racial intolerance, religious diversity and sexual promiscuity. Letters to the editor were fiery, and even included several anonymous submissions by faculty members about their own sex lives. As Harper noted, many articles "pushed conventional boundaries," such as "Abortion: Where To Go and What To Do in Poughkeepsie."[228] This new publication sparked some interest with its radical approach to news, but it lacked the editorial muscle of the *Miscellany*. The *Chronicle* essentially hoped that the shock value of its liberal content would replace hard-hitting journalism. But by 1978, submissions had dramatically decreased and the staff seemed to quickly change gears, suddenly morphing the paper into a monthly literature review. The final issue was published on April 28, 1978. The *Miscellany News* outlived a second *Chronicle* and remained Vassar's only newspaper.

Still, the paper struggled like never before. But despite its lackluster appearance and tired articles, the *Miscellany* did manage to attract many freshmen in 1974 and 1975. By 1976, there was a respectable pool of 20 reporters, in addition to a full team of editors. However, these writers did not last for long; comparing the staff boxes year to year, students fluctuated significantly. Writers rarely repeated from semester to semester and, unlike today, very few writers remained on the paper long enough to seek full editorial positions.

As the staff lost interest and respect for the paper, so too did the community. In Spring 1980, several students began stealing columns from the paper's office as a practical joke. During this time, writers were asked to leave printouts of their typed articles in a box outside of the College Center office. Andy Seiler '80, who wrote a column entitled "Flicks for Film Fans" for two years, remembers dropping his work off in that box each week. One night, however, after Seiler dropped his article in that hanging plastic folder, a group of students stole it and replaced it with a parody article. "The parody mocked my writing style and claimed erroneously that there were lots of Bruce Springsteen songs in one of the movies being shown on campus that weekend, and that Bruce fans should definitely go to see it," Seiler recalled. "There were certainly no Bruce Springsteen songs in the movie. You can imagine my reaction." Embarrassingly, the editors did not notice the obvious changes, stylistic errors and misspellings. The revised "Flicks for Film Fans" column was published. The pranksters struck multiple times, reversing Seiler's attitude on a variety of other movies, editing them to reflect that he "liked the movies I hated and hated the movies I liked."

But that incident was just the prelude. One week, the entire newspaper was stolen. The same group of students who stole Seiler's article drove to the *Miscellany*'s local printer about an hour after the editors had dropped off the completed layout. The students then convinced the workers that they were a second set of editors, and that they needed to rearrange a few articles before publication. The printer gave the students the plates, and the pranksters promptly drove away with them. Because it was the last issue of the year, the thievery was never reported or noticed. The final issue of the 1978 school year had disappeared.

Seiler was able to put the events of his senior year behind him, becoming a successful entertainment reporter for *USA TODAY*. But he still remembers the tremendous unprofessionalism that infected the paper during the late 1970s and early 1980s. "In all my days as a journalist," he said, "I never witnessed the level of chicanery that went on [at the *Miscellany*]."

But the paper's adventures, misadventures and unprofessionalism were not always so comical. In September 1978, College President Virginia Smith wrote a lengthy letter to the editor complaining about the disturbing number of factual errors.[229] "The problem," she wrote, "is not a lack of communication so much as it is *miscommunication*." Smith then gave a lengthy list of "fallacies" reported in the previous week's issue: the paper had misspelled a professor's name, confused an administrator's job title with that of his wife, and said that an English professor was a Russian professor. Further, she found numerous mistakes and simplifications in an article on the Jewish Chaplaincy. "The article… concluded that I had already decided not to give space to Hillel, even though the meeting to discuss… [the plan] was not scheduled until four days after the date of the paper," she wrote. Smith also took issue with the article's statistic of 800 Jewish students on campus: "Stated as a simple fact, it must in reality be a gross estimate since statistics on religious faith are not regularly collected on campus."

The apparent lack of journalistic standards exploded into more serious controversy when several student organizations complained about the paper's coverage. In Fall 1982, the Student Afro-American Society (SAS) and the Gay People's Alliance (GPA) met with *Miscellany* editors to discuss the ways in which coverage was "ignorant, racist, sexist and homophobic."[230] Later in the semester when *Miscellany* reporters snuck into an SAS meeting "despite the group's insistence that the meeting remain closed," the SAS demanded the resignation of the editors. The Student's Association intervened, and the matter was settled with a formal reprimand of the newspaper. The paper expanded the space it gave to campus opinions, hoping that, by including more voices, they would be subject to less criticism.

The Calm After the Storm

After the lack on interest in the early 1970s, the aesthetic nightmares of the mid-1970s and the journalistic disasters of the late-1970s, success slowly began to return to the *Miscellany* throughout the 1980s. Numbers help to illustrate the paper's rebound. Of the nine publications that sprouted up in the late 1970s and 1980s, the *Miscellany* remained the most frequently published at 21 issues each year, as well as the most widely circulated, with about 3,500 weekly copies of about 12 to 16 pages each. In addition to the $20,000 budget awarded by the Vassar Student Association, the paper raised about $18,000 each year on its own through advertisements and subscriptions. Advertisements appeared more frequently by the mid-1980s, which showed recovery from the advertising drop-off of the 1970s. This budget cushioning allowed the paper to maintain its equipment, print longer issues and even publish special editions. This was quite a change from the decade prior, when declining revenues and debt threatened the paper's suvival.

Although the pains of coeducation were ostensibly healed by the 1980s, articles in the *Miscellany* suggest the College remained very concerned about its image. The President's Advisory Committee on Coeducation continued to examine the matter well into the decade, as this September 28, 1984 piece shows.

Readership grew as well. *Miscellany* staffers personally stuffed every student and faculty mailbox with an issue of the paper (a tradition discontinued in the late 1990s). The paper also witnessed a healthy climb in letters to the editor. Perhaps most importantly, editors once again developed a strong sense of their role in the College's history, a sense that had been disrupted by the tumult of coeducation. "There's a sense that the *Misc* must go on," quipped former Editor in Chief Jennifer Harriton '90 in an interview with the *Vassar Quarterly*.[231] "I think that sense of tradition is reflected in the commitment people make to the paper. We're the history of the campus." As we have seen, a sense of legacy among editors is highly correlated with enhanced professionalism and attention to detail.

The frequent feedback that Harriton received—which ranged from "complimentary letters and phone calls to verbal assaults by screaming students in the College Center"—proved that the Vassar community was once again reading the paper. Harriton offered the *Vassar Quarterly* her own unscientific method for determining readership: "This year, there haven't been so many papers in the garbage bins, so I can assume that people are taking them home. Or else they're not throwing them in the garbage just so that they can burn them at night."

While many of the adults at Vassar were uninterested in, even embarrassed by the sloppy *Miscellany* of the 1970s, these attitudes seemed to change by the early 1980s. For the first time in decades, the *Vassar Quarterly* dedicated significant amount of space to an article about the paper. A Fall 1982 piece by Lisa Klein '78 presented the experiences of several past *Miscellany* editors and discussed the weekly production cycle. The article acknowledges that while "its reporting sometimes falters and its spelling doesn't always pass muster," the paper is the clearest window into student life.[232] The Alumnae/i Association stood by this sentiment, and started to print a regular section in its magazine called "Excerpts" that featured snippets from the *Miscellany News*, along with a few other campus publications. The section remained in the *Quarterly* for a decade. The fact that these excerpts were reprinted verbatim demonstrates that the adult employees of the College began to regard the student newspaper as a publication worthy of showing off to alumnae/i.

The Continued Climb of the 1990s

It took time and effort, but the newspaper of the late 1980s and early 1990s showed marked improvements. Layout was the most noticeable improvement; the paper rejected the cartoonish header font it had employed during the 1970s and began to pay more attention to the ways in which articles were arranged. Greater staff recruitment and retention was another accomplishment. Throughout the 1990s, the paper made a concerted effort to attract submissions, even beginning a column to "showcase students', professors' and administrators' non-fiction prose."[233] Every issue included at least one large advertisement for new writers "of any experience level." At the beginning of each school year, editors made stalwart pleas to freshmen to submit their work. "The *Miscellany News* does not exist within a vacuum," read a September 1996 editorial.[234] "Without members of organizations informing us of events and news, our coverage cannot be complete." With a larger staff, the paper was able to improve in other ways as well. The number of investigative stories expanded to unprecedented levels, touching on topics like Vassar's investment portfolio, disability access and the tenure process. Coverage of the Hudson Valley increased too, and sports coverage went from about two, often-ignored pages per issue to three or four pages with more timely and in-depth coverage of athletic events. The *Miscellany* also added a variety of regular columns, ranging from horoscopes, to weekly student quotations, to poetry.

The paper seemed to offer more of everything as the size of the paper ballooned from an average 14 pages per issue in 1985 to an average of 19 pages in 1994. This tactic succeeded in boosting readership. However, the paper's physical expansion placed a tremendous burden on the budget. By 1994, increased costs, shrinking subscriptions and the negligence of the treasurer plunged the paper into debt. By the winter, the situation had become so dire that the Vassar Student Association (VSA) was forced to absorb the paper's financial liabilities. In trade, the student representatives would exert much control over the *Miscellany*, deciding the length of each issue and examining ways to curb spending. This was the first time since the 1870s that the student government exercised such direct editorial control over the *Miscellany*. The February 25 issue, for example was cut from the 24 pages proposed by the editors to 16 pages; the March 4 issue was only 12 pages. When the VSA Council tried to slice the April 1 issue from 16 pages to 8 pages, the dedicated editors refused. Instead, they each paid $100 out of pocket to have the full issue printed. After an angry staff editorial claimed that the Council had treated them too harshly, the student representatives reevaluated their position and returned control of the page count to the *Miscellany News* Editorial Board.[235]

Unprofessionalism Persists

But the paper's financial troubles were indicative of deeper problems. Between the 1920s and the late 1960s, the *Miscellany* had a fairly strict set of policies. It had constant layout, a method for handling advertising and a lengthy style manual. There was a single copy of this thick manual—lost sometime between 1969 and 1970— which included "detailed advice for handling a variety of different editorial situations and common problems," according to an editor from the early 1960s. "It was a huge old book, with extra appendices paper clipped into it frequently, that we kept on a coffee table in the office and consulted constantly." Editors had added tidbits to the manual for years, updating policies and procedures where necessary. This stylebook accounts for the *Miscellany*'s relative consistency over five decades; the *lack* of this stylebook also accounts for the frequent changes in appearance and policy that occurred after 1970. Rules were not written down.

Although the editors of the late 1970s and 1980s seemed to fix the haphazard layout of the earlier 1970s, rebuilding consistent editorial and business policies proved more difficult. In the spring of 1994, just as the paper was recovering from their budgeting fiasco, they underwent a storm of criticism for printing an advertisement from a Holocaust-denying organization. The advertisement was accepted without much critical analysis. After all, the editors had no set standards—it was simply an exchange of advertising for revenue. Angry letters to the editor and campus-wide complaints forced the Editorial Board to reassess the paper's advertising policies. The Board adopted, and wrote down, new guidelines to ensure no advertisements that were in violation of Vassar's own regulations, specifically thinking of the College's policies against harassment and discrimination. Giving the College administration even indirect control over the paper's policy was debated vigorously, but the editors went with the safer course and modeled its own set of policies for selecting advertisements on College procedures. These same guidelines, incorporated into the Bylaws in the later 1990s, have been continuously reevaluated since then, most recently in 2001 and 2007.

Editors of the late 1980s and 1990s made a concerted effort to record their policies and procedures. Eric Robinson '89 was an instrumental figure in overhauling the Bylaws of the *Miscellany News*. Robinson had been involved with the *Miscellany* for all four of his Vassar years, culminating in a position as Senior Editor. In Fall 1988, the new Bylaws went into effect and helped to standardize many editorial policies. The document described the responsibilities of each position, enumerated the rights of Editorial Board members, and spelled out the procedure for constructing the weekly staff editorial. The Bylaws also described some financial caveats and regulations—but this still did not seem to ensure prudent management of the budget. Robinson recalls the paper running through its entire annual budget in a single semester. Apparently, editors never bothered to collect revenue for advertisements that had run throughout the fall. For a time, it looked as if the paper would not be able to publish in the spring. Fortunately, a donation from an alumnus and some work with the VSA Council solved the financial trauma.

The *Miscellany* was still not the professional machine that it once was. Indeed, the Editorial Board of the 1990s was incestuous and amateurish in a number of ways. "We were rather clubby and self-involved and didn't always encourage new people to join," said Cricket Cooley '93, who served as a writer and Opinions Editor. The period from about 1990 to 1996 saw a decrease in advertisements in the paper requesting new reporters and editors; one editor from the period noted that "we usually asked specific students to join, to ensure that they were our kind of person." This stands in contrast to the frequent open meetings and requests for new staff of the 1980s. And although there were advertisements requesting "opinionated submissions" from the student body, there were fewer requests for permanent members. The editors were certainly dedicated, but also insular. "We tended to hang out in the office at all hours, there was a rather incestuous hooking up thing going on, and we often held our staff meetings in the Mug," Cooley said, remembering a great deal of "office drama" that resulted from editors' romantic encounters. "We weren't so good with the journalistic standards either," he continued. "My friend… the Sports Editor often assigned my name to his articles about the games he played in to avoid the appearance of conflict of interest. I was just at the house of the former News Editor… who swore we used to steal money from the Classifieds to buy food and beer."

Incidents such as these—which the careful editors from the 1950s and 1960s do not recall—serve as a reminder that the *Miscellany*'s standards of professionalism were in constant flux. The very idea of "professionalism," advocated by editors like Robinson in an effort to recover from the disastrous 1970s, was questioned in the 1990s. What exactly did professionalism mean in the context of a student newspaper? Some argued that emulating 'real' newspapers was the wrong direction. After all, the *Miscellany* was an amateur student publication, and deviating from this identity would be dishonest. This sort of thinking led directly to the creation of the "Backpage" in 1995.

The Backpage, the final two pages of the newspaper, was the *Miscellany*'s attempt at a humor section. For a time, it included classified ads along with a large calendar of events. Writers would add short lines mocking various lectures, plays and parties. Soon, the classifieds disappeared and the section was downsized from two pages to a single page on the back of the newspaper. The satirical calendar occupied the bottom half of the page, while the top half was reserved for some sort of topical lampoon. The Backpage has continued to the present, still dividing the page evenly between a marked-up calendar and some sort of satirical commentary. Letters to the editor over the past decade suggest that many have found the Backpage offensive and childish. Russ Hasan '04 summed up several of the arguments that students have leveled against the humor section:

> Every time I read the *Misc*'s Backpage, I feel a new sense of having been insulted, and this week's Backpage was the last straw… You may think it's funny to use "gayest" as a derogatory adjective, as you did on Tuesday, April 16, but I disagree. And that is only one of many examples of the kind of humor that would be juvenile from a 12-year-old, let alone college students. Has it ever occurred to you that more people might read the activities page (which would improve not only the *Misc* but the state of Vassar activities) if the central source of activity information was written to inform instead of to showcase your immaturity and insultingly stupid

jokes? In my opinion, you should give your Backpage to a serious writer to write in a serious way—better *no* humor than *bad* humor. One of these days, your Backpage will slip up and seriously offend someone—it probably would have already if that many people bothered to read it.[236]

While the Backpage has been popular with many students, Hasan is hardly alone. "I just don't know why the *Miscellany News* wastes such prime space on crap," said journalist Theresa Keegan during a Summer 2008 critique of college newspapers sponsored by Bloomberg News. Columbia University Professor Nancy Beth Jackson agreed. "The content is so excellent everywhere else, but this Backpage feels clubby and amateurish," she said. "The editors are obviously sophisticated, but the content is so beneath them. It feels like everything is an inside joke that most students wouldn't get. Why does the paper make fun of and dismiss legitimate Vassar lectures and events on the calendar, for example, rather than actually use the space to cover them?" Numerous editors from other college papers, and well as journalists and professors who attended the conference, lauded the overall 2008 *Miscellany*, but considered the Backpage to be childish, distasteful, and unable to effectively satirize the College in any meaningful way.

The reaction in the 1990s was similar. Several Backpages sparked angry letters to the editor from students and faculty alike. These letters often complained that the section was offensive, especially because it lacked the reflection necessary for effective social satire. While views on the Backpage differed, its creation in 1995 signals the unprofessionalism that remained part of the paper's staff—and the questioning over the very goal of professionalism. Though the Editorial Board had come a long way from the upheaval of coeducation, rebuilding a unique style and identity was a lengthy and difficult process.

A Revolution in Printing

Printing technology was one element of the paper that *did* seem to become more professionalized in the 1980s and 1990s. A 1984 "Friends of the *Miscellany News*" campaign raised $6,000 for the paper, funding a Rainbow 100A computer. A decade later in September 1994, the paper began using its first e-mail account, *misc@vassar.edu*. The new computer allowed the staff to move away from their typewriters and employ more innovative layout and typesetting. Amanda Spielman '96 began working for the paper in 1993 as a freshman layout editor.[237] "We used to drive over to the publisher in Wappinger Falls every week," recalled Spielman, whose elder brother had also attended Vassar and held a student employment position entitled *"Miscellany News* Typist." He was responsible for retyping the handwritten stories that writers would produce each Friday. Editor in Chief Jessica Barron '97 was also frustrated by the slow and old-fashioned manner of production. "The Editor in Chief and the Senior Editor would drive to the printing place with the [article] print-outs in one hand, and a folder containing ads and photos in the other," she said. Barron described staying at the printer for hours with "nothing but glue sticks, scissors and straight knives" to layout each issue. It was a ridiculous process by professional standards. "We would have to bring dozens of clippings over there and show the printer exactly how we wanted them to appear," added Spielman. By that time, many college and university papers ranging in size from the *Harvard Crimson* to the *Oberlin Review* had turned to digital newspaper printing. Vassar's process was, by contrast, almost identical to the manner in which the *Miscellany Monthly* was produced nearly 130 years earlier.

Spielman worked to change that. She had been editor of her high school's newspaper, which used PageMaker software for desktop publishing. Once she was elected Editor in Chief in 1996, she asked the Wappinger printer if they would be willing to go digital. They refused. Undeterred, Spielman, along with fellow editor Joseph Goldman '96, contacted numerous other local printers. Eventually, they found Walden Printing, who was the most technologically capable in the area. The editors quickly negotiated a contract. "The people at Walden had technology on their end that allowed us to just bring them a disk containing the PageMaker files," Spielman recalled. Using a single PowerMac running the first version of Adobe PageMaker, the *Miscellany News* had gone digital.

Later that year, the paper purchased a scanner and disk drive, and began to use Adobe PageMaker for layout and Adobe Photoshop for graphics. "Going desktop was part of the *Misc*'s long-term plan of increasing production technology," said Managing Editor Jonathan Tischler '98. "Once adopted, it really increased the efficiency of our production process and allowed us greater control over our final product."

A New Medium for an Old Publication

Digital print publication was not the only technological revolution of the 1990s. The *Miscellany News* established its first presence on the World Wide Web at *http://misc.vassar.edu* in 1994. 1994 was the birth year of Netscape and modern Internet. That year also saw the founding of the World Wide Web Consortium, the primary standards organization for the Internet. Technologies that had been largely restricted to scientists and major research universities had now become public and commercial. Newly popular coding standards allowed individuals around the country to craft their own Web site. Vassar, always progressive, was one of the first schools in the country to put its student newspaper online. Indeed, looking at the *U.S. News and World Report* rankings of the top twenty liberal arts colleges and national universities from that year, only eleven of those 40 institutions had their primary student newspaper online. Vassar was proudly among them.[238] Michael Dillon '96 designed the site, and ran it directly out of the newspaper's office on an old Macintosh computer. To manage the site, the Editorial Board created the positions of Technology Editor and Assistant Technology Editor.

Gabe Anderson '99 became involved with the paper during his freshman year as Assistant Technology Editor. Along with Shreyank Purohit '99, Anderson worked hard at streamlining the young site between 1995 and 1997. In 1997, he purchased a newer computer that could support greater graphical elements. Anderson went on to become Editor in Chief during his junior year in 1998, continuing to develop the *Miscellany*'s online presence. The paper's original Web site was all hand-coded HTML. After the layout was completed on PageMaker for the print edition, text would have to be manually transferred into the raw code using BBEdit, a simple HTML editing application. Every article had to be manually coded and formatted. "Looking back on it, I don't even know how I managed to do that for the paper's 30 or so articles every week," Anderson reminisced. "It was really, really slow." At the time, the Web site was run off of a single, low-end Performa (an early Macintosh computer) using AppleTalk to connect to the Internet. AppleTalk, a type of connection slightly faster than the 56k modem, ran at less than one-third the speed of present-day Ethernet lines.

Since it first launched in 1994, the newspaper's Web site has gone through several iterations. Though the first HTML coding has been lost, the four designs above represent some of the most significant redesigns. These homepages pages are from April 1998 (upper left), February 2000 (upper right), and December 2003 (lower left). The final image from May 2007 (lower right) depicts the design that lasted from 2004 through 2008. This emphasized the paper's new tabloid layout by highlighting a single story with a predominant image.

As Editor-in-Chief of The Miscellany News, I have no life other than the paper; I sleep, eat, dream and breathe the Misc. I am responsible for all aspects of the paper, both as an organization and a publication. I coordinate weekly Editorial Board meeting s, oversee editors as they layout their sections, and don't leave the office until early Thursday morning each week when the paper has reached a level of perfection so extraordinary that everything else in my life seems meaningless. (But usually, after a lack of sleep has made me delirious, I just reach a point where I stop caring and then pass out halfway between the Misc. office and my room.)

Anderson saved only one page of the old site, which was the second-generation online home of the *Miscellany News*. The newest version of the site, which launched in 2008, employs a red and black motif to gently recall Anderson's original design.

Nevertheless, Anderson was the proud guardian of the paper's budding Web presence site. "The Internet was very different back then," he recalled. "Netscape was everyone's primary browser, and the capabilities were severely limited." During Anderson's tenure, the Web was quickly expanding and he worked to give the site constant facelifts. "Still, our page looked really boring by today's standards. But it was nonetheless so cool to be on the paper at a time when this whole new medium was emerging. I remember thinking even back then that within a decade, news would travel in a whole different way."

Explosions of Controversy

The improving technologies for the newspaper—print and digital— were happy achievements in an otherwise trying decade. Polls from the period showed that students of the 1980s and 1990s increasingly identified as "liberal."[239] Perhaps corresponding to the "increasingly politically correct climate" of Vassar (according to one 1995 graduate), the 1990s and early 2000s saw frequent campus controversies surrounding matters of race, gender and class. Occasionally, students took offense at certain items in the *Miscellany*, accusing the paper of failing to attract a broad range of ideas. Cricket Cooley, who served as Opinions Editor, found it difficult to satisfy critical readers. "We were known as the center of the road publication," Cooley said, noting that the conservative *Spectator* and liberal *Unscrewed* appealed more to the political fringes on campus. Cooley felt that, although the Opinions section had a slightly liberal slant, the majority of the paper was largely unbiased, which annoyed many on campus. "It was pretty hard to get any conservative viewpoints, however, since there were like three conservatives on campus at the time and they all wrote for the *Spectator*. Very polarized," he recalled. For some students, there were not enough radical voices either. For them, the paper's insistence on relative objectivity rendered it far too conservative in its approach to journalism—even offensively so.

Race was a particularly sensitive topic on campus, a sensitivity that the *Miscellany* had to adjust to more than ever. During the 1990s, competition among selective colleges to enroll highly qualified minority students increased dramatically.[240] Vassar's admissions officers conducted far-reaching campaigns, travelling to predominantly black high schools and asking minority alumnae/i to aid recruiting efforts. Their efforts were beginning to pay off; the Class of 1996 saw a 111 percent increase in the number of black freshmen enrolled. In its vigorous effort to recruit students of color, some students openly questioned the policies of affirmative action in the *Miscellany*. Two letters to the editor in the spring of 1996 argued that it was unfair for the College to admit minority students at a much higher acceptance rate than white students. This caused a firestorm of backlash. Many were enraged that the campus newspaper would publish such pronounced opinions against affirmative action policies.

Outrage would continue over other issues. In 1991, Cooley had a cartoonist lampoon a speech given by civil rights activist Jesse Jackson at Vassar. The cartoon showed Jackson with a suitcase saying, "I'm on my way to Hymietown," satirizing his alleged anti-Semitism. Editor in Chief Joanna Pearlstein would not let Cooley publish it, thinking it would stir up people in the "insanely [politically correct] culture that was Vassar in the early nineties." Some editors questioned this decision, and remained unsure about the role of such self-censorship. Pearlstein was likely airing on the safe side after an incident involving Senator Daniel Patrick Moynihan's Vassar speech a year earlier, in which he insulted a professor's Jamaican wife by telling her to "Go back to your country if you don't like it here." At the time, the campus shut down for a week with protests.

But the *Miscellany* sidestepped only one landmine. Controversy broke out in 1995 when an offensive comic was printed involving Ebonics. Amanda Spielman was Junior Editor at the time. "That was a huge deal, and a big uproar," she recalled. "People called the *Misc* racist, even when none of us had any bad intentions in printing the cartoon." The incident sparked an in-depth discussion on the relationship between freedom of speech and political correctness. "Where does paper stand on that balance? We had never really though about it before," said Spielman. "We sort of took for granted that we could print whatever we wanted in the paper." Such conversations also occurred after the *Miscellany* printed the aforementioned advertisement from the Holocaust-denying organization. "We hadn't really though about declining advertising before, and so we had that conversation," she said. "And then after the [Ebonics] cartoon ran, we had to have even lengthier conversations about how we made those sorts of editorial decisions."

Fortunately, the newspaper was not always at the center of these controversies. But the *Miscellany* did cover countless such incidents throughout the 1990s and early 2000s, which manifested in angry letters to the editor between different members of the community. These frequent "mini-explosions," as former News Editor Chris Seaman '02 described them, followed a predictable format: some Vassar person, organization or office would do or say something offensive and "the entire campus would get up-in-arms about it." Letters to the editor would fly into the *Miscellany* office, both condemning and defending the accused person or group. After two weeks, all memory of the event seemed to have been erased and the situation would rarely be followed up by the editors, or talked about again by students.

Even comedy groups were not immune. A controversial comedy skit performed by the now-defunct group "Laughingstock" caused a storm of protest due to the use of racially charged language during the show. In this case, the aftermath was long-lasting; even today Vassar holds an annual All-

College Day, which was the direct result of student outcry following the skit. There were many community forums following the show, often emotionally raw. "It was my job to help cover these events," said Seaman, who was News Editor and Acting Editor in Chief for a time. "As people voiced their opinion, I was struck by how few people had actually seen the skit in question or were familiar with its content. Interestingly, the skit satirized the very response that it generated. I realized that students on both sides of the debate were formulating opinion without knowing the facts." The politically correct culture of the College seemed strange to Seaman. "In many ways I found the fallout to be troubling. The Vassar Student Association (VSA) subsequently derecognized the comedy group. Any vocal support for the group was forcefully shouted down." As a writer and student journalist, Seaman was personally concerned about the implications on free speech and academic freedom. "I think it's ironic that All-College Day claims to be a source of dialog, when in fact, the administration was complicit in squashing dissenting opinion [that the skit was okay]."

Several alumnae/i from the period described the hostile climate as being thorny for the newspaper. One alumna, who gave her reflections on the condition of anonymity, complained that the environment was "oppressively" politically correct. "Someone would make some innocent comment, and it would be blown out of proportion by the campus's radical left," she said. "While I would describe myself as a fairly liberal person, living at Vassar during [the 1990s] was like tiptoeing through a field of landmines. A perfectly nice person could say one thing that would be taken out of context, and suddenly the *Misc* had it splashed all over its pages as the scandal of the decade. It was ridiculous." More often than not, she felt these events did not deserve to be printed as news. "I always complained to my fellow editors that we were just fanning the flames," she said. "It wasn't responsible journalism."

Whether or not these "mini-explosions" were overly reactionary, they were a distinctive part of campus coverage at the end of the 20th century and the beginning of the 21st. And because of its own role in covering these controversies, the *Miscellany* was often a target of complaint. If the paper printed letters of one particular persuasion or another, editors would be inundated with accusations of racism, sexism or classism. Editors during this period almost universally recall feeling as if they were on "pins and needles" whenever an issue came out, for fear that someone would misinterpret an article as offensive. To Seaman, the climate seemed bizarre. "We were willing to print letters of almost any opinion. In fact, one of our most vocal critics was given his own column," he recalled. "Many students thought that we weren't sufficiently liberal in our reporting, a claim that I think is specious. After all, our goal was not to promote a particular political stripe, but rather to provide information." Seaman himself wished that more conservative voices had written for the paper. "Though I identify myself as a liberal, I often find conservative op-ed pieces to be the most intellectually challenging. I would have liked to see more of this debate in our content."[241]

The *Miscellany* found itself at the center of one particularly ugly controversy. Not surprisingly, this storm originated with the Backpage. During graduation weekend in May 2004, there was an extremely controversial Backpage feature on actor Samuel L. Jackson who spoke at that year's Commencement. "It was a fake interview with a lot of vulgar language that was, I believe, based on his movies," recalled Jorge Sierra '04, a writer for the *Miscellany* at the time. In the satirical piece, Jackson is "spoofed as giving college speeches filled with profanity, sexual innuendos and descriptions of violent acts."[242]

Many students were outraged that the paper would print race-based jokes about an African American speaker. Soon after the newspaper hit the stands, a meeting was organized between Vassar's Director of Affirmative Action and the two editors directly involved in the Backpage. The editors apologized and the paper agreed to reprint the issue with the article deleted. Still, anger on campus persisted. During the graduation day festivities, there were several protests against the racist depictions of Jackson. These protests were disruptive enough to make Page One of the *Poughkeepsie Journal*. While some students spoke of their outrage to the *Poughkeepsie Journal*, others told the paper that the Backpage was just the latest in a series of incidents that have exacerbated racial tensions. Hannah Weinstock '04, one of the protest organizers, said she hoped the demonstrations would help spark better dialogue between members of the campus community. "The writers and the editors apologized for the article and they even helped us in planning the protest," she said. "We just to want make sure that this doesn't happen again." Others defended the Backpage. "I felt that it was an attempt to make fun of the College's tendency to fawn over celebrities and in doing so, it perpetuated a lot of age-old stereotypes," said Michael Awusie '04. Nevertheless, many students attended graduation with multi-colored armbands as a sign of support, and others made a "black power sign" with their hands as they received their diplomas. Even one of the editors, Brian Belardi, also wore a multi-colored armband. "I was [one of] the only [people] who [publicly] contradicted the protesters," said Sierra, who did not find the Backpage particularly offensive. "I had e-mailed the Backpage Editors my thoughts earlier. At my best friend's suggestion, I had walked around campus doing an informal poll on random students. I [then] told the Director of Affirmative Action... that most of Vassar does not view the article as outrageous or racist. It's hard to write something you know can be controversial or that people will disagree with in a campus like this, especially when you live and work with the people who read your articles, some of whom are very powerful, very well connected. This protest happened 1-2-3 and the tone escalated to something pretty ugly."

Like Russ Hasan had predicted in his letter to the editor two years earlier, the Backpage was destined to stir up trouble and distract students from the otherwise improving *Miscellany*.[243] Vassar's increasingly politically correct climate made life for the editors even more challenging.

Turn of the Century, and Turn of Luck

As we have already observed, the period after 1969 was somewhat of a rollercoaster for the *Miscellany*. At some moments, the paper was professional, popular and heavily staffed, and at other moments, its quality sank. The next unfortunate moment in the paper's history came between roughly 2000 and 2002. Those years were essentially 1970 all over again; the layout, quality of writing and overall tone hit sudden lows of sloppiness and unprofessionalism. There can be little doubt that Rose Friedman or Marty Smith, Editors in Chief in the late 1940s who enforced tight standards for layout and content, would have been horrified to read the paper that kicked off the 21st century. On a single page of the first issue of 2001, there were eight misspellings, three grammatical errors, and one instance where an article cut off because of sloppy layout.[244]

The style of the *Miscellany News* changed dramatically in 2001, when two editors "armed with a box of crayons, a highlighter... and some back issues of the *Village Voice*," redesigned the paper into tabloid format over winter break.[245] Their models were the *Village Voice* and

Helicon, Vassar's literary publication. Away from the traditional front page with news and pictures, the redesigned *Miscellany* sported a single cover image. The editors felt that they had fashioned a paper for the new millennium, with sleeker fonts, an airier layout and shorter pages. In reality, this new format was difficult to manage. Staffers who entered Vassar directly after this redesign complained that the tabloid appearance looked childish and unprofessional.

Stylistic standards seemed to decrease with physical standards. Part of the problem was yet another loss of legacy. As we saw after the *Miscellany's* long-standing stylebook vanished in the early 1970s, the paper underwent a decade of constant change and uncertainty. Policies shifted quickly. A similar occurrence came in 2001, when the paper's digital archives suddenly disappeared. In 1998, the Vassar Student Association (VSA) had purchased a heavy-duty Unix-based server to run its Web site, and the *Miscellany* decided to take a similar course. "When we left Vassar in 1999, we had accumulated six years of consistent online archives," site designer Gabe Anderson recalled. That server remained online for four years, until it crashed in 2001 and all online archives were lost. This proved to be a tough challenge for the editors, who had become accustomed to using the paper's Web site to find background information and policy precedents.

Journalistic standards decreased precipitously as well. The clearest evidence of this came with the coverage of the September 11 terrorist attacks. The September 14, 2001 issue of the paper showed a shocking level of insensitivity and childishness. Directly following the deaths of thousands of Americans, the paper included two sets of comics, a cursory article about "Summer Break Adventures," and a large collection of photographs about Serenading. These pictures displayed dozens of carefree students engaging in the traditional Serenading food fight, hurling ketchup and chocolate syrup as if nothing were the matter. The staff editorial from that issue was short, only about 200 words, and tersely urged students to give blood and "support those around you." There was also an advertisement for editors, which read, "Abstain from gratuitous premarital sex and write for the *Misc!*" Even more shockingly, the issue even included a Backpage provocatively titled "Tickle My Ass." Printing this sort of newspaper only three days after 9/11, particularly given the number of Vassar students and families who were personally affected by the attacks, seems unimaginble.[246]

In this April 13, 2001 cover story about heightened restrictions on alcohol, the cartoonish nature of the redesign is evident. Making the comparison between 1970 and 2001 even more readily apparent, the editors briefly changed the name of the paper to "the *Misc*."

Moreover, a larger-than-usual number of the paper's top editors graduated in 2001. This erased much of the human capital that had accumulated over the 1990s. Adding insult to injury, Editor in Chief Katie Pontius '02, one of the few remaining editors with multiple years of experience, resigned from her position because of health issues. "This really left the ship without a captain," recalled Emma White '05, who entered Vassar as a freshman in Fall 2001. White applied to the vacant Features editorship on a whim during her first few weeks on campus. It was not until she joined the Editorial Board that she began to understand the grave issues facing the paper. After Pontius, Ben Silverbush '02 very briefly took control of the paper, but his leadership was not able to fully restore the organization to health. The *Miscellany* even failed to print two issues—an almost unheard of interruption in the paper's production.

Even more serious were the paper's concurrent financial burdens. Just like the *Miscellany*'s quality in general, the paper's financial status had been in constant flux since the 1970s. In 2001, thanks to a series of miscommunications between the editors, the printing company and the College's accounting office, the printer had not been paid for nearly a year. This meant an accumulated debt of over $20,000. The Vassar Student Association (VSA) and the College administration held extensive discussions with the *Miscellany*. To summarize these problems and plead for the help of the community, the newspaper published the following editorial:

> Dear Vassar Community,
>
> The *Miscellany News* would like to address recent campus attitudes toward the school paper that have alarmed and upset us. The general consensus on campus seems to be that the paper neglects the community and does not represent the student population or its concerns. At last week's VSA meeting, there were several 'digs' and negative comments about the *Misc*. These comments can be heard anywhere on campus. We ask of you, why?
>
> Several rumors are circulating that we would like to address; among them, our financial status. Currently, the *Miscellany News* is approximately $15,000 in debt. This debt was incurred, and continues to accumulate, from weekly printing costs. You may have noticed that we discontinued color on the Backpage and cover for this reason. As our debt grows, we are forced to ask ourselves, is this worth it?

The *Miscellany News* was founded in 1866 and has since been a vital part of the Vassar community as a starting place for ideas and action. Over the years, the *Misc* has teetered on the edge of debt, at times plunging feet first into the red. Each year, however, the *Misc* appears on newsstands, offering students a forum to make their voices heard, however makes the students seem unpopular [*sic*].

Writers and editors of the paper have prided themselves on their commitment to this purpose. For posterity's sake, one wall in the *Misc* office is covered with the wisdom of former Editors in Chief. Jennifer Higginbottom reminds us that "The *Misc* writes the history of Vassar College, and we are responsible for whose history gets written."

The goal of a student newspaper is to represent the student body and College community. If we are not even able to give our papers away, is there any point? Every week, the editors put in late nights to get the paper on the stands. We are completely open to criticism; we welcome it. Yet week after week, people fail to bring their complaints to our Paper Critique or write letters to the editor.

Beyond this, all we hear is the faceless grumble "The *Misc* sucks." Vassar is a community that prides itself on initiating change. How does anyone expect to change the world without first making the tools of change your own? If the *Misc* is not all you expect it to be, we urge you to tell us, to work with us, to make it your own. "Never forget what you do matters. You can make a difference in people's lives," another former Editor in Chief reminds us all. We welcome any criticisms that you might have, whether you are student, faculty staff or community member [*sic*].

We ask for your reassurance that what we do is worth it. We ask for your grievances, for your suggestions, and for your help. If we can not secure this show of support, we have to reconsider our place in the community. "We are the student newspaper of Vassar College and we mustn't ever forget what that means. Report fairly, report accurately… we are members of this community and shouldn't shy away from working with groups, organizations and people any more than we should shy away from criticizing them." Help us make this happen.[247]

Without changing many words, this editorial could have easily been published in 1970. The tone of determined hopelessness and of embattled ideals is nearly identical. But the editors' pleading did not bring them the "show of support" that they hoped for. Even political moderates began to attack the content of the paper as sloppy and one-sided. One letter to the editor by Jorge Sierra, a former writer, said that he "never even looks at the *Misc* [any more], unless I'm in a masochistic mood."[248] Sierra complained that the paper was too liberal, taking "radical stands and then stating or implying that this is what all members of the Vassar community should think and do." The *Miscellany*, he accused, is "a proponent of values that are more liberal than the mainstream College community's, and [will] always alienate significant minorities." The paper was embattled from all directions.

More pressing than the battles for student engagement and support—battles that editors had been fighting for a century—was the crushing debt. College administrators worried about the long-term feasibility of the paper's management. Fortunately, because of the paper's historic position on campus, Vassar's Board of Trustees stepped into the fray to cover the debt and ensure that the *Miscellany* was able to resolve its financial issues. Besides another, relatively small dip in 2002, the paper has since enjoyed relatively stable finances. For the most part, subscription and advertising revenue have remained constant, along with a steady VSA budget.

The Recovery Effort

Clearly, the paper of 2002 was in trouble. Compared to a decade prior, the staff was still cripplingly small and hopelessly inexperienced. Editors did not have a firm grasp of the layout software; Quark had recently replaced the previous PageMaker software, which had been used for about five years. Many of the young section editors had never used the software before, a problem that is clear from the awkward layout that continued into 2002 and 2003.

Fortunately, the financial situation was beginning to ease. Upon their election, Editors in Chief Mike Healy '03 and Marcie Braden '03 immediately began working with the VSA Council to ensure the financial stability of the paper. They also trimmed the size of the paper and increased advertisements, taking precautions to keep the paper in good health. Braden had stayed in Poughkeepsie during the summer of 2002 for an internship. She was able to use some of that time to prepare vigorously for the coming semester. The office, which had been covered in old issues, was completely cleaned out and rearranged. By the end of the summer, the paper's financial outlook was even bright enough that the editors were able to purchase several new computers, along with digital cameras.

Little did the young Emma White know when she became Features Editor that she would soon join the Executive Staff and help to rescue the *Miscellany* from obsolescence. Beginning in 2002, a number of local and personal factors combined over the next three years to return the paper to the prestige it had enjoyed in the 1990s. A section editor herself, White was forced to deal with the technological and staffing dilemmas. With such a small workforce, she was forced to take control of both the Features *and* News sections. "People just weren't applying to work for us," she recalled. "Writers wouldn't get their articles in on time, and I had to write many last-minute articles myself. Put together, it was just a tremendous amount of work." Even when writers did manage to complete their articles, they were often poorly written. "We just weren't obeying journalistic practices—not in terms of style and certainly not in terms of quality or ethics."

The following semester, White took the reigns as Editor in Chief with Larissa Pahomov '05 as her co-editor. The pair was able to complete the work of Healy and Braden, putting the paper back on track. "When we began our term, I remember that it was difficult to even get section editors to attend our Editorial Board meetings," White said. "Over the semester, the two of us really pushed for stricter standards in our applicants. We really began a system of quality control that I think was lacking for the previous few years." Their more rigorous screening process included more structured applications for editorships, longer interviews and more training for new staff writers. White and Pahomov also began initiatives to recruit more freshmen to work on the paper. In Fall 2003, the *Miscellany News* held a special event during freshmen orientation. "This was such a great idea," White recalled. "We were the first faces that these students saw. They started to make friends with each other and apply to work on the paper."

All of this was part of a larger strategy to raise public awareness of the *Miscellany* on campus, and strengthen the student body's trust in the paper. White wanted to eliminate the notion that the *Miscellany* was an amateur, unreliable source. "The question I was really trying to deal with was, how were we going to make this publication relevant again?" she said. "One thing that we noticed was the ridiculous amounts of coverage given to national and international news. We really took a step back, and decided that for the *Misc* to be relevant, the coverage had to be limited to campus." This decision essentially moved the editorial policy of the *Miscellany* back to where it had been before the Great Depression. Contradicting the efforts of Vivian Liebman to become a "newspaper of the world," the Editorial Board of 2003 moved the paper in just the opposite direction—to become a paper solely of the community. Outside news would be brought in only when it pertained to Vassar students or faculty. This unofficial policy remains with the paper today. Unlike the *Miscellany* of the 1930s or 1980s, the newspaper ceased printing stories purely about national events unless they somehow connect to Vassar.

Journalistic standards also rose. When a student was nearly expelled from Vassar and the campus shut down with protests, the *Miscellany* printed a special edition that was by all accounts fair, thorough and accurate. Slowly but surely, the campus responded to the more relevant, more accurate newspaper. Readership and staff returned. As younger applicants joined the ranks of the *Miscellany*, computer expertise also began to swell. Before long, editors were comfortably using Quark, able to control more formatting details and produce a crisper publication— although the tabloid formatting and cover story approach continued.

Students were not the only ones to notice the positive changes; alumnae/i subscriptions rose significantly between 2003 and 2004. College administrators also became more willing to work with the paper (much like they had waited for the storms of the 1970s to settle). "It is so key to have good relationships with the people that you are interviewing," noted White, who served as Student Assistant to the College President during her senior year. White also worked with the Development Office to arrange a series of panels featuring alumnae/i journalists. In organizing those panels, she became close with Director of Regional Programs John Mihaly '74. Mihaly eventually gave her the opportunity to interview Academy Award-winning actor Tom Hanks, who came to speak at Vassar. "It was a fabulous experience. I sat with him, had lunch and conducted an amazing interview," recalled White. "But most importantly, it was a sign that the College now trusted us again. They were willing to have us sit down with this incredibly prestigious visitor."

Once again during this period, we see the strong correlation between an interest in the paper's legacy and the paper's professionalism. When

Marcie Braden cleaned the office, she also revamped the filing system of the paper's archives. New filing cabinets were purchased and archives from the 1970s through the beginning of the 21st century were carefully catalogued into folders. This system was expanded and maintained by White when the old print photography space was transformed into a room dedicated to the archives of old issues. Deborah Temkin '04, who served as Sports Editor, Arts Editor and Contributing Editor, even planned to compile the paper's archives by topic in order to create general topic timelines. Ultimately, however, the project proved too time-consuming with her other responsibilities on the paper. But just the fact that she considered such a massive indexing project suggests a deep recognition of the paper's legacy on the Editorial Board—a recognition that had weakened between 2000 and 2002.

White seems to have been a common thread between all of these various changes. According to many of her co-workers and staffers, she was instrumental in changing the *Miscellany's* image on campus. White connected with graduates, solicited faculty submissions and garnered interest from a previously apathetic student body. But beyond all of that, White created a system of succession, institutionalizing the changes made by her and her colleagues. The Bylaws and stylebook saw their most dramatic expansions since they were entirely rewritten in 1989. "The last thing I ever wanted was for this paper to become *mine*," she said. "It wasn't my paper, it was the College's paper. And all that I wanted was to make sure that it continued after I graduated."

Professionalism and Lack Thereof

Sure enough, the changes implemented by White and Pahomov were sustained. In large part, they laid the groundwork for success in the post-2004 period. But the Editors who graduated in 2004 and 2005 were not able to fix all of the Editorial Board's problems. The increasing professionalism of the paper's content did not always correspond the increasing professionalism of the Board itself. One of the faults recognized by average writers and staffers during this period was that the editors were very cliquish—a habit that developed in the 1990s.

This manifested itself in various ways. According to some editors, the Editorial Board often ignored the Bylaws, allowing certain individuals to advance to higher positions on the paper despite lackluster qualifications. Some editors never even read or knew about the Bylaws in the first place. One editor, who spoke on the condition of anonymity, noted that the majority almost always drowned out dissenting voices during debates over the staff editorial. Another editor, who also preferred to remain anonymous, complained that the staff was not always kind to new members, despite recruitment efforts. Some perceived the paper's Executive Staff to be too close to one another, and too commanding of section editors. One section editor recalled "an overly authoritative executive, who had a singular vision of what the paper needed to look like. If it didn't match their vision, it had to change."

Other administrative issues existed as well. While peer newspapers such as the *Bowdoin Orient* and the *Yale Daily News* maintained digitized minutes of their meetings starting in the late 1990s, the *Miscellany* never did so. Apart from the Bylaws, institutional memory seems to have been preserved mostly orally, making continuity of style and policy somewhat difficult.

Even with these problems behind the scenes, there can be little doubt that the paper had improved significantly in both content and style since 2003. Moreover, the *Miscellany* had once again become institutionalized in the College community. Students seemed to love reading about the frequent, often melodramatic campus controversies.

The following years would be pivotal for the *Miscellany News*. Thanks to a talented and dedicated group of students entering the College in 2004, the Editorial Board was able to codify and perfect the recovery efforts that had been quickly implemented by White and Pahomov. Without the crucial changes and foresighted fixes implemented in 2003, however, the newspaper's contemporary history might have unfolded very differently.

203 Elizabeth Daniels and Clyde Griffen, Full Steam Ahead in Poughkeepsie: The Story of Coeducation at Vassar, 1966-1974. (Poughkeepsie: Vassar College, 2000), p. 98.

204 Lila Matsumoto, "Sarah Gibson Blanding," edited by Elizabeth Daniels. 2005. http://vcencyclopedia.vassar.edu/index.php/Sarah_Gibson_Blanding (accessed June 3, 2008).

205 Rosalind Rosenberg, "The Limits of Access: The History Of Coeducation in America," *Women and Higher Education: Essays from the Mount Holyoke College Sesquicentennial Symposia*, John Mack Faragher and Florence Howe. (New York: Norton, 1988).

206 Lila Matsumoto, "Alan Simpson," edited by Elizabeth Daniels. 2005. http://vcencyclopedia.vassar.edu/index.php/Alan_Simpson (accessed November 9, 2008).

207 Elizabeth Daniels and Clyde Griffen, *Full Steam Ahead in Poughkeepsie*, (Poughkeepsie: Vassar College, 2000).

208 "Editorial," The *Vassar Miscellany News*, May 10, 1950.

209 "Coeducation–A Bold New Challenge," The *Vassar Miscellany*, October 4, 1968.

210 M.A. Farber, "Vassar Going Coed," The *New York Times*, October 2, 1968.

211 The transition to coeducation was a shaky one for Vassar. Even into the tenure of College President Frances Fergusson (1986-2006), gender proved to be a difficult hurdle. "It takes time in academia, meaning a generation, or 25 years, for people to change their opinions about an institution," Fergusson said in a 2002 interview with the *New York Times* ("Women's Colleges Learning How to Get a Man," December 4, 2002). She added, "I got here 16 years after the moment when the change occurred, and there were still people who would forget we were coed, even those who were doing our recruiting. When I came in, admissions material was done in pastel colors," she recalled. "It didn't work so well." Then there was the issue of the Vassar's colors. "They were a soft pinky-rose and gray," she said. "They are now a deeper maroon red and gray. We saturated the colors a little, which seems appropriate."

212 "The Misc's Demise: Take It, It's yours!" The *Misc,* December 2, 1969.

213 "New Businesses in Store," *The Poughkeepsie Journal,* July 23, 1970.

214 "*Misc* Suspends Publication," The *Misc,* November 20, 1970.

215 *Ibid.*

216 Of course, this does not count the period between 1866 and 1872 when the paper was intentionally annual.

217 "*Misc* Suspends Publication," The *Misc,* November 20, 1970.

218 "Student Interest," The *Misc,* April 9, 1971.

219 Evidence presented in Susan Poulson and Leslie Miller-Bernal, *Challenged by Coeducation: Women's Colleges Since the 1960s*, (Nashville: Vanderbilt University

Press, 2006) suggests that, despite a general decline in interest, men quickly overran the student government. This worried many in the administration, who feared that men would soon dominate what little campus engagement remained.

220 Sarah Riane Harper, "The Modern *Miscellany News*," edited by Elizabeth Daniels. 2006. http://vcencyclopedia.vassar.edu/index.php/The_modern_Vassar_ *Miscellany*_News (accessed May 3, 2008).

221 "*Misc* Suspends Publication," The *Misc,* November 20, 1970.

222 "Editorial," The *Misc,* September 22, 1971.

223 "Editorial," The *Vassar Miscellany News*, March 3, 1969.

224 Sarah Riane Harper, "The Modern *Miscellany News*," edited by Elizabeth Daniels. 2006. http://vcencyclopedia.vassar.edu/index.php/The_modern_Vassar_ *Miscellany*_News (accessed May 3, 2008).

225 "The Great Experiment," The *Misc,* October 1, 1971.

226 "Letter to the Editor," The *Vassar Miscellany*, March 3, 1947.

227 Sarah Riane Harper, "The Modern *Miscellany News*," edited by Elizabeth Daniels. 2006. http://vcencyclopedia.vassar.edu/index.php/The_modern_Vassar_ *Miscellany*_News (accessed May 3, 2008).

228 Sarah Riane Harper, "The Modern *Miscellany News*," edited by Elizabeth Daniels. 2006. http://vcencyclopedia.vassar.edu/index.php/The_modern_Vassar_ *Miscellany*_News (accessed May 3, 2008).

229 "Virginia Disappointed," The *Miscellany News*, September 28, 1978.

230 Sarah Riane Harper, "The Modern *Miscellany News*," edited by Elizabeth Daniels. 2006. http://vcencyclopedia.vassar.edu/index.php/The_modern_Vassar_ *Miscellany*_News (accessed May 3, 2008).

231 The *Vassar Quarterly interview with Harriton in 1990?*

232 "The Beat Goes On," The *Vassar Quarterly*, Fall 1982.

233 "Editor's Note," The *Miscellany News*, March 1, 1995.

234 "Editorial," The *Miscellany News*, September 13, 1996.

235 "Editorial," The *Miscellany News*, April 9, 1994.

236 "Letter to the Editor," The *Miscellany News*, April 26, 2002.

237 Spielman, who graduated *cum laude* with Independent Major in Communication and Culture, put her experience with *Miscellany* publishing to good use. She has since worked for numerous publications including *Food and Wine Magazine* and *Martha Stewart Living*.

238 *U.S. News and World Report, 1994 America's Best Colleges*, October 4, 1993. I define "primary student newspaper" simply as the oldest and best-known newspaper of record of the college or university in question. Large universities such as Harvard often have multiple student publications with news and analysis, but in almost all cases, there is usually a clear newspaper of record, like the *Crimson*.

239 "Student Views in the 1992 Election," The *Miscellany News*, October 9, 1992.

240 "Disappointed About Black Enrollments? Vassar College Shows How to Do It," *The Journal of Blacks in Higher Education*, No. 1998, pp. 78-79.

241 After completing New York Medical College, Seaman is now in his third year of residency at the University of California, Davis. He credits his experiences on the *Miscellany* for teaching him concentration and vital time management skills.

242 Poughkeepsie Journal article about the situation

243 "Letter to the Editor," The *Miscellany News*, April 26, 2002.

244 The *Miscellany News*, September 19, 2001.

245 "Hot Off the Presses: New Improved *Miscellany News*," Vassar Quarterly, 2005, Volume 101, Issue 3.

246 The most appropriate and comforting post-9/11 article ran in the September 21, 2001 issue. This thoughtful piece by Jon Cruz (who wrote the "Vassar Chronicles" column) compared the campus's response to 9/11 with its response to the attacks on Pearl Harbor 60 years earlier. On December 7, 1941, "students found themselves awash in a wide range of feelings… [about] the radically altered world around them." Both in 2001 and 1941, students flocked to the Chapel to hear the reflections of their fellow community members and sit in silent contemplation.

247 "Editorial," The *Miscellany News*, February 8, 2002.

248 "The Misc's Attempts at Inclusiveness Fail," The *Miscellany News*, February 15, 2002.

Chapter Five:
The Contemporary *Miscellany News*, 2004-Present

I n Fall 2004, the Class of 2008 stormed through Vassar's gates with a talented and enthusiastic group of student journalists. While the previous generation of editors did a great deal to restore the image of the paper after the sudden meltdown of 2000-2002, this next generation emphasized high-quality writing and proper journalistic practices, while maintaining financial stability and growth. Just as 2003 had seen a tightening of visual style and formatting, 2004 saw a tightening of journalistic standards.

Vassar's increasingly competitive admissions standards seemed to correlate with better quality writing.[249] While 42 percent of applicants to the Class of 2002 were admitted, only 28 percent of applicants to the Class of 2012 were offered a spot. Average SAT scores climbed. Between 2004 and 2008, the number of in-depth feature stories increased; investigative articles were generally longer and contained more interviews. More detailed policies on letters to the editor and anonymous submissions emerged too. The Bylaws were continually revised to maintain higher levels of continuity as editors came and went.[250] The Bylaws were also amended to include more stringent policies banning conflicts of interest. Vassar Student Association (VSA) Council members were no longer allowed to join the Editorial Board, and Student Assistants to the President could sit on the Editorial Board only as non-voting members.[251] The paper as a whole became more selective than it had been in the past decade; while occasional slackers remained, editorships became more competitive.

Continuing the trend that began in 2003, College administrators remained proud of the newspaper, viewing the *Miscellany* as a legitimate source of communication. The *Vassar Quarterly*, for example, profiled the newspaper's staff in 2005, reaffirming the significance of the publication to Vassar's alumnae/i. The Office of College Relations also used sections of a Miscellany article in its April 2006 *On Campus* publication. Perhaps their unattributed quoting represented the ultimate form of flattery; the paper's writing had finally become decent enough for the College to quote directly in their publicity materials.[252] Even faculty began to use the paper for research and classroom activities. Students enrolled in the introductory "Readings in United States History" course are asked to write a research paper on the history of

Vassar or the Hudson Valley. Those who write on Vassar inevitably use the *Miscellany* as a source. According to Professor of History James Merrell, students have used the newspaper most extensively when writing about Vassar's response to the Great Depression, reactions to World War I and World War II, and the Vietnam protests.

Editor in Chief Aaron Biberstein '06 and Contributing Editor Judy Jarvis '07 work at the storyboard in the *Miscellany News* office in College Center 303. The *Vassar Quarterly*.

Professor of English Donald Foster required the freshmen in his English 101 course "Inside Story: What's News?" read the paper each week. The class was Vassar's first freshman English course in journalism. Early in the semester, students had to select an article from the *Miscellany* and make copies for the class to discuss. "The articles served that day as a focal point for our section on local beats," explained Foster. "Several students in that class have already written for the *Misc*, and found it a valuable experience."

In short, the newspaper's recovery that began in 2003 restored the newspaper's image in the minds of the adults on campus. Subsequent Editors in Chief Aaron Biberstein '06 and Judy Jarvis '07 worked diligently to give consistency to the paper's new design. In an interview with the *Vassar Quarterly*, Jarvis remembered the period "when the paper's financial insolvency and lackluster student interest almost doomed it to obsolescence."[253] She "made a concerted effort to improve its quality," she noted. "Thanks to the dedication of its recharged staff," the paper was measurably better than it had been in the early 2000s.

The alumnae/i magazine's article also seemed to imply that the 2005 Editorial Board created the paper's first Web site, thanks to Web designer Ian Crowther '04. As we saw in Chapter 4, Crowther's site was merely an overhauled version of *http://misc.vassar.edu*, which had existed since 1994. Gabe Anderson, who worked on that original site, caught the 2005 *Quarterly* article and was annoyed with the implication that the paper had only become successful thanks to the "stewardship of its dedicated new editors." Anderson wrote a testy letter to *Quarterly* for its Fall 2005 issue. "What is frustrating for us former editors is to see not only misleading details, but also that the institutional knowledge that we worked so hard to preserve seems to have been lost some time after the class of 1999 graduated," he wrote.[254] "The implication that this is the first time the *Misc* has been online saddens me." He recalled his diligent Web work during his years at Vassar, as well as the high advertising and subscription revenues garnered by Managing Editor Jonty Yamisha '99. Anderson contended that his Editorial Board produced a "quality newspaper" with in-depth reporting by News Editors Jennifer Deane '99 and Stephanie Litos '99, and Senior Editor Jennifer Higginbotham '99. The group, he wrote, "earned not only the interest, but dare I say the respect of the student body." Moreover, Anderson noted that he was well trained by his predecessors, Amanda Spielman '97, Joe Goldman '98, and Hill Anderson '98, "who took the newspaper and the journalistic responsibility that went with it very seriously, setting high standards for those of us who followed in their footsteps; we did our best to maintain that same level of quality."

It seems clear that when the 2005 editors interviewed with the *Vassar Quarterly*, they had no conception of this history. For them, the success of the 1990s was removed from their mental radar; it was the hardship of 2000-2002 that constituted the *Miscellany*'s past in their minds. This disagreement also shows the damaging effects of rewriting much of the paper's stylebook and Bylaws in 2000. When the paper was redesigned in the tabloid format, the rules that had guided it since the late 1970s were discarded. Policies were forgotten without recognition of the past. History was lost.

Major Areas of Coverage

Much has changed at Vassar between 2004 and the present. This change has meant exciting times for the *Miscellany*. Several trends have dominated coverage. First, construction has been a central focus in this period, as the College continues to build and renovate at unprecedented levels. Beginning with the restoration of Jewett House in 2003, the paper has written about renovations of the Town Houses, Terrace Apartments, Davison House, Students' Building, Kenyon Hall, Old Observatory and Art Library, just to name a handful of locations. The *Miscellany* has kept tabs on all of these projects, even conducting video tours of the Davison and Town House construction sites.

Second, since Catharine Bond Hill became Vassar's tenth President in 2006, financial aid has also been a frequent topic in the *Miscellany*. Hill, an economist, spent much of her academic career researching the economics of higher education. Specifically, she has studied the accessibility of higher education for low-income, high-achieving students. During her tenure at Williams College, she was a leading researcher for the Williams Project on Higher Education, founded in 1989. The Project examined issues of socioeconomic diversity among student bodies at a variety of selective colleges. At Vassar, she immediately prioritized financial aid spending. At the 2007 Commencement, Hill announced that Vassar would return to need-blind admissions. The following year, the College replaced loans with grants for students with calculated family incomes under $60,000. The *Miscellany* has not only covered these changes, but also wholeheartedly endorsed them in lengthy editorials. The same was true with plans to attract and admit low-income students from Poughkeepsie High School, as well as undocumented immigrant students.

THE MISCELLANY NEWS

Since 1866 | misc@vassar.edu

College President Fran Fergusson
finishes final year at Vassar
pages 10 and 11

4.28.06 | Volume LXXX | Issue 21

Fran Fergusson retired in 2006 after two decades at the helm of Vassar. During her tenure, the campus landscape was renewed and Vassar once again became highly selective. Memories of her eventful and productive tenure filled the pages of the *Miscellany* for months, seen clearly in this final retrospective from April 28, 2006.

Third, campus controversies—"mini-explosions" in the words of News Editor Chris Seaman '02—have continued to dominate the newspaper. Just like they did in the 1990s, these controversies would follow similar patters: an issue would rile or offend segments of the community, that group would hold meetings or petition the student government, and there would be a series of emotional forums and discussions. One particular news story that dominated coverage during the 2004-2005 academic year involved the *Imperialist*, a conservative magazine affiliated with the Moderate, Independent, Conservative Alliance (MICA). Controversy erupted over an article entitled "Race and Freedom" that many viewed as racist. "How is diversity achieved," read the anonymous article, "is [by minorities students] voluntarily confining themselves to ghettoes of cultural centers. I find the objective of diversity to be utterly meritless, suggesting that our colleges should become some zoological preserve in some paternalistic attempt [to] benefit our 'non diverse' students." The article implicitly targeted the multi-cultural ALANA Center, as well as Blegen House, a center for gay and lesbian students.[255] Angelic Sosa '08, an African American student, wrote an irate letter to the *Miscellany News*. Sosa was furious at the use of "ghetto" to describe buildings designated for particular communities. "These are places where students of color and homosexual students can feel comfortable," Sosa said. "Now they're uncomfortable." But the article was not the only element of the *Imperialist* that outraged students; a cartoon depicting an angry-looking black woman yelling at an innocent-looking white girl was also decried as intolerant. The caption read, "Black student confronting a white supremacist on campus."

Many students demanded that the Vassar Student Association (VSA) Council formally punish MICA, and that the *Imperialist* lose its right to publish with student funds. "To ignore the historical and social connotations of a word like 'ghetto' is inflammatory," said James Cantres '08 at a Council forum on the publication. "I feel like I'm being hated when I hear something like that." Even after MICA issued a brief apology, Tiera Rainey '08 remained unsatisfied. "It is not our jobs as minorities to educate MICA on common sense," said Rainey. "This is definitely not a dead issue." Rainey was among those who asked the Council to cancel MICA's funding. "I think they should lose their privilege to publish with student money," Rainey said at the forum. "They like to rabble rouse. It's not about public dialogue." Many were also upset that the author of the *Imperialist* article remained anonymous—yet one of MICA's leader's referred by name to the anonymous author of a piece in the *Miscellany News*. The article, written by a black student, was critical of the "inherent hostility toward diversity at Vassar College."

Students grew increasingly angry with MICA's attempt at self-defense. MICA President Matthew Ambrose '07 tried to argue that that this was only the third issue of the *Imperialist,* and that the incident was simply part of the publication's "growing pains." *Imperialist* editor Graydon Gordian '07 defended the meaning of the inflammatory cartoon. "When black students accuse a white student of being racist, that student is as helpless as a little girl," he tried to explain. When he first saw the cartoon, he said he thought it was "stupid, but innocuous," and let it into the publication. Eventually, the Council forced MICA to hold an open forum on the controversy. The student government was reluctant to freeze their budget or decertify their organization, given the lack of conservative voice on campus.

The incident loomed large in the *Miscellany* for months. Coverage was generally seen as fair and balanced, and the paper's ability to handle this delicate situation by printing and soliciting letters from varying points of view supported campus-wide dialogue. Faculty, students, Council members and members of MICA wrote to the newspaper in droves. Though the College was divided over the *Imperialist* affair, there seemed to be some unity over the *Miscellany* as the *de facto* forum for discussion. The MICA affair was certainly the largest campus controversy during the post-2004 period. Still, other similar controversies have arisen and have dominated the *Miscellany*'s news and opinions coverage for weeks, sometimes months.

Stylistic Progress

The period between 2004 and 2008 saw gradual but significant improvements in the paper's physical appearance. In Spring 2007, co-Editors in Chief Sam Rosen-Amy '08 and Amanda Melilo '07 changed the paper's font from the amateurish Veranda to the more newsy and professional Miller-Roman. Office records show that the paper paid $450 for use of the font, an investment that was well worth the facelift. Editors had complained for years about Veranda, a font more often found in old Microsoft Word documents and cheap tabloids than in newspapers; it gave the *Miscellany* a wholly unprofessional appearance. Miller-Roman, by contrast, is similar to the body text of major papers such as the *New York Times* and the *Washington Post*. This simple font change made a world of difference in the paper's professional appearance.

Another important formatting change came the following year when the paper transitioned from a three-column to a four-column format. Like the font change, this also gave the paper a boost of professionalism. Since the tabloid redesign, each page was designed like a magazine with pull-out quotations and three thick columns. Most major newspapers print at least four columns per page, and often more.

A third stylistic change was the introduction of 'planters' onto the cover in Spring 2008. Planters are short descriptions of exciting stories inside the newspaper. Placing them on the bottom of the front page, editors were able to show more than a single story on the paper's monolithic cover. Again, planters are commonly found on professional newspapers in order to attract readers with a variety of interests.

The new font, four-column format and cover planters moved the *Miscellany* further away from the slapdash tabloid appearance of 2000-2001. The *Miscellany*'s design was dramatically tightened as the editors developed increasingly specific guidelines for digitally designing the paper.

Spring 2008 also saw another significant change, though it was less visible to readers. For the first time, copy editors and section editors experimented with digital copyediting. Quark Copy Desk—copyediting software that worked with the paper's layout application—allowed on-screen corrections to articles, rather than having to print the entire paper and write corrections by hand. This saved time for both copy editors and section editors, who no longer had to enter corrections manually. Though the paper abandoned the use of Copy Desk the following semester, the idea remained. Editors began to copy edit solely on the computers rather than on printed pages. This procedure saved ink, paper, money and, most importantly, great amounts of time.

Looking Ahead: Vassar Journalism in a New Century

In April 2008, I was elected Editor in Chief and Emma Mitchell '09 and Alexandra Matthews '11 were elected Senior Editors. Excited to further the progress of our predecessors, the three of us spent the final months of the 2007-2008 year considering the major challenges that the *Miscellany*

News faced. We identified a number of personal goals, and began efforts to build on the growing professionalism of the past few years.

An Overhauled Web Site

The most significant project that we identified was a complete overhaul of both our Web site and our Web philosophy. The last redesign of the site in 2005 served the paper well for several years, but ultimately proved too inflexible to adapt to more recent Internet trends and coding protocols. Layout was clunky, and the site was rarely visited or discussed by members of the College community. Installing a rudimentary counter into the site's HTML code, I determined that only 52 visitors came to our site over the course of two weeks; 34 of them came from IP addresses of computers inside the *Miscellany News* office. In other words, the old site was used largely as an archival reference for editors and not as a source of information for the student body. Moreover, the site was updated only once each week. A staffer had to copy and paste the contents of each week's issue, a tedious process that took hours. Only rarely did editors post mid-week article updates to provide the campus with more timely coverage.

This lack of timeliness became increasingly problematic as the *Miscellany News* began to face increasing competition from amateur student blogs.[256] Most of these blogs began during the 2007-2008 academic year and initially focused on campus gossip. But by the spring semester, some blogs began to post more newsy items about issues such as financial aid, Vassar's relationship with Poughkeepsie and residential life. These postings sometimes contained blatant inaccuracies about College governance and policies. One blog post began a rumor that Bill O'Reilly—the conservative television newscaster—would be Vassar's 2008 Commencement speaker. Many students became angry about the choice before realizing that the information about O'Reilly was entirely incorrect. Despite such inaccuracies, student-run blogs became ever more popular.

Our new Web site, *http://www.miscellanynews.com*, is based on state of the art HTML, XML and CSS. With capabilities ranging from audio and video embedding to a live RSS feed, it is among the most powerful and functional college newspaper Web sites in the country.

Much of their success was due to anonymous commenting, a feature that allowed users to post anonymous thoughts. Numerous visitors wrote racist, classist, or sexist comments under the cover of anonymity; the debates that ensued over such controversial statements attracted hundreds of students and sparked much conversation within the College community about the relationship between free speech and the Internet. These thoughtless comments, while popular, were also worrisome to administrators. Indeed, President Catharine Bond Hill devoted a sizable portion of her 2008 Spring Convocation speech to the topic of anonymous, hateful messages.

Upon seeing such blogs arise, *Miscellany* editors became worried about the potential decline in the importance of the student newspaper. Though the publication was the oldest at Vassar, some feared that its weekly publication schedule seriously diminished its ability to report and editorialize on campus happenings, especially compared to blogs that could receive a tremendous amount of attention for pithy rumors and misinformation.

It was clear that the old Web site, *http://misc.vassar.edu*, was unable to meet the challenge of the 24-hour news cycle. The new Executive Staff—myself, Matthews and Mitchell—were determined to launch a Web site suitable for the next generation of Vassar students. After extensive discussions with Matthews and Mitchell, I spent the summer coding and designing an entirely new online home for the *Miscellany News*. For the first time, the paper would no longer be located on the College's server, but rather on its own server at *http://www.miscellanynews.com*.

The new site, launched in August 2008, boasts countless new features light years ahead of the former site. Perhaps the most significant change is the flexible formatting; the entire site can be rearranged within minutes depending on the news of a particular day. This was certainly not the case with our previous site, whose rigid homepage layout displayed only a single story from each section. This design could not be easily changed for breaking news, since the designer had long since graduated. The flexibility of *http://www.miscellanynews.com* allows editors tremendously more creativity in the ways that they can display content.

The new site also offers immeasurable increases to functionality. Not only can users post comments and discuss articles, but they can also share articles via e-mail, Facebook, MySpace, or through a host of other social networking sites with the click of a button. They can also send letter to the editor directly from the Web site homepage, or send anonymous news tips. Within minutes, students can even fill out an application to join the paper's staff. For the first time, the *Miscellany* produces an RSS feed, meaning that users can subscribe to our RSS and track our stories through third-party applications like Google Reader. The site can also track the popularity of particular articles and prioritize them on the homepage accordingly. Our new online home is constantly changing and fully interactive.

The inclusion of multimedia is another major leap forward. Unlike our previous site—and the sites of many other college papers— *http://www.miscellanynews.com* seamlessly presents slideshows, high-resolution photography, video and audio. Online Editor Molly Turpin '12 has used video to interview the Dean of the College, tour through the Davison House construction site, and record one of the College's swimming and diving meets.[257] Like most newspapers, the *Miscellany* will no-doubt rely increasingly on these forms of multimedia and interactive Web content in the years ahead.

The Miscellany News Guide to Poughkeepsie

One of Catharine Bond Hill's primary objectives at Vassar has been to improve the uneasy relationship between the College and the surrounding community. For the past two years, the administration and the Vassar Student Association (VSA) have pushed students to leave campus and experience Poughkeepsie. Their most notable and successful effort was the introduction of the Community Shuttle in Spring 2008. The shuttle leaves from Main Building and loops around several local shopping areas. This program, advocated strongly by VSA President James Kelly '09, proved to be very popular. Nevertheless, many students still did not feel the need to leave campus. After all, most of what students need is available within walking distance of the dorms. Some continued to view the stores and people beyond the so-called "Vassar Bubble" as foreign and even frightening. As a result, many graduated from Vassar without visiting the many cultural and natural attractions of the Hudson Valley.

We always fear what we do not understand. I strongly believe that if students knew more about nearby businesses and attractions and saw that Vassar students have successfully made use of them, they will be inclined to do the same. This two-pronged strategy—information plus the Vassar connection—is the goal of the *Miscellany News Guide to Poughkeepsie*. The first entries of the *Guide* were compiled over Summer 2008 and have been bolstered every month since. The *Guide* includes restaurant reviews, descriptions of local stores and sketches of the many cultural resources of the Hudson Valley. All of these narratives are written by Vassar students and include their own opinions about each of the locations.

Is this restaurant a good place for an anniversary dinner? What sandwiches are the tastiest? Which hiking trails can be completed in just a few hours? Which local museums contain the Hudson River School paintings from Art History 105-106? By answering these very student-centered questions, the reviews in the *Miscellany News Guide to Poughkeepsie* will spark interest in the outside community through knowledge and information. The *Guide* will also include a list of restaurants that make deliveries to Vassar, along with their phone numbers and scanned copies of their menus. All of this will be a permanent feature of the new Web site, and will be continually updated as new businesses and local attractions open.

Redecoration of the Office

The *Miscellany News* office has been located on the third floor of the College Center, room 303, since the building's completion in 1972. When I first began my tenure as News Editor during my freshman year, I was surprised at the unfortunate state of the office. Tables were arranged obstructively, closets were full of obsolete equipment and the workroom was dusty and dark. Upon my election as Editor in Chief,

I began to sort through the files and papers that clogged the office. I found old advertising checks from 2003 totaling over $3,700. I found a broken-down fax machine. And I found bundles of dust just about everywhere. With these discoveries, a major redecoration project began. The tables were rearranged, the files were sorted, and piles of garbage were quickly discarded. Emma Mitchell '09 repainted the walls to create a lighter and more cheerful atmosphere. Significantly, we have added many historical images to the walls of the office. These images range from

Senior Editor Emma Mitchell '09 repaints the tattered walls of the *Miscellany News* office during the summer redecoration.

an original, antique watercolor of the College, to various reprints of photographs and images of early Vassar. We have also adorned the walls with old front pages of the *Miscellany News*, which range from the very first issue of the *Weekly* to the more contemporary issues of the paper. My personal hope is that by surrounding ourselves with historical images and newspapers, we will be constantly reminded of our role in literally writing the history of the College. Editors will also be reminded to look to the newspaper's tremendous archives as a resource for their stories.

Installing new high-speed Internet lines, lighting, furniture and ventilation, the *Miscellany News* office has transitioned into a professional-looking, 21st century newsroom.

Archiving and Historical Research

As a history major at Vassar, I have a deep interest in the history of the College and its newspaper. Unfortunately, access to the archives of the *Miscellany News* is difficult. Most issues of the paper exist on microfilm in the basement of the Thompson Memorial Library, but few students (or even editors) can find and view them. Editor in Chief Sam Rosen-Amy '08 advocated the full digitization of the paper's archives. Many other college newspapers, such as the *Harvard Crimson*, the *Barnard Bulletin* and the *Yale Daily News* have been professionally scanned and digitized into searchable online documents. These were freely available not only to their respective communities, but also to scholars and the general public.

The cost of this scanning is significant. However, we have begun conversations with the Associate Director of the Libraries for Special Collections Ronald Patkus as well as the Development Office and about the best ways to undertake this project. My hope is that, within a few years, these truly significant historical documents will be made available for students and researchers across the country. Though the national economic depression of 2008-2009 is not working in our favor, I still hope to push this project to completion. Until the digitization is complete, we hope to make the *Miscellany News*'s history as accessible as possible and to use our impressive archives to add historical angles to our investigative stories.

The End of Weekly Covers and the Return to Broadsheet

Weekly covers began in 2001 as part of a general redesign of the paper into a tabloid format. After extensive conversations with the Executive Staff and the Editorial Board, the *Miscellany* decided to transition back to broadsheet—the format used between 1914 and 2000—beginning in Spring 2009. The consensus among the editors was that the cover and much of our layout made the paper look amateurish. Besides the *Miscellany*, our only peer papers that use covers are the *Chicago Weekly* and the *Swarthmore Phoenix*. Broadsheet papers such as the *Williams Record* and *Amherst Student* look far more professional and far more inviting to readers.

"Our goal this semester has really been to look more newsy," said Eric Estes '11, Design and Production Editor, who led the move to broadsheet. "With the cover, the *Miscellany News* looked a lot like something you might pick up at the front of the supermarket, rather than a professional newspaper. If we want our readers to take our news seriously, we have to realize that formatting matters." He added, "That sort of artistic look of a cover brings in a lot of uncomfortable subjectivity. It's really difficult to find a single 'most important' story each week, much less one that lends itself to a large image. Now the headlines and the articles will speak for themselves."

Indeed, our hopes for our redesign were based in a commitment to higher quality journalism. Broadsheet allows us to display each week's news in a more democratic fashion. That is, the new format can present numerous articles on the front page rather than choosing a single story each week. As the paper has discovered over the past eight years, the 'most important' story in a given week cannot always be represented with a large photograph. Placing multiple stories on our front page— whether they concern the men's basketball team or the Vassar Student Association or a faculty member—attracts a wider array of readers. Though we sacrificed a unified creative image, we created a space for eclectic disunity, where readers can see varied aspects of life at Vassar.

The idea of returning to broadsheet is not a new one; it had been discussed occasionally at least since my arrival at Vassar in 2006. To see it through, the move took a great deal of planning and effort, but the Editorial Board believes that those efforts paid off.

The Miscellany News

Since 1866 | miscellanynews.com | JANUARY 29, 2009 | Volume CXLII | Issue 12

Vassarions descend on D.C. for inauguration

Charlie Dobb
STAFF WRITER

Millions packed onto the National Mall in Washington, D.C. on Tuesday, Jan. 20 to witness President Barack Obama's historic inauguration. Scattered throughout the crowd were dozens of Vassar students and alumnae/i faculty eager to catch a glimpse of the nation's 44th President.

Students changed plans, skipped classes and endured various hardships to attend what Christine Cruz '11 called "a mind-blowing event." Cruz, like many students, was forced to miss the first day of classes. She traveled on overcrowded trains and stood in long lines for everything from restrooms to food for the opportunity to watch the moment on large screens, since, despite having arrived at the National Mall at 5 a.m., she could not see much from her seat. "It wasn't 'live,' but I was there, and there was an energy about it," said Cruz.

Andrea Banks '11 described it as "somewhat organized chaos," noting that several times after asking anxiously what she should do, she was told by inaugural personnel that they were just as unsure as she was. Crowded and facing a shortage of bathrooms, Banks called her time spent on the Mall "uncomfortable to say the least." But she was quick to dismiss the discomfort,

calling it "simply all worth it."

Perhaps the most difficult aspect of the whole event was simply getting in and out of the capital. The U.S. Department of Transportation released claims that extra trains had been added to the schedule between D.C. and major eastern urban areas such as New York, Philadelphia and Boston. When she returned back home, she found it crowded due to "capacity" and recalls a "throng of people" waiting outside. "They shouted 'farm to lines' and I looked around and thought, 'You have got to be kidding me. Do you see how many people are out here?'" said Banks.

Vassar Student Association President Jimmy Kelly '09 attended the event with Vice President for Student Life Nate Silver '10, Vice President for Academics Camille Friston '09, Alex Meade '09, Riley Greene '11 and Lauren MacLean '12

Excited for political change, dozens of Vassar students and alumnae/i braced the cold to witness the historic inauguration of Barack Obama as the 44th President of the United States.

Kelly said that he will keep with him always the image of an "elderly woman who stood next to me throughout the inauguration—she was so personally moved by the moment of his oath. I didn't know her story, nor did she know mine, but at that moment we hugged and knew that change is here and that America might regain its standing in the world."

Back in Poughkeepsie, students gathered in the Villard Room to watch the inauguration at an event sponsored by the Africana Studies Program, the Political Science Department, the Women Studies Program, the Office of Campus Life, the Vassar College Democrats, the African Students Union, the Asian Students Alliance and the Feminist Alliance. The room was packed with students and faculty who watched the proceedings on a big TV at the front of the room.

Debate over faculty cuts leads to a tentative compromise

Julianne Hertz
NEWS EDITOR

In an effort to cut costs in the wake of the national recession, the Vassar administration decided this fall that they would not rehire several adjunct and visiting professors whose contracts expire in the spring. However, in the midst of a great deal of protest from students, faculty and alumnae/i associated with the English Department, the administration was able to put together a plan that will allow two of these professors to teach at Vassar part-time during the 2009-10 academic year.

The College's endowment decreased by about $195 million during 2008. According to President Catharine Bond Hill, these monetary losses necessitate a $750,000 cut to faculty salaries next year, resulting in 60 to 80 courses being cut from the curriculum in Fall 2009.

In a Dec. 11 e-mail to the College community, Hill explained that the English Department, which submitted a proposal to add 11 new course sections for the 2009-10 academic year, was instead asked to reduce the number of sections offered next year by two, which meant that some professors in the Department could not have their contracts renewed.

However, alumnae/i and students alike protested that by not re-hiring English professors—specifically Visiting Associate Professor of English M. Mark and Adjunct Assistant Professor of English Julia Rose—the administration was reducing the number of creative writing courses offered at Vassar. Mark currently teaches Literary Nonfiction, which teaches students to write nonfiction genres ranging from memoirs to travel essays. Rose specializes in American literature and fiction writing. Upon hearing that these professors were being forced to leave, many members of the Vassar community started Facebook groups, held meetings and sent e-mails to the administration to express their concern.

English Department co-Chairs Michael Joyce and Peter Antelyes issued a joint statement on Dec. 12 protesting the faculty cuts: "Like most liberal arts colleges, Vassar depends for much of its curricular diversity and innovation on its pool of non-tenure-track faculty," they wrote. "We believe the administration has the creative writing program has not been specifically targeted for

Continued on page 3

Students await musical thrills of Beirut in ViCE kickoff

Gillian Demikay
ASSISTANT ARTS EDITOR

Imagine your favorite rock band came to Vassar and wanted to play with you in a live performance. It would most probably be a dream come true for a Vassar musician. For students who are fans of the unique indie band Beirut, this dream is far from unrealistic. Vassar College Entertainment (ViCE) is bringing Beirut to Vassar in a concert featuring a group of Vassar musicians on Saturday, Jan. 31 at 8 p.m. in the Chapel.

Beirut has its roots in the music that 23-year-old Zach Condon composed in his bedroom during his teens. Condon, who plays the trumpet, horns, ukulele, accordion, piano, percussion, clarinet and mandolin, was introduced to music by his family, especially his father, who wanted all of his children to play the guitar. After dropping out of high school and music than one college, Condon decided that being a student was not right for him and went to Europe with his older brother. "I felt like that was the first place I needed to see if I was going to drop out of school,"

Beirut's Zach Condon has created a sound unique to the indie rock world.

Condon said in an interview with The Miscellany News.

Condon stayed mostly in Paris, where he found inspiration for his

early songs, including the popular "Postcards from Italy." He was particularly affected by the French youth, who listened to Eastern European artists and progressive Balkan folk, along with mainstream French bands like Air and Justice. When he returned back home, Condon composed music inspired by his European journey and recorded the scores in his bedroom. Condon admitted that he never expected his songs to get as popular as they did. But "Postcards from Italy" and Condon's other early music got extensive attention on the Internet even before Beirut's first record came out.

After Condon finished recording his songs in studio with assistance from early members of Beirut, he signed to Ba Da Bing! Records, run by Ben Goldberg '95. Beirut's debut

album Gulag Orkestar gained immense success after its release in 2006 and was selected as the best album of 2006 by indie label Rough Trade Records. Released in 2007, Beirut's second album, The Flying Club Cup, proved that the band was not a one-album wonder, reaching the top of the album of the year lists in a number of European publications including The Sun, The Telegraph and Uncut.

The band will release the double EP March of the Zapotec/Holland on Feb. 17 on Condon's own Pompeii Records. The Vassar Chapel is the first stop on the band's new tour, after Vassar they will visit New Mexico, Hamburg, Amsterdam, Brussels, London, Paris and Minehead, UK.

Director of ViCE Anabel Graff '09 said, "I wanted to bring them here forever because we had the connection and [Goldberg] went to Vassar. I thought it would be great to use the connection and have a great show." Goldberg said that neither the band nor Ba Da Bing! had initially expressed an enthusiastic interest in playing at

Continued on page 14

Inside this issue

The current design of the *Miscellany News*, implemented in Spring 2009, replaced the tabloid-style cover design with a more traditional broadsheet layout. The front page is printed in color. The Editorial Board believes that the result of the redesign is a far more professional newspaper.

A Master Plan

A major administrative goal is to adopt a long-term Master Plan for the *Miscellany News*. This plan would serve as a guiding document for the general direction in which the paper should move over the next decade. As far as I can tell, such a plan has never existed, and as a result, long-term planning has historically been far from 'long-term.' Instead, ideas have passed orally from graduating seniors to younger Editorial Board members. Though this system has admittedly worked for nearly 150 years, it leaves incoming editors with confusion about exactly what major projects they should prioritize. Should we follow the casual advice given to us by graduating editors? Should we maintain the status quo? Or should we conceive new projects, new styles and new ideas entirely? It has never been clear.

In May 2008, the *Miscellany News* was fortunate enough to be invited to the Bloomberg College Editors' Workshop, hosted by Bloomberg News at the Columbia University School of Journalism.[258] Twenty college editors from across the country are invited to discuss common problems, directions and ideas. Several papers reported having lengthy five or ten-year plans to guide current editors. Out of this conference and these plans, it was clear that the *Miscellany* needed to take three major steps. The first two have already been accomplished in Fall 2008, while the third is a longer-term goal:

1. *Switching from the outdated Quark layout software to Adobe InDesign*: InDesign is the new industry standard for desktop publishing, and is fully compatible with our new Web site, which can upload InDesign articles automatically. InDesign works seamlessly with Photoshop, Illustrator and Adobe Creative Suite 4 (CS4). Of the 20 newspapers represented at the conference, all but three were happily using InDesign. After speaking with Mitchell and Matthews, we decided to transition away from Quark beginning in Fall 2008. Additionally, we will continue the trend of the last couple semesters toward paperless copyediting. Printing the entire newspaper on ledger paper was an old-fashioned and outdated method for correcting errors. Instead, the switch to Adobe InCopy allows for spelling and grammar checking within the layout document. This

dramatically reduced typos and careless grammatical mistakes during the 2008-2009 school year.

2. *Restructuring of Editorial Board responsibilities:* When we decided to eliminate the cover design, the Executive Staff also took a hard look at the structure of the Editorial Board. Before the changes that we initiated in Spring 2009, each section editor was not only responsible for writing and editing weekly articles, but also for laying out their section on our computer software. The combined workload was tremendous, and we discovered that editors were forced to spend a great amount of time fixing details of layout. Almost no other newspapers at the Bloomberg Conference gave such tremendous layout responsibilities to their section editors. As a result, we noticed, their quality of writing was often higher than ours since their editors focused solely on content. The *Miscellany News* decided to follow a similar course. Beginning in Spring 2009, editors for News, Opinions, Features, Arts and Sports became responsible for meeting extensively with their reporters and producing top-notch pieces. The Executive Staff, in conjunction with our Design and Production Editor, became responsible for laying out the paper. Estes, a Computer Science major and aspiring designer, felt that the switch to broadsheet professionalizes the paper's operation. "It will help with consistency. The paper will have a unified artistic vision, rather than five editors all with slightly different layout standards. It's also a huge advantage for editors, who can now focus on content and stop wasting time on formatting. They should be worried about the journalism."

3. *Establishing an independent endowment:* An independent endowment is one of our long-term dreams. Different college newspapers have different ways of covering their production costs. Large daily papers like the *Harvard Crimson* and the *Stanford Daily* run much like real businesses. They profit from advertising and subscriptions, and use that revenue to print the paper, pay staff and purchase equipment. Smaller papers like the *Bates Student* receive funding entirely through the

student government or the college administration. Either source of funding represents an inherent conflict of interest, since it makes criticizing either the administration or the student government somewhat awkward. If the paper's words are too harsh, there is a risk that funding could be cut. Such repercussions can be exercised more subtly too. At Amherst, for example, a prominent administrator felt that he had been misrepresented in a newspaper article. As a result, some members of the administration were asked not to speak to the paper. The *Amherst Student* quickly faced difficulties in finding sources for their stories. A similar situation occurred at Alfred University, where the paper's office space was dramatically downsized after a year of hostility with the college's administration. In other words, when the administration controls the paper financially and owns its offices and equipment, life can easily be made difficult for editors. A similar concern exists with the student government. If the Vassar Student Association (VSA) decided to cut the *Miscellany*'s funding, it could easily impinge on our editorial creativity. Our paper might have to shrink, and we would be forced to increase advertising and decrease our use of color printing. For this reason alone, it is necessary for the *Miscellany* to have a reserve of funding outside of the VSA or the College's control. I believe that, as a long-term goal, we must work toward an independent account that can be used to ensure continuity of the newspaper in financial hard times.

249 In the first decade of the 21st century, colleges across the United States became more selective, thanks to an increasing number of applications from the children of the Baby Boomer generation. Students' test scores and grade point averages increased dramatically at many institutions including Vassar.

250 "Bylaws," The *Miscellany News*, 2004.

251 To clarify, Contributing Editors (who do not control specific content and serve at the direction of the Editor in Chief) are permitted to be Student Assistants to the President of the College. Contributing Editors are the only editors who may have that job, and if they do, they forfeit their vote the Editorial Board, although they may participate in all meetings and discussions.

252 The April issue of *On Campus*, the monthly publication of College Relations, included four quotations taken directly from a March 31, 2006 *Miscellany News* article entitled "The World According to TC" by Walter Padilla '07. In the June issue of *On Campus*, College Relations acknowledged its error and apologized for the unattributed quotations.

253 "Hot Off the Presses: New Improved *Miscellany News*," Vassar Quarterly, 2005, Volume 101, Issue 3.

254 "*Miscellany News*," Vassar Quarterly, 2005, Volume 101, Issue 4.

255 The ALANA Center is located in the Old Laundry Building, directly behind Main Building; Blegen House is located on Collegeview Avenue. The Afro-American Cultural Center (AACC) was originally housed in Blegen until the ALANA Center opened under the presidency of Frances Fergusson. Blegen then became a resource center for lesbian and gay students, until the aging building was closed for in 2008 for not meeting building codes.

256 It is fair to say that few print publications have challenged the *Miscellany News* in any significant way since the 1980s. Given the student government's limited budget, it is difficult for them to recognize an organization that would essentially duplicate the function of the *Miscellany*. Without being recognized, wet-behind-the-ears publications cannot receive funding, obtain office space, or even reserve meeting rooms. The Daily Brew, a short daily publication that existed between 2000 and 2002 is a useful case study. The Brew, which focused on Poughkeepsie and national news, remained unrecognized by the student government for nearly a year, and even after it was recognized, it was not technically *authorized*—another level of red tape that prevented it from having a regularized budget. Instead, the publication had to survive off the meager Media Publishing Fund. The editors struggled to pay about $15 per day to print about 200 copies; by the end of 2001-2002 academic year, the group was nearly $2,000 in debt. Like many startup publications throughout the College's history, the *Brew* folded once its founders graduated in 2002.

257 Turpin had signed up for the *Miscellany*'s Freshmen Orientation event, and expressed interest in helping to operate our new Web site. The Editorial Board quickly amended the Bylaws to create the position of Online Editor; she quickly filled it, and was introduced into the site's management and began thinking innovatively about different multimedia approaches. For example, she worked with Photography Editor Kat Mehocic '12 to post 5-10 Photos of the Week in high resolution. She also worked with Contributing Editor Juliana Kiyan '09 to cover the VSA's Meet Me in Poughkeepsie event using video, slideshows and articles.

258 The paper had also been invited the previous year and attended by then-Senior Editor Kiyan.

Chapter Six:
Personal Experiences

To depart for a moment from the narrative history of the *Miscellany News*, it might be useful to offer my own personal experiences on the paper and at Vassar to illustrate the lifestyle of an editor. In explaining my own beginnings on the paper, I hope to better illuminate the *Miscellany*'s current practices, problems and procedures and correct for any biases that have crept into this history.

My first taste of journalism came in high school. I worked on the *Horace Mann Review*, a tri-annual magazine of investigative reporting. A stronger student in English and history than in math and science, I naturally gravitated toward extracurricular activities that involved writing and research. My involvement on the *Review*, however, began mostly as a venture to build my résumé for the rigorous college admissions process. My high school, Horace Mann, was intensely focused on college admissions and our counselors warned us repeatedly to grow our list of extracurricular activities. And so we did. Many of my friends and I tried to put as many hours as we could into as many campus organizations as we could—whether we were genuinely interested in the activity or not. On the bright side, this gave us broad experience; on the darker side, our schedules were unimaginably crowded.

Horace Mann is often referred to as the "ultimate pressure cooker" of New York City's schools; a common joke is that students are so overwhelmed with academic and extracurricular work that graduates can be identified by their nervous ticks, always checking their watches and agonizing over unfinished assignments. Though generalized stereotypes about schools are rarely true, these characteristics of Horace Mann could not be more accurate.

But with all that said, I have never seen a more intelligent, self-motivated and opportunistic group than the students with whom I graduated. As a student there since the age of three, it was impossible to appreciate the education I was receiving. Though I always knew that my classmates were bright—and cutthroat and sneaky—I did not fully realize that other schools did not also instill these qualities of unrelenting self-advancement in their students. At Horace Mann, one did whatever one had to do to get ahead. We stalked our college counselors at all hours of the day and night, we ingratiated ourselves to our teachers and we flipped through our flashcards until the moment an exam was dropped in front of us. Those who were admitted to the Harvards and Yales were revered; those who were not were gossiped about and ridiculed.

From this ruthless, fast-paced, winner-takes-all environment, I came to Poughkeepsie. As a lifelong New Yorker, an escape to the open spaces of Vassar was an interesting change. But several aspects of College life quickly clashed with my Horace Mann background. The first that I noticed was that students travelled across the campus at a snail's pace. At Horace Mann, students raced to and from their classes, zipped into the library to study for an exam and never showed up late for any sort of meeting. Not so at Vassar. During my first few days as a freshman, I noticed that students rarely walked anywhere directly. They stopped for chats, and blissfully sat on the grass listening to music. I would walk right behind people on a narrow pathway trying to pass them, and they would mosey slowly along without a care in the world. On the third day of school, my new friends and I planned for dinner at 6:15 p.m., and I arrived exactly on time, maybe even one minute early. To my shock, they strolled over to the Dining Center at 6:23 p.m., barely acknowledging their tardiness. In retrospect, I can see that it was my upbringing—and not their disrespect—that agitated me. But during my first few weeks, I faced the difficult task of slowing down my inner clock to match the relaxed pace of Vassar.

During my time on the *Horace Mann Review*, I had no plans to continue with journalism or writing after I was admitted to college.

But even before entering Vassar, my focus was already on post-college life. Since April, my friends and I had been actively considering career paths. I even remember talking with two of my closest friends a week before our graduation about the specific graduate programs we intended to pursue; we had already downloaded and reviewed several graduate applications. I knew that I would pursue a law degree after college, and only needed a concrete plan—and what better time to begin formulating these plans than on the third day of Vassar freshmen orientation.

During our first week in Poughkeepsie, the Career Development Office (CDO) advertised office hours for members of the Class of 2010 to come and discuss their career plans. Prepared with a binder and a list of 15 detailed questions, I marched over. Entering the office, I was shocked to find it empty. I checked my calendar to make sure it was the right day; it was. If college counselors at Horace Mann had announced such office hours, every student would have been fighting outside the door since 5 a.m. to be the first in line. The CDO administrative assistant looked up at me gleefully from her novel—I think it was *Harry Potter*, but I could not be sure—and she announced that I was the only person to attend. After waiting for two minutes and making small talk, I was brought into a back office where the career counselor, Bertha, greeted me and offered various types of tea.[259] I politely refused. After five more minutes of chitchat, she invited me to sit down at her desk. I did so, opening my binder to my typed list of questions. I began my inquisition. The conversation went something like this:

> *Brian:* I want to attend a top-25 law school for the year following my graduation, and I have a few questions. First, does your office correlate law school admissions success of graduates with the applicant's major? Which discipline has statistically had the most success coming from Vassar?
>
> *Bertha:* Umm. I don't know if we do that. If you're looking for classes to take, though, sociology is really interesting. I've heard great things about Vassar's sociology classes. If you like to read, you might enjoy the sociology major.
>
> *Brian:* Yeah, maybe, thanks. But I'm wondering if past law school applicants have any statistically higher success rate coming from any particular department. Do you know if anyone keeps hard numbers?
>
> *Bertha:* That's a good question....

Brian: Oh, okay. Let me ask this—

Bertha: You know what you should take? Anthropology. I've heard great things. You can learn about the origins of different languages and linguistic patterns.

Brian: Do law schools look favorably on anthropology students?

Bertha: That's a good question. I'm not sure.

Brian: Okay. Well, maybe I can Google that… Let me ask you this—in your experience, have any specific extracurricular activities helped Vassar's past law school applicants?

Bertha: Well, Vassar has a whole bunch of extracurricular activities that are just wonderful. Everything from jazz bands to experimental theater.

Brian: Oh. Okay. Great. And do top law schools tend to prefer any specific extracurricular?

Bertha: You know, that's a great question. I'm not sure.

The conversation was going in circles. Getting anything useful from this woman was like trying to nail jelly to a tree. I cared not an iota about anthropology or experimental theater, and sitting there, I grew increasingly frustrated. (To be fair, I should say that on the whole, the CDO and its staff are extremely helpful and know their subject well. Bertha no longer works for the office, and since freshman year I returned to the CDO multiple times. I cite this example only to highlight the generally relaxed attitude that I had quickly come up against). After that meeting, I questioned whether Vassar was the right environment for me.

It would be a nice story to write that after some time at Vassar, I have mended my opportunistic ways and now enjoy exploring the curriculum—experimental theater and all. But no such metamorphosis has occurred. I still consult graduate school rankings, still have no interest in linguistics, and have been practicing for the LSAT since freshman year. At times, my need to plan for life beyond graduation has made me feel like somewhat of an outcast at Vassar. The students that I met during my first year seemed willing to experiment will all sorts of activities, even the campus circus troop. Perhaps Vassar students are simply motivated by different goals than the Horace Mann crowd that I was accustomed to, or perhaps they were just unsure of their goals.

Either way, I remember feeling that although students studied hard, most had no real sense of what profession they wanted to pursue.

As a freshman, it bothered me that the College seemed to coddle such indecisiveness, allowing students to leave Vassar without a profession or a plan. Convocation speeches by faculty, for example, often focused on the joys of intellectual discovery and the merits of "just learning for the sake of learning" in a liberal arts setting. Certainly I was a strong supporter of a liberal arts education—otherwise I would not have attended Vassar. But I believed equally strongly in the utilitarian nature of education. Even if one entered college without a definite career path, one should certainly *leave* college with concrete plan. Vassar should not be in the business of graduating aimless wanderers. It should foster energetic personalities, citizens with a strong desire to break from lethargy and become the movers and shakers of society. That sense of deeply rooted motivation seemed absent from the environment, at least as far as I could tell in those first weeks.

These were the thoughts that churned in my head following my frustrating conversation with Bertha. I quickly realized that I would have to take matters into my own hands. I began calling admissions offices of top law schools and compiling their answers to my questions. Though I could not find statistics tailored to Vassar graduates as I had initially hoped, I *was* able to find data for similar liberal arts colleges. Among the answers I found was that law schools—although they will deny it—look favorably on history majors and on students with backgrounds in political science. Economics was another statistically successful discipline. Without any of the curricular exploration that Bertha had pushed for, I was prepared to declare a double major in history and political science and minor in economics that very afternoon, before the first week of classes was even complete.

The other matter I needed to research was extracurricular activities. Do law schools even care about anything beside LSAT scores and grade point averages? I discovered that they do. I tracked down answers from several admissions officers. Sure enough, I found that competitive law schools tend to favor students involved analytical writing activities. Given the level of commitment associated with daily or weekly student publications, in addition to the clarity of expression that they require, several admissions officers told me that student newspapers were an excellent extracurricular preparation for law school, particularly if I ever planned on joining a law review publication.

The very next day, I e-mailed Vassar's weekly newspaper, which I remembered was called the *Miscellany News*—the unusual name stuck in my head. Horace Mann's paper was called the *Record*, which I considered to be a much more suitable name for a newspaper. Nevertheless, I heeded the advice of the admissions officers and began writing for the *Miscellany*. By the middle of the semester, I had applied and been accepted to the position of Assistant News Editor.

As Assistant News Editor, my job was three-fold: first, I wrote one article each week. Second, I collected the weekly News Briefs—a few paragraphs of Security's adventures and misadventures patrolling the Vassar campus. Lastly, I was responsible for manually entering into the computer all of the corrections that had been handwritten by copy editors onto article printouts. This part was horribly boring. It made little sense to me why the Editor in Chief, Senior Editors and Copy Editors could not simply correct errors on-screen, editing them directly themselves. It also bothered me that our layout software was unable to correct spelling automatically, making my job all the more time-consuming. Nevertheless, I had to sit in the office for hours, entering countless spelling and grammatical errors.

Most of the job, though, was surprisingly fascinating. I soon found that I thoroughly enjoyed working on the paper as more than just a line on my résumé. As an assistant editor, I was able to write about a wide variety of topics; I interviewed the Dean of the College, the Director of Campus Dining and numerous campus guests. I began to take great pride in the *Miscellany*, especially the News section, and started to feel that I was part of an organization much larger than myself. I even found myself cutting my studying short so that I could spend additional time researching a particular article or conducting an extra interview.

Equally engaging were the people that I met. The editors were very different from many of the students I had encountered in my first few weeks. As a whole, they tended to be extremely goal-oriented and organized. The editors were always scurrying from place to place, calling sources and meeting with reporters. Because they were so concerned with deadlines, they were also extremely punctual and efficient—qualities that impressed me, given my Horace Mann background. My few months as

Assistant News Editor introduced me to a highly talented and ambitious group. It did not take me long to realize that I had found more than an extracurricular activity; I had found my niche at Vassar.

And the *Miscellany* seemed happy to accept me. In January 2007, News Editors Katie Paul '07 and Juliana Kiyan '09 approached me about applying for a full editorship. I did so immediately, honored that they had asked, and was accepted after an interview with the Editorial Board. That semester, Kiyan had herself been elected Senior Editor, leaving me to run the section with Paul. I spent the spring semester of my freshman year as Paul's co-editor, and learned a great deal about the production of the *Miscellany*. Given that she was a senior and I was a freshman, I naturally took my cues from her. She seemed so experienced with newspapers that I remember later being shocked to learn that she had worked on the paper for only a single semester. Regardless, she taught me a great deal about management, journalism and digital layout using the Quark design software. Most of what I learned was by watching—she took the lead on most tasks, which was probably for the best since I was still inexperienced. We faced a number of challenges with our staff; our pool of writers was small, and a number of them had difficulties stringing together complete sentences, much less providing analytical and dynamic news coverage. As a result, Paul and I had to write a great deal ourselves in addition to our usual layout duties.

My training wheels came off when Paul—a history major—began intensive work on her senior thesis toward the end of the semester.[260] Previously, I had come into the office on Tuesday nights (production night) between about 5:00 p.m. and 11:00 p.m. She then took the later shift from 11:00 p.m. onward. When her thesis deadline approached, she needed to miss several Tuesdays. This meant that for the first time, I had ultimate responsibility for putting the section together from beginning to end. For most of the semester, Paul had e-mailed and called negligent writers and fussed with layout details. Suddenly, I was left on my own to resolve such issues. Although she was only a phone call away, I began to feel a weight of responsibility on my shoulders that I had not yet felt during my time on the *Miscellany*.

Once Paul graduated, Hayley Tsukayama '08, one of our most talented and reliable writers, joined me as co-editor. With a semester of experience behind me, I was able to take on a great amount of the workload. I felt much more confident in both the editorial and management aspects of the section. We worked together for the entire 2007-2008 academic year assembling more than 20 issues together. Together, we faced a variety of challenges. Perhaps the most annoying, and persistent, was that our pool of interested writers remained low and seemed to decrease steadily each month. For some reason, freshmen were mostly interested in Arts and Life, leaving us high and dry. This meant that Tsukayama and I were often forced to write two, sometimes three articles ourselves each week in addition to editing the entire section. Fortunately, the two of us had a firm grasp of the College administration and student government; by the second semester, we had our management of the section down to a science.

I assigned articles, and came into the office on Saturdays, Mondays, and on Tuesdays until 11:00 p.m. Tsukayama came in on Sundays and on Tuesdays from 11:00 p.m. onward. She worked intensively with writers on style and corrections to articles that had been submitted over the weekend. In general, I was not very good with details. I did a poor job of entering copy corrections into the layout software and lacked knowledge about *Miscellany* style. A running joke in the office was that I could never remember whether the photographer's name should go on the left or right side of a picture. But I remained enthralled with the larger enterprise of producing the weekly paper.

By the spring, we had a new Assistant News Editor, Julianne Herts '11. Herts was a fantastic asset to our team, especially as Tsukayama—also a history major—was forced to spend increasing amounts of time on her thesis. Herts was a strong writer, and much more careful than I had been about entering copy corrections. At the end of the semester, she was the natural choice to replace the graduating Tsukayama.

For me, however, that semester would be my last working on the News section. One day in early April, Editor in Chief Acacia O'Connor '08 called me into the office and asked me about my plans for the upcoming Editorial Board elections. She suggested that I apply for Editor in Chief. That spring, a significant number of editors on the Executive Staff were graduating—a major loss, since the members of the Class of 2008 had been instrumental to the paper's growth over the previous four years. For many younger editors, the prospect of running the *Miscellany News* without them seemed impossible. April saw a great deal of discussion and gossip about who would take the reigns. I felt surprised and honored that my name arose from those no-doubt contentious discussions. Before O'Connor approached me, I had intended to apply for Senior Editor, assuming that I was not yet ready to become Editor in Chief. But when she broached the possibility, after a moment of shock, I happily applied.

My visceral desire to lead the *Miscellany News* had nothing to do with résumé-building or graduate school. I simply loved the paper; in my mind, it was as simple as that. It was a feeling I had never felt before, certainly not at Horace Mann. It was a feeling of ownership and pride, of serving something larger than myself. I wanted to improve the paper, make it more professional and build on the legacies of my predecessors for the good of Vassar.

That very night, I prepared a seven-page application for Editor in Chief. Although I was the only person running for the position, my interview was a source of stress for several weeks. Insecure, I went to bed each night worried that I would not be elected, or would be somehow forced off of the Editorial Board. I am not quite sure why the thought of being Editor in Chief made me so nervous—perhaps because the seniors above me spoke of the position as an enormous mantle of responsibility. My application focused on two long-term projects: overhauling of the Web site and beginning the process of digital archiving. Both of these projects had been pipe dreams of staffers for years, and I hoped to make them come true. During the interview I was asked about virtually everything: my feelings on layout changes, my desire to increase staff diversity and my hope for a more 21st-century, tech-savvy *Miscellany*.

After a 30-minute interview, I left the meeting room sure that I would be rejected. And then, about an hour later, I was overjoyed to receive a phone call from O'Connor, congratulating me on my election. At the time, I was with Copy Editor Emma Mitchell, who had herself interviewed for the position of Senior Editor. We received our notification calls one after another. Nervous at the prospect of losing, we left the room as soon as our phones rang in order to speak privately with O'Connor. We then returned to share the good news with the other. By the end of the night, Alexandra Matthews '11, Mitchell and myself had all been elected as the *Miscellany* Executive Staff.

The three of us instantly bonded over our mutual fear for the year ahead. We ran the final few issues of the spring semester very successfully. I half-expected that some major catastrophe would force us, with our tails between our legs, to call the graduating editors for help. But everything ran smoothly. The only serious problem we encountered could be blamed on technology. In the moments before we were about to send the entire graduation issue of the paper to the printer in late May, our entire office lost Internet connectivity. Myself, Mitchell and Matthews literally had to carry an iMac computer to a working Ethernet port in order to complete the issue. With this problem fixed for the short term, we were able to convince Vassar's Computing and Information Services to rewire the office, which had cables lying every which way across the floor in order to connect each computer to our network. Proud that we had overcome this glitch, we felt excited and anxious for the future.

As soon as our graduation issue was finished, we began long-term planning. We discussed our poorly maintained Web site, our efforts at digital archiving and the many production inefficiencies that we hoped to solve. We were all very excited to implement changes that would modernize and professionalize the *Miscellany*. We would spend that entire summer thinking about, worrying about, and planning for the paper's 142nd volume.[261] For my part, I spent months interviewing former editors, coding a new Web site and bouncing around ideas with Mitchell and Matthews. We were all energized for the year to come.

The jobs that we entered in September were undoubtedly more difficult than we could have imagined. During my first semester on the job, I spent more time in the *Miscellany News* office than I ever thought possible. My academic and social lives became afterthoughts. During my freshman and sophomore years, I saw my friends every day. Once I became Editor in Chief, I barely saw them two days each week—even then I often had to cancel because of a meeting or a sudden problem. There was always some sort of crisis—an article was missing, a writer was misbehaving, or an advertiser was 'forgetting' to pay. This description of the job must sound fairly miserable—no time to sleep, no time to study and certainly no time for much of a social life. Yet the job was a thrill like none other. The excitement of seeing students read the paper every Thursday and watching them visit our new Web site by the thousands was extraordinary. All of us felt a tremendous sense of accomplishment.

The *Miscellany*'s 2008-2009 Executive Staff, from left to right: Emma Mitchell '09 (Senior Editor), Brian Farkas '10 (Editor in Chief) and Alexandra Matthews '11 (Senior Editor).

After involving myself in the newspaper, I became much more comfortable at Vassar. I had found my niche, a group of like-minded individuals who were as goal-directed as I was. Bertha's laissez-faire approach to college was not my cup of tea—but I suppose I absorbed at least some of her message, albeit accidently. In the *Miscellany*, I had found *my* anthropology class, my experimental theater program, and my passion. Though I doubt I will pursue a career in journalism, producing a weekly newspaper has taught me a great deal about media, writing and administration. It has also taught me the meaning of deep and abiding commitment. The *Miscellany* has ensnared me heart and soul; I have given more time and energy to the paper than I have to any other organization in my life. In this way, I suppose I have experienced the magic of a liberal arts college. Where else could a person have the freedom to take a leap of faith and stumble upon an unforeseen passion—becoming the editor of a 150 year-old publication—and still be able to follow an unrelated career after graduation? Horace Mann taught me to identify and achieve goals; Vassar taught me that life's twists and turns might not always be so bad. Although I do wish that people would walk a little faster.

259 Name has been changed for the sake of anonymity. Bertha no longer works at the Career Development Office (CDO), and the CDO has improved dramatically since my freshman year.

260 Speaking with former *Miscellany* editors, I found (unscientifically) that certain majors have been more common than others on the paper's staff. The two most commonly reported majors were history and English. Perhaps not surprisingly, Business Managers and Managing Editors (the members of the Editorial Board who have been responsible for advertising and subscriptions) have been overwhelmingly economics majors.

261 One early change that the Executive Staff decided to make in Fall 2008 was to standardize the newspaper's founding year and volume number. As mentioned in the Introduction, the *Miscellany News* had gotten into the habit of printing its founding year as 1866 while concurrently printing a volume number indicating that it began in 1915. 1915 was the year that the *Vassar Miscellany News Supplement* simply became the *Vassar Miscellany* Weekly. The *Weekly* became the *Vassar Miscellany News* in 1917. The inconsistencies surrounding these dates and names have been frustrating, and the average reader might have simply assumed that the editors lacked basic math skills. Beginning with the September 11, 2008 issue, the Executive Staff decided that the 2008-09 year would be the 142nd volume of the *Miscellany News*, taking 1866 as our founding year.

Chapter Seven:
Change and Continuity Over Time

When I set out on this project, I imagined a simple title—
Miscellany News: A History. But even a cursory look into the
archives shows that this title would have been somewhat
misleading. As we have seen, Vassar's student newspaper has gone through
a host of names and name changes, including the *Vassar Miscellany
Monthly*, the *Vassar Miscellany News Supplement*, the *Misc*, and only most
recently, the *Miscellany News*. So much for the working title.

But looking back on papers past, there is more continuity over
time than these varied titles suggest. For example, although "*Misc*" did
not become the paper's official title until 1970, this nickname can be
traced back to 1891. That fall, Juliet Wilbur Tompkins '92 wrote a brief
piece for the *Monthly* using this sobriquet to refer to the publication.[262]
Tompkins even hints that "*Misc*" had been common parlance for many
preceding years. Writers and editors remembering the paper over the
20th century almost universally refer to it as the *Misc*. Even today, few
students use "the *Miscellany News*" to refer to the paper. This small
example of the newspaper's moniker demonstrates the *Miscellany*'s
complex relationship between change and continuity.

On one hand, the paper undergoes constant change. After all, its
staff experiences a 100 percent turnover every four years. With no
faculty advisor and few administrative records, institutional memory
has always been haphazard at best. In theory, the Bylaws and Stylebook
should hold jurisdiction over editorial content and ensure continuity

over the decades. In practice, however, most editorial rules of thumb are passed down orally from older editors to younger ones. If there is ever a question on 'policy' or style, editors immediately jump to previous weeks' issues to resolve the dispute, rather than consult the Stylebook. This is not to say that the Stylebook or Bylaws are completely ignored—far from it. But both of these documents are unable to reach the level of detail that editors require when making daily decisions. As editors graduate, institutional memory fades and policies evolve, often accidently. Thus, perpetual change is built into the *Miscellany*'s structure.

But on the other hand, despite these constant shifts, an issue of the *Miscellany* from a century ago somehow remains entirely recognizable. Many elements of style and content are very similar—the role of the staff editorial, the types of stories that editors prioritize, the level of coverage given to stories about Poughkeepsie, even the internal debate over the role of the newspaper itself. All of these represent continuities over time.

Change itself represents something of a continuity. Nearly every former Editor in Chief that I interviewed claimed responsibility for a major revival of the newspaper. Virtually all of them made a case that their Editorial Board rescued the *Miscellany News* from obscurity and obsolescence. "We really took the paper to a level of professionalism never before seen," recalled Hilda Scott Lass '36 of her fellow editors. "We left the *Misc* a professional and well-read publication." An editor 60 years her junior echoed her sentiments almost verbatim. "I think we saw the *Misc* through a golden age of quality and respectability," said Amanda Spielman '97, Editor in Chief in Spring 1996. "Before us, the paper was not very well read on campus. The students in my class were really the ones to enforce journalistic integrity and dramatically improve the poor quality of the writing." Even within the same decade, different Editorial Board members have claimed that their cohorts single-handedly delivered journalistic excellence to the *Miscellany*. Indeed, I even caught myself falling into this historical trap after we produced the October 30, 2008 issue of the paper. "This is the best issue of the paper I can remember," I confidently exclaimed to my fellow editors at our weekly Paper Critique. "We really produced one of the best issues in *Misc* history." In unexpected ways, history repeats itself on the *Miscellany News*.

Though the memories of editors might be exaggerated, the paper has indeed gone through constant transformation. What began as an annual 4-page pithy publication transformed into a 36-page monthly collection of literature, and this morphed into a 24-page modern weekly newspaper. Despite these changes, staffers from the 1930s and staffers from the 1990s speak about the same challenges and complain about similar journalistic, budgetary and ethical concerns. Through constant evolution, more unites the *Miscellany* over its history than divides it. This chapter synthesizes some of the most pronounced continuities and evolutions over nearly 150 years.

Commitment of Editors

The steadfast commitment of *Miscellany* editors to their publication is undoubtedly the most unifying continuity over time. As we saw in the Introduction, Grace Margaret Gallaher's portrayal of late 19th-century *Miscellany* editors in her book *Vassar Stories* provides a vivid account of the early staff's commitment.[263] The editors willingly gave up their sleep and their studies to ensure the health of the newspaper. So it was then, and so it has been since. Regardless of the hour, regardless of other responsibilities, editors have always felt a deep responsibility to put the paper first. Gabe Anderson '99, who served as Editor in Chief in the late 1990s, put this historical truism in modern terms. "Caffeinated Mountain Dew and coffee with lots of sugar are your only friends," he reminisced. "I remember when I first applied for the job, my predecessor sat me down and told me, 'You realize that after you get this position, you will no longer be Gabe Anderson; you will be the Editor in Chief.' He was right."

The time-consuming nature of editorial work is hardly unique to the *Miscellany News*. Charles Thwing wrote in 1878 that "The first evil [of student publications] is that the student's editorial duties are likely to exhaust his energies and thus to unfit him for his regular college work." Thwing worried that if the paper took too much of an editor's time, he would be "compelled to neglect his Greek and mathematics." Thwing's words certainly ring true in the 21st century; it is hardly uncommon for editors to fall behind on their coursework—or even skip their Greek class—in order to put the paper to bed.

Creating a weekly newspaper is a full-time job. It is often difficult to imagine that editors must concurrently take four or five courses. "It really gets easier after you do journalism in college," said Victor Navansky, former Editor in Chief of the *Swarthmore Phoenix* and publisher emeritus of the *Nation*, speaking to a group of college editors in May 2008. "Once you leave college, you can devote everything you've got to your craft. But when you're still stuck in school, your attention has to be split seven ways. You can never give your publication the 110 percent that it deserves."

That is not to say that many editors do not *try* to give it everything. Former *Miscellany* Senior Editor Eric Robinson '89, now a lawyer specializing in First Amendment issues, recalls skipping his LSAT preparation classes, "much to my mother's dismay," because they conflicted with production night. But Robinson could not have cared less. In his mind, college was all about learning responsibility, and the newspaper taught him more responsibility than any class or standardized test ever could. Robinson now credits the paper with teaching him to think, to write and to manage his time effectively. "I wouldn't trade [my *Miscellany* experience] for anything," he asserted, "even if my friends thought I was crazy." Friends of *Miscellany* editors rarely view their newspaper friends as anything but fanatical. "My closest friends, they just didn't get it," said Gabe Anderson. "Why? Why would he stay in that office for 40 hours every week? Why won't he just come and hang with us?" These are all reasonable and familiar questions.

Interviewing former editors, one of my standard questions was the approximate number of hours they recall giving to the newspaper. The chart below lists these hours, which represent the unscientific, self-reported numbers. The first number is the smallest number of hours an interviewee reported, and the larger number is the maximum reported hours:

Position	Range of Reported Hours Per Week
Staff Photographer	1-2
Staff Writer	2-4
Section Editor	5-15
Copy Editor	8-11
Managing Editor	2-6
Photography Editor	6-9
Senior Editor	8-15
Editor in Chief	15-40

Being the editor of a section can take up to 15 hours each week; the role of Editor in Chief can take up to 40 hours. Consider that in 2007, the average American worked 46 hours per week, without taking academic credits concurrently, for an average annual income of about $40,000.[264] *Miscellany* editors do nearly that much work purely out of devotion to the paper. "We all recognize that we are obsessed with the *Miscellany News*, which may be unhealthy for us, but it certainly benefits our readers!" quipped former Editor in Chief Judy Jarvis '07 in a 2005 interview with the *Vassar Quarterly*.[265] When Vassar President Frances Fergusson announced her retirement hours before the *Miscellany* had to be sent to print, editors put their lives on hold to "conduct interviews, compose articles, and reshuffle the news section in order to break the story in the *Miscellany News* on the same day as the *New York Times* did." This sort of commitment has occurred every week for over a century, as editors routinely sacrifice personal and academic commitments for the good of the newspaper.

Lack of Monetary Compensation for Editors

Editors for the *Swarthmore Phoenix* create a very similar product as the editors of the *Miscellany News*. Both papers are weekly and run about 20 pages per issue with a circulation of 2,000. Their annual budget structure is nearly identical. Both staffs work equally hard to write and edit a newspaper that accurately reflects the constituencies on their respective campuses. Yet editors for the *Phoenix* can expect something that editors for the *Miscellany* cannot: upwards of $2,500 each year. Not only does Swarthmore College pay them under work-study, but the newspaper itself also uses ad revenue to pay individual writers and photographers for freelance work.

The practice of paying writers and editors is fairly common among student papers, particular those at larger schools such as Stanford, New York and Princeton universities. Another incentive that some institutions offer is academic credit for work on the paper. Editors of the *Fox Journal* of the University of Wisconsin can earn credit in the Communications Department, under the rationale that staff members "gain valuable experience in reporting, editing, photography, graphic design, and advertising sales."[266] Editors at the *Pace Press*, the paper of Pace University, can choose between cash or credit for their labor.

At no point in the nearly 150 years of the *Miscellany News* has Vassar offered money or credit to its editors. Although few liberal arts schools are willing to give academic credit (since journalism and communications usually do not qualify as liberal arts disciplines), many of Vassar's peer schools *do* offer editors paid positions under work-study.

This discrepancy has not gone unnoticed by the fatigued staff. In the March 1892 issue of the *Vassar Miscellany Monthly*, Edith Colby Banfield '92 wrote a six-page essay entitled "A Plea for College Journalism" bemoaning the difficult position of her fellow student journalists. Banfield had written both poetry and prose for the *Miscellany* during her freshman and sophomore years, and took her work very seriously. In the spring of 1892, she seems to have been promoted from "Contributor" to "Senior Contributor," a distinction not previously found. Banfield might have applied for an editorship, however, if the position offered her anything but a byline. Banfield's essay argued that Vassar should incentivize participation by either paying writers or by offering academic credit. She based her argument on a *New York Evening Post* article by Henry Finck. Finck had suggested that colleges should "accept editorial work [on school papers] as equivalent to a regular course of lectures and recitations."[267] In other words, he offered similar reasoning to the University of Wisconsin and the *Fox Journal* in recognizing the value of the on-the-job education that newspapers offer.

Banfield agreed. "Is there not some way by which the College can promote the work of its own paper?" she asked rhetorically in her essay. After all, she reasoned, students were being pulled in so many different directions between the rigors of coursework and the commitments of extracurricular activities. "As the demands of the curriculum become more exacting," she wrote, "the College paper has increasingly harder work to live to its ambition." As Vassar grew, so did its academic and extracurricular offerings. How could the *Miscellany* get better, indeed how could it survive at all, if its editors' time was being stretched more thinly each year? Her description of the chaotic lives of editors would hardly inspire students to become involved with the paper:

> *I do not know whether the students of the earlier days [in the 1860s] could run a magazine comfortably in their leisure moments; I do know that they cannot do so now. Inquire of the editor of to-day—victim of the modern rush that has possessed the College halls no less than Wall Street—and you will hear a tale of overwork, weariness and discouragement that would be black indeed if through it did not flicker the light of unquenchable enthusiasm.*

Her words have continued to ring true in the 20th and 21st centuries. "We applied to receive academic credit last year," wrote the editors in a melancholy 1969 staff editorial.[268] "We were turned down." They went on to complain that they often have to pay sundry *Misc* bills out of our own pockets" and that the editors had little time to balance their many activities. The same is true today. Editors are frantically overworked, and must often choose between the *Miscellany* and a variety of other activities. Mike Newmark '08 served as Arts Editor during the 2006-2007 school year, and although he loved the job, decided to give it up in 2007-2008 to work for CARES, Vassar's 24-hour peer counseling service. Both activities required significant time commitments, and Newmark was forced to make a choice. Although he was able to continue working on the paper in a less time-consuming role as a weekly columnist, many students simply cannot find the time to juggle the newspaper with their academics, campus jobs, and the "maelstrom of activities" that Banfield described over a century ago.

Editorial Trends

Staff editorials are the institutional voice of any newspaper. Without exception, every issue of Vassar's student publication since 1866 has included an editorial. These editorials have run the gambit of political and social opinion, at times staunchly liberal and at other times vigorously conservative. The Editorial Board has never been quite satisfied with the role of the student government, sometimes pushing it to be more active and sometimes cautioning it against micromanagement and false representation of student voice. They have both praised and condemned various College presidents, and both lauded and criticized various American presidents. They have advocated both war and peace.

Clearly, staff editorials grow from unique historical moments. Although this leads to great contradictions between different Editorial Boards, there are also distinct consistencies in the Board's opinion over time. Below are several striking continuities that bridge decades of editors:

Lack of Student Engagement

One consistent goal, in the words of Diane Gersoni '66, has been to "criticize students' lethargy and try to arouse an active interest in the happenings of the outside world." Perhaps because editors are so knowledgeable about campus events and the affairs of the College administration, they become quickly annoyed when their fellow students are unaware or oblivious.

This annoyance has been apparent since 1914, the year that weekly publication began. A December 11 editorial decried the lack of student interest in creating a club to champion women's suffrage.[269] Though many of the students expressed vague interest in the idea, few were willing to commit time and energy. Worse still, many students were apparently unaware of ongoing national efforts to give women the vote. This infuriated the *Miscellany*'s editors, who had themselves reported on such efforts and endorsed the inherent right of women to participate in the political process. "Why not organize?" questioned the headline.[270] "Women of other colleges, for example Smith, Barnard, Wellesley, and Bryn Mawr, have already felt their responsibility in this matter. They have already formed organizations for the study and promotion of the political freedom of women. Why should *we* not organize?"

Ever since this incident, there has been a strong tradition of urging students to be informed and active members of their communities—whether that means participating in student organizations (as a 1953 editorial nudged) or staying informed about American involvement in Iraq (as a 2008 editorial pushed).

Expanding Financial Aid

The *Miscellany News* has supported the expansion of financial aid for most of the Vassar's history, even before extensive aid became a widespread and politically correct policy. "We must throw open our educational facilities to those who earn their way," the Editorial Board declared in 1925.[271] "Distinction according to wealth should exist as little as possible in a group where intellectual attainment is the ideal criterion." This sentiment was echoed more than 80 years later when a 2007 editorial congratulated College President Catharine Bond Hill on returning Vassar to a need-blind system of admission. Hill, an economist who studied higher education and affordability, pushed for the College to no longer consider applicants' ability to pay tuition in making admission decisions. "The *Miscellany News* applauds this decision... because a need-blind policy reflects one way (of many) in which the College is putting words about commitment to all types of diversity into action," editors wrote in September 2007.[272] "Hill... has clearly put accessibility at the top of her agenda."

On numerous other occasions, the editors have confirmed their commitment to extensive financial aid. After the 2008 economic recession resulted in a $200 million hit to the College's endowment, the Board asserted that financial aid should be one of Vassar's most important priorities.[273] "Despite the expense such policies entail, it is imperative that they continue so that all qualified students have the opportunity to attend Vassar, rather than only those from the ever-shrinking pool whose families can afford to pay," wrote the editors in November 2008.

National and International Politics

We have already seen the complicated political leanings that have existed on Vassar's campus. Politics can be split into two categories: political *awareness* and political *persuasion*.

Political consciousness was low for the first 50 years of the College's history. Consequently, *Miscellany News* editorials have historically avoided national and international politics, instead focusing on campus issues. Student interest in global affairs was minimal between the early days of the College and the 1920s. As we saw in Chapter 2, the Great Depression caused an explosion of interest in politics beyond Vassar's gates. Suddenly, the Editorial Board began to frequently offer opinions on countless policies, especially those related to welfare and the economy; within a decade, World War II expanded interest into the arena of foreign policy. Discussion of national issues continued into the 1950s and 1960s, particularly regarding the Vietnam War and the civil rights movement. After the 1970s, however, editorials once again avoided national and international subjects.

Today, the Editorial Board tends to take positions almost exclusively on events at the College. After all, many editors contend, readers do not look to the *Miscellany News* for thoughts on global issues; readers look to the paper for its views on Vassar. This philosophy has generally held strong over the past four decades. Though staff editorials will often frame Vassar issues in a broader context, the Board rarely editorializes on a solely national situation. Two notable recent exceptions have included a 2001 editorial on the 9/11 terrorist attacks and a 2003 editorial condemning American presence in Iraq. In most cases, editors work to frame national issues as problems affecting the lives of students. This approach is very different from the editorial style of the 1930s, in which editors argued for specific national policies from a nationalist point of view, much like the style of professional newspapers like the *New York Times*.

In terms of political persuasion, the Editorial Board has generally been more liberal than the student body as a whole. Almost immediately after September 11, the Board took a strong stand against the retaliatory rhetoric of George W. Bush's administration, even at a time when many were rallying around the flag and pushing to support the administration:

> President Bush's recent addresses to the nation conveyed, implicitly and explicitly, his administration's intent to respond to this crisis by rallying for nationalism and retaliatory violence. This political position is dangerous because it is generated in direct response to the abruptly formed emotions instilled, purposefully and carefully, by the terrorists themselves. Political actions of retaliatory violence will only serve the terrorists' true intent... Yet another possible danger stemming from our government's recent responses to the terrorist attacks is that nationalism will fuel racism and race-based violence against Arab Americans domestically. If our government preaches the politics of division and war and if Americans are told to fear the invisible enemy that lurks within our very borders, there is the distinct possibility that racist groups and other radical individuals may

> take advantage of the situation by [committing] acts of violence... The death of so many people is something that we as a country may someday recover from, but the death of the American dream, a place where all people have equal rights to life, liberty and the pursuit of happiness would be something from which our country would never recover.[274]

Throughout Bush's tenure, the *Miscellany* constantly questioned the "War on Terror," particularly the practice of holding enemy combatants without due process.

However, the Board has also advocated fairly conservative policies over the 20th century and has not shied away from criticizing the Democratic Party. Although Vassar is known today for its fairly liberal student body, the College had strong conservative elements for much of the 19th and 20th centuries.[275] Liberalism grew slowly among students, and Vassar's politics were often bitterly divided. *Miscellany* voting polls—administered sporadically between 1920 and 1968 before presidential elections—consistently indicated that more than 50 percent of the student body favored the Republican candidate. Nevertheless, the Editorial Board has generally supported more liberal policies and more liberal presidential candidates. Since 1916, the *Miscellany* has endorsed a presidential candidate in every national election, and has chosen a Democrat in 19 out of 24 contests. Since 1960, the paper has consistently endorsed the Democratic candidate. This political tendency intensified after the resignation of Richard Nixon in 1974, whom the Board vehemently criticized in three separate staff editorials. Two of the most emphatic endorsements were for John F. Kennedy in 1960 and for Barack Obama in 2008. In both cases, the candidate was younger and appealed to students hungry for new political perspectives. The editors of 2008 noted the similarities, and even scanned a microfilm copy of the Kennedy endorsement and placed it side-by-side with the Obama endorsement on the *Miscellany* Web site. After eight years of the Bush administration, the Editorial Board condemned the Republican's divisive approach to governing, and looked for new approaches to the nation's problems:

> The past eight years have been unsettling ones for the United States. Americans have witnessed the erosion of civil liberties, the disastrous effects of an unregulated economy and the unapologetic expansion of executive power. President George W. Bush has led the country through

a misguided war in Iraq, trampled on Constitutional rights and taken a unilateral approach to foreign policy that has alienated America's allies and wounded, perhaps irreparably, the perception of America as a beacon of opportunity and justice.

But the most insidious political maneuvering has perhaps been the polarizing and divisive dialogue perpetuated by the Bush administration and members of the Republican Party. The politics of fear and xenophobia run counter to so many of the values that we on the Vassar campus espouse and practice. The importance of knowledge, of debating ideas and of appreciating different perspectives—all of these values have been dangerously and embarrassingly absent from our Executive Branch over the past eight years. More than war, economic collapse or failed social policy, the implicit and explicit shift of our national discourse to an "us" versus "them" dichotomy—regarding blue states and red states, Muslims and Christians, "pro-America" and "anti-America"—poses a deep threat to the fabric of this nation.

In light of these dark national trends, we welcome the leadership and sound policies of Senator Barack Obama. He vows to withdraw all combat brigades from Iraq within his first 16 months in office. He supports subsidized, voluntary national health care for those without employer-based or existing coverage, and would mandate health care for all children. He supports *Roe v. Wade* and the Freedom of Choice Act. Obama would end the wrongheaded Don't Ask, Don't Tell policy, and favors federal civil union legislation…

Obama's is a stirring and historic candidacy. In the political theater of American narratives, Obama's life follows a somewhat unconventional story arc, complicating the conceptions of the American experience and the "Everyman." He has inspired and brought together millions of Americans from all walks of life who identify with his message. And as the potential first black American president, Barack Obama's implications for civil rights and grassroots change in our country are huge.

At the end of this long election cycle, we must look forward to a world that requires more than experience with military might, a world that is increasingly technological, interconnected and complex. The next leader of the United States must be able to think critically and act transparently, to believe in our country's past but also envision its future. Obama embodies the complexities of the United States as it is, and represents the opportunity of this country as it aspires to be.

Because of his ability to inspire, his thoughtfulness, intellectual curiosity, and his inclusivity, Obama is exactly the leader and ambassador that our country so desperately needs at this perilous moment in our history.[276]

Without doubt, the 2008 editors hoped for a new tomorrow, much as the 1960 editors had. The table below provides a summary of the candidates whom the *Miscellany* has endorsed. Through these endorsements, one can begin to understand the political philosophies, hopes and fears of the editors at various points in American history.

Year	Candidate Endorsed	Party
1916	Woodrow Wilson	Democrat
1920	Warren Harding	Republican
1924	John Davis	Democrat
1928	Alfred Smith	Democrat
1932	Franklin D. Roosevelt	Democrat
1936	Franklin D. Roosevelt	Democrat
1940	Wendell Willkie	Republican
1944	Franklin D. Roosevelt	Democrat
1948	Thomas Dewey	Republican
1952	Dwight Eisenhower	Republican
1956	Dwight Eisenhower	Republican
1960	John F. Kennedy	Democrat
1964	Lyndon Johnson	Democrat
1968	Hubert Humphrey	Democrat
1972	George McGovern	Democrat
1976	Jimmy Carter	Democrat
1980	Jimmy Carter	Democrat
1984	Walter Mondale	Democrat
1988	Michael Dukakis	Democrat
1992	Bill Clinton	Democrat
1996	Bill Clinton	Democrat
2000	Alfred Gore	Democrat
2004	John Kerry	Democrat
2008	Barack Obama	Democrat

Lack of Issues to Editorialize On

The creation of a weekly paper in 1914 added a new challenge: the Editorial Board somehow had to come up with a campus issue to editorialize on each week, rather than just each month. At a school as small as Vassar, this task is easier said than done. Every few weeks when news was slow, editorials were weakly worded or irrelevant. The challenge became even greater when the *Miscellany* adopted biweekly publication a few years later, which continued until World War II. Rarely were there enough "juicy controversies" as one editor from the late 1930s put it, "to merit two passionate staff editorials each week." The Board sometimes had to result to sleepy pieces encouraging students to volunteer, to read newspapers and even to keep tidy rooms. Though many issues during this period featured fiery arguments, others were clearly the product of slow news weeks. After the return to weekly publication, a staffer from the late 1940s said that the single best part of the new schedule was "no longer having to come up with a mediocre editorial."

But even since then, devising a weekly editorial topic has not become much easier. Opinions Editor Cricket Cooley '93 recalled the painful process for writing the weekly piece. "We took turns writing the staff editorial, a job we all hated, since there was usually nothing to really take a stand on." Even today, some of the longest discussions of Editorial Board meetings occur on weeks when nothing really angers the editors enough to write about. In those cases, editors are obligated to find something, anything, to throw their institutional voice behind. This seems to be a dangerous practice; the Board is sometimes forced to take strong positions on fairly trivial matters. This potentially diminishes the paper's ability to be taken seriously on the issues of greater importance.

Relations with Alumnae/i, Faculty and Student Government

The *Miscellany News* has always maintained a somewhat awkward relationship with the rest of Vassar. At various times, it has been criticized as an "organ of the faculty," an "organ of the alumnae," and an "organ of the student government." At other times, the paper has also served as a bully pulpit for the views of its editors. Letters to the editor have accused the paper of unfairly advancing certain points of view (of faculty, alumnae/i, student representatives, or editors) at the expense of the student body as a whole. Many editorial boards have been forced to deal with the central question of whom the *Miscellany* should serve: should it be a newspaper *by* students and *for* students, or should it be aimed at the Vassar community more broadly?

Alumnae, in addition to students, played an active role in the quarterly *Miscellany* and the *Miscellany Monthly*. Between 1901 and 1906, the paper even set aside an entire issue each year solely for the alumnae to write and edit. By the beginning of 1907, alumnae demanded a more constant connection with the *Miscellany*. The publication was their primary means of communication after graduation, and hundreds of alumnae subscribed. As a result, the "Alumnae Department" was founded—a section that filled approximately 25 percent of each issue with the letters, poetry and essays of graduates. By February 1909, the Alumnae Association recognized the *Miscellany* as its "official organ" for communication.[277] An alumnae editor and five associate editors enjoyed complete control over the Alumnae Department within the ostensibly student-run publication. It is difficult to say the exact working relationship between the student and the alumnae editors; most likely, the alumnae simply submitted their finished materials. It was the students who controlled the layout, along with the financial matters of advertising and printing.

Nevertheless, the two groups of editors worked well together—at least on the surface. During the second annual meeting between the two editorial boards in 1914, serious questions about the "size and character of the Alumnae Department were discussed."[278] Concerns were expressed on both sides. Alumnae and students both felt "increasing difficulty in having two magazines and possibly two policies between a single pair of covers." Although the *Miscellany* benefited by having renewed and constant interest from graduates, there were grumblings that a separate alumnae magazine should be established, "at no distant date."

This hope soon came true. The Alumnae Department disappeared from the *Miscellany* in 1916 when the *Vassar Quarterly*—the first magazine independently published by the Alumnae Association—was founded. Its goals were fully tailored to informing and communicating with alumnae. The magazine was, ironically, more of a newspaper than the *Miscellany Monthly*, since the *Quarterly* focused mostly on College events. It strived to keep graduates abreast of "changes in equipment, in curriculum, [and] in student thought."[279] It would serve as a "meeting place in thought" for alumnae "so widely scattered throughout the world." So, by 1916, the voices of graduates had been largely removed from the newspaper. For most of the 20th century, the *Miscellany News* no longer had to cater to alumnae.

Faculty influence proved more difficult to shake. As we saw in Chapter 1, faculty paid close attention to the student publication in its early days. Sources indicate that the *Vassariana, Transcript* and *Vassar Miscellany* had faculty advisors. This practice was not discontinued until the mid-1890s. However, even then, professors maintained a fairly active voice in the publication. Since the paper's founding, professors submitted essays on academic topics, such as "Our Obligations to France," an article by Professor James Orton in July 1872.[280] They continued to author pieces well into the 1920s, including small items about themselves and their own scholarly activities. Beginning with weekly publication in 1914, faculty began writing frequent letters to the editor, responding vigorously to the previous week's coverage.

The faculty wrote a tremendous amount of material, compared to today's standards. While today's staff occasionally receives a letter from a professor or administrator, faculty involvement in the paper dropped off significantly in the early 1960s. Perhaps it was the culture of the 1960s—one that was skeptical of authority—that demanded the publication express purely student voice. Ever since, faculty members are more likely featured as subjects of articles rather than authors.

Historically, student government has actually held deeper influence over the paper than have the alumnae/i or faculty. Student government began at Vassar in 1868, when a group of girls "politely disinvited" President John Raymond and the faculty from a meeting. The students began by organizing Founder's Day—a surprise birthday party for College founder Matthew Vassar. But soon, the group began to establish student organizations, ranging from the Choral Society to the Debating Society. In 1902, the faculty formally granted the government limited control over social affairs, asking elected officials to "discourage objectionable dancing and activities." This task eventually translated into budgeting and organizing all of the varied student groups.

The exact place of the *Miscellany News* in the student bureaucracy, however, has never been quite clear. Until the 1950s, the so-called "big five" dominated extracurricular life at Vassar. These umbrella organizations were the Students' Association (student government), the Christian Association, the Athletic Association, Philaletheis (a dramatic and literary society) and the Political Association (formed in 1922). All activities originated from these larger organizations, and students usually had enough time to commit to only one. They were financed and controlled by the student government.

The *Miscellany* existed outside of this structure.[281] Perhaps because its membership had always been smaller—between 30 and 50—it was not considered to be its own umbrella organization. Nevertheless, the student government financed the paper and was theoretically responsible for its management. Student Association records show random and odd categorizations for the paper.[282] Between 1872 and 1889, the student government did not list the *Miscellany* as an extracurricular activity at all. In 1892, it was listed under the header of Philaletheis (probably because it related to literature), but this mantle was dropped just one year later. Between 1893 and 1914, the financing for the paper was marked as "Miscellaneous Expenditures"—the same budget they used to purchase "floral arrangements for assemblies" and "tea for [Association] meetings."[283] With the advent of weekly publication in 1914, the student government finally listed the *Miscellany* alongside the four umbrella organizations. However, they used smaller handwriting and put the publication at the very bottom of their ledger.

Today, the paper is considered to be a Vassar Student Association (VSA) organization. The *Miscellany News* receives an annual budget from the VSA and complies with the rules that apply to other VSA organizations. At least in theory, then, the student government holds considerable power over the paper. The VSA also can formally "reprimand" the paper, as it did several times in the 1990s for writers' questionable ethics. Formal regulations for student publications are spelled out in Article IV, Section 21 of the VSA Bylaws:

Publications
A. Student publications must submit bylaws stipulating the mission and purpose of the publication, the roles of the editor, the process for the

inclusion of submissions including, but not limited to, letters to the editor and other responses to published material.

B. Publications shall enjoy the full right to publish without prior review or editorial control by the VSA Council.

C. Libel and other forms of defamation will not be tolerated by the VSA.

D. Publications shall be considered open source, allowing for the copy and redistribution of printed content with proper citation.

E. Editors in Chief shall assume responsibility for articles published in their respective publication.

F. Publications are defined as published written documents with editors, not including flyers.

Despite these stipulations, the Editorial Board of the *Miscellany* has a great deal more freedom from the student government than other organizations. Because of its history, its advertising revenue and its loyal body of alumnae/i supporters, the paper enjoys considerable autonomy.

According to the Bylaws, the paper is "independent." In other words, its opinions do not express those of the College or the student government, but only of its Editorial Board. It is true that the paper was financed by the College for its first few decades of publication, and financed by the student government ever since. But it is difficult to say exactly how much of an effect this financing has had on editorial decision-making. Today, financial matters never enter into discussions of content and editors seldom consider the financial ramifications of their reporting. The *Miscellany News* remains a publication for the entire Vassar community, but from the distinct perspective and authorship of students.

Commitment to Student Voice

Despite incursions from faculty and alumnae, editors of the *Miscellany* have always resisted. Since at least 1893, we can see their staunch desire for the publication to be a conduit of student voice.[284] This commitment intensified in the 20th century. In the 1916 anthology of poetry from the *Vassar Miscellany Monthly*, the editors made "no apology for including nonsense verse" in the volume.[285] By "nonsense verse," they meant poetry about "silly" or "hysterical" topics deviating from the strict academic style that they would have learned in literature classes. Representing students honestly, they felt, was far more important than creating a literary magazine that purported to be intellectual or professional. "To understand the life of a college without understanding the whimsies of its citizens is impossible," they wrote in the preface to the anthology. Their volume would "represent a definitive phase of life"; any critic who "condemns us for a sacrifice of dignity also condemns the truthfulness of our volume."

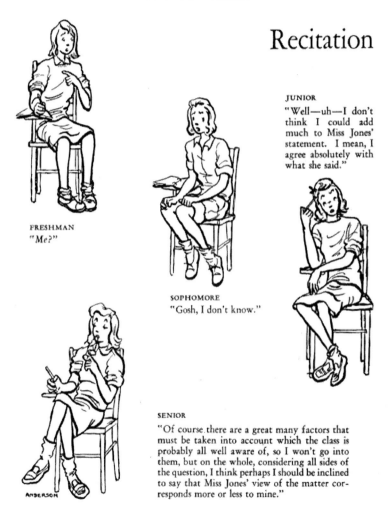

Recitation

FRESHMAN
"Me?"

SOPHOMORE
"Gosh, I don't know."

JUNIOR
"Well—uh—I don't think I could add much to Miss Jones' statement. I mean, I agree absolutely with what she said."

SENIOR
"Of course there are a great many factors that must be taken into account which the class is probably all well aware of, so I won't go into them, but on the whole, considering all sides of the question, I think perhaps I should be inclined to say that Miss Jones' view of the matter corresponds more or less to mine."

Continuities over time can be found everywhere at Vassar, even in the verbosity and bloviating corresponding to increasing class years. *Jean Anderson, Vassar: A Second Glance.*

Vassar's student publication was certainly not unique for its focus on the "whimsies" of student life. The *Harvard Lampoon* began in Spring 1876 as a collection of stories and cartoons about Harvard life. It quickly became one the most famous satirical publications in the country. Yet it was also tasteful. According to one critic, "It has been, as a whole, remarkably free from objection in point of moral taste."[286] The *Lampoon*, now the world's longest running humor magazine, was the first of its kind to be written entirely by students. As early as the 1880s, editors at other colleges followed suit, publishing humor magazines of their own. Like the *Lampoon*, other humor magazines—or humor sections of student newspapers—were "free from vulgarity" but instead aimed to poke fun at their fellow students. What *was* unique about the *Miscellany*, however, is that it attempted to integrate more "frivolous" content—satirical and humorous descriptions of student life—with the 'real' content. In the 1920s, the paper often published "joke issues" that parodied the newspaper. In 1923, the *Vassar Millennium News* appeared; in 1924, the *Vassar Miscellany Snooze* appeared, followed by the *Vassar Miscellany Muse* (1926), and the *Vassar Misused News* (1923). All of these publications offered a satirical look at Vassar life, particularly mocking the student government, administration and especially the Editorial Board. They made fun of the "incessant typos, frequent errors, and false quotations of the College president" found in the *Miscellany*. Eventually, the paper even tried to lighten its "highbrow" approach to writing by including occasional jokes. Modeling these jokes on the *Wellesley Weekly*'s "Parliament of Fools" section, the editors reserved a small space for "humor on the general failings of the community in a witty and satirical manner."[287]

But beyond the silliness of jokes and satire, the *Miscellany* editors throughout the 20th century have worked to make their newspaper as representative as possible. Although staff editorials are historically liberal, the paper regularly prints letters and submissions of all political persuasions. The editors have always tried to capture multiple perspectives of campus issues.

Tension Between Editorial and Business Content

According to the 2008 Bylaws of the *Miscellany News*, the Managing Editor is "responsible for the financial management of the paper" and reports directly to the Editor in Chief. Yet for the past three decades, Managing Editors have held relatively short tenures. Often, they have been economics majors looking for a position that would give them financial experience and join the Editorial Board in their senior year. These individuals rarely contribute to the content, design or production of the paper. Their responsibilities are largely limited to advertising and subscriptions. This stands in contrast to other members of the Editorial Board, who tend to remain on the Board for three or four years, contributing to many different aspects of the publication.

The strange relationship between the business and editorial sides of the *Miscellany* has deep historical roots, which can be traced back to 1872. When the quarterly publication first began, the "Business Department" was separated from the editors. Business Managers worked incredibly hard, often performing the job themselves, with little appreciation. Not much changed for much of the 20th century. Anne Susswein '61 served as Business Manager from Fall 1959 until her graduation. "Most of what I remember was arguing with the editor to get all the advertising in, so that we would get the revenue," she recalled. The 1960s Bylaws spell out a co-equal power structure between the Editor in Chief and the Business Manager. Yet Susswein and others involved in the paper's financial management described themselves as being subservient to those working on the editorial side. She remembers being instructed to help the Circulation Manager whenever she was short handed, having to personally stuff papers into mailboxes in the old post office in Main Building.

It is not that the editorial staff did not appreciate the efforts of the business managers. The first page of the May 11, 1966 issue featured a special note thanking the Advertising Department. "Advertising is a more vital area of a newspaper than most readers realize," the editors wrote.[288] "It is no understatement to say that without them, we could not exist." But although this note shows thanks, it also proves the distance of the business managers from the rest of the staff. After all, one would never find a note thanking a copy editor for their diligent work; such thanks would have been understood. The editorial staff was in the dominant position of thanking the subservient advertising staff for their work.

The importance of business staff seems to wax and wane with the state of the paper's budget. When the budget is fairly stable, editors have generally given minimal thought to financial concerns. But when a shrinking budget has threatened the existence of the *Miscellany*— as in the early 1970s and the early 2000s—the importance of fiscal management became a priority. Editors from these periods of crisis recall that the business staff was more heavily involved in publication, working closely with the editorial staff on cost-saving measures and guiding the general direction of the paper.

"Bombast, Slovenliness, and Looseness of Expression"

It is no secret that the *Miscellany News*—like all student newspapers—has suffered from sloppy reporting, questionable journalistic ethics and blatant unprofessionalism. Certain historical moments saw particularly high numbers of errors and carelessness. The paper of the early 1970s, for example, was often sloppy. During this tumultuous period in Vassar's history, the College had just adopted coeducation and the student government's shrinking budget meant limited resources for the paper. In this case, financial and social factors are correlated with awkward layout, typographical errors and weak editorial writing.

Other incidents of carelessness, however, cannot be so easily justified. As any student editor will admit, the rush of the production schedule often necessitates cutting corners. Unfortunately, this means that issues of the paper will sometimes include errors in spelling and grammar—or worse, errors in dates, quotations and basic facts. Carelessness can sometimes become ingrained into reporters' routines; as a writer, I certainly remember submitting articles that were poorly edited, simply because I had an economics test the following day. Editors generally see writers' articles get weaker during midterms and final exams. These external factors, which ideally would have no correlation to the quality of the journalism, in reality weigh heavily on the writers and editors.

None of this is unique to the *Miscellany News*. As early as 1878, Charles Thwing worried that production rush would lead editors to adopt "faulty style."[289] Editors of other college papers report similar concerns, and across the country student newspapers are stitched together in the early hours of the morning before they are due to be published. As Thwing noted, "the rapid writing that [an editor] is sometimes compelled to do cultivates superficiality of thought, and the necessity under which he labors, of 'filling up space,' fosters bombast, slovenliness, and looseness of expression."[290]

Lasting Personal Relationships

Nearly every former staff member that I have interviewed—whether from 1937 or 2007—keeps in touch with his or her fellow editors. Many have fond memories of pulling all-nighters to watch the paper come together at four in the morning. As we saw earlier, Editors in Chief universally recall spending between 15 and 40 hours in the newsroom each week surrounded by Senior Editors, Copy Editors, and various section editors. Not surprisingly, the connections made on the

Miscellany News often last a lifetime. Indeed, many lifelong friendships have been born and nurtured in the

Nineteen former editors from the 1990s met for brunch at Phillip Marie Restaurant in Manhattan on June 8, 2008. Nakiso Maodza, Evan Greenstein, and Joe Goldman sit at the end of the table reminiscing. Goldman invited me to join the group and record their recollections. *Jonathan Kang.*

newsroom. Editors from the 1890s complained that there were "untold numbers of alumnae contributions [especially] from former editors, because these women continue to talk to one another religiously and speak about the College and the newspaper."[291] Award-winning writers Mary McCarthy '33 and Elizabeth Bishop '34 and remained lifelong friends. These strong staff connections continued in later periods. Joan Gunn '51 served as Distribution Manager for two years, leading efforts to dispense the paper each week. "We gathered and folded each edition. Warm friendships are still shared, even 50-plus years later," she recalled. "After all, what do you do with an active mind as you sit hypnotically folding hundreds of the latest edition?" Gunn sees her fellow *Miscellany* staffers regularly, and describes them as some of her closest friends.

Romantic connections—which more can be surmised than proven—have also had their place in the newsroom. Gabe Anderson, Editor in Chief in 1998, made such a connection with News Editor Jen Deane '99. Anderson and Deane were married in 2005. "She had been trying to get involved with the paper for a long time, and before I was Editor in Chief, she sent an e-mail to someone and didn't hear back from them," he recalled fondly. "She was frustrated, and stormed over to the [newspaper] office. She burst through the door, and there I was, sitting there working on the Web site. We just looked at each other. And the rest, as they say, is history."

Success of *Miscellany* Graduates

Many of Vassar's most famed graduates have worked for the *Miscellany News*. Since its beginnings as a literary publication, writers for the *Miscellany* have enjoyed much success after College. Given the personality type that the paper attracts—hardworking, studious, determined—this is not surprising. Even if the paper does not *create* the work ethic of its editors, it certainly fosters it. As one historian of higher education noted, college papers serve as "admirable training ground" for professional journalists. "Quickness of thought and action, coolness of judgment and purpose, and attempted impartiality" are all hallmarks of success, and are all learned on the *Miscellany*'s Editorial Board.

Indeed, *Miscellany* staffers must learn to manage their time, express ideas concisely and attract readers with literary flair. Editors must also learn to manage a large staff and control a budget of tens of thousands of dollars. For some, this management experience is just as valuable as the journalism experience. For others, the quick writing skills they acquired proved invaluable. "[The *Miscellany*] was where I first learned the 'bead' approach to reporting a story," recalled former Editor in Chief Peter Cohen '78, now Vice President of Product Marketing at Authoria, one of the country's largest management consultants. "Put the biggest, most important 'bead' in the first paragraph, the second most important bead in the second paragraph, etc. It's a practice that's served me well in my career in marketing and public relations."

The success of *Miscellany* graduates manifests itself most immediately in graduate school and fellowship acceptances. In the past few decades, former editors have been admitted to top journalism schools including Columbia University and the University of Missouri, as well as top law schools including Harvard, Yale and Georgetown Universities. They have also been awarded prestigious fellowships, including at least three Watson Fellowships and one Rhodes Scholarship. *Miscellany* graduates can currently be found at some of the country's largest news organizations such as the *New York Times*, the *Washington Post*, the *Boston Globe*, and MSNBC, to name only a few. Some of the most common careers, based on alumnae/i interviews, are academia, journalism, publishing and law.[292]

Below is a small, chronological sampling of the careers of former writers and editors after their graduation. Far from being exhaustive, these mini-professional biographies represent only a handful of some of the most interesting and varied career paths that began on the pages of the *Miscellany News*.

Jeanne Webster '01

An English and economics major, Jeanne Webster entered Vassar in 1897 with a passion for just about everything. She took courses in penal reform, education, social justice, and writing, and soon became involved in the College Settlement House that served poor communities in New York. Webster vocally supported the socialist candidate Eugene Debs in his 1900 presidential bid, despite the fact that women were not able to vote, or encouraged to participate in politics.[293] Her family lured her into writing; Mark Twain was her great uncle, and her father was the successful publisher Charles Webster.

When she entered Vassar, Web-

Daddy-Long-Legs follows a young girl named Jerusha "Judy" Abbott through her college years at a school that is almost certainly based on Vassar.

ster became a regular contributor to the *Vassar Miscellany Monthly*. After reading her short stories in the *Miscellany*, her sophomore English professor recommended her to the editors of the *Poughkeepsie Sunday Courier* to write a weekly column of Vassar news and events. At least two of her stories from the *Monthly* seemed to have been picked up by the Poughkeepsie paper, including "Villa Gianini," a piece about her travels in Italy during her study abroad. The piece was popular, and she later expanded it into a novel entitled *The Wheat Princess*, published in 1905.

Webster forged numerous close relationships with fellow students, and her social experiences at Vassar provided the material for her successful novels *When Patty Went to College* and *Daddy-Long-Legs*. After graduating from Vassar in 1901, she moved to New York City and worked as a freelance writer for various magazines. During her long career, she wrote eight novels, numerous plays, and countless short stories. *Daddy-Long-Legs* is among her most popular works, which since Webster's death has been translated into 18 languages. It is especially popular in Japan, where it has been adapted into a television series and movie. In the United States, it was made into a movie as well, staring Fred Astaire and Leslie Caron.

Although Webster's works were humorous and playful, some scholars see them as "subversive commentaries against the patriarchal Victorian society of the early 1900s."[294] Many of Webster's works addressed national problems that defined the Progressive Era in America, including the condition of asylums, prisons and schools.

Edna St. Vincent Millay '17

Poet, dramatist and renowned author, Edna St. Vincent Millay is among Vassar's most highly regarded graduates. But before she became the first woman to earn the Pulitzer Prize for Poetry in 1922, she was a regular contributor to the *Miscellany Monthly*.[295] Her poem "Interim" won the *Miscellany* Poetry Prize Contest on May 14, 1914, for its "direct and powerfully imaginative appeal."[296] The piece was reprinted in the 1916 anthology of the best *Miscellany* poetry:

(A man speaks)

The room is full of you!—As I came in
And closed the door behind me, all at once
A something in the air, intangible,
Yet stiff with meaning, struck my senses sick!—

Sharp, unfamiliar odors have destroyed
Each other room's dear personality.
The heavy scent of damp, funereal flowers,—
The very essence, hush-distilled, of Death—

Has strangled that habitual breath of home
Whose expiration leaves all houses dead
And wheresoe'er I look is hideous change.
Save here. Here 'twas as if a weed-choked gate
Had opened at my touch, and I had stepped
Into some long-forgot, enchanted, strange,
Sweet garden of a thousand years ago
And suddenly thought, "I have been here before!"

You are not here. I know that you are gone,
And will not ever enter here again.
And yet it seems to me, if I should speak,
Your silent step must wake across the hall;
If I should turn my head, that your sweet eyes
Would kiss me from the door.—So short a time
To teach my life its transposition to
This difficult and unaccustomed key!—
The room is as you left it; your last touch—
A thoughtless pressure, knowing not itself
As saintly—hallows now each simple thing;
Hallows and glorifies, and glows between
The dust's grey fingers like a shielded light.

There is your book, just as you laid it down,
Face to the table,—I cannot believe
That you are gone!—Just then it seemed to me
You must be here. I almost laughed to think
How like reality the dream had been;
Yet knew before I laughed, and so was still.
That book, outspread, just as you laid it down!
Perhaps you thought, "I wonder what comes next,
And whether this or this will be the end";
So rose, and left it, thinking to return.

Perhaps that chair, when you arose and passed
Out of the room, rocked silently a while
Ere it again was still. When you were gone
Forever from the room, perhaps that chair,
Stirred by your movement, rocked a little while,
Silently, to and fro...

And here are the last words your fingers wrote,
Scrawled in broad characters across a page
In this brown book I gave you. Here your hand,
Guiding your rapid pen, moved up and down.
Here with a looping knot you crossed a "t,"
And here another like it, just beyond
These two eccentric "e's." You were so small,
And wrote so brave a hand!
        How strange it seems

That of all words these are the words you chose!
And yet a simple choice; you did not know
You would not write again. If you had known—

But then, it does not matter,—and indeed
If you had known there was so little time
You would have dropped your pen and come to me
And this page would be empty, and some phrase
Other than this would hold my wonder now.

Yet, since you could not know, and it befell
That these are the last words your fingers wrote,
There is a dignity some might not see
In this, "I picked the first sweet-pea to-day."
To-day! Was there an opening bud beside it
You left until to-morrow?—O my love,
The things that withered,—and you came not back!
That day you filled this circle of my arms
That now is empty. (O my empty life!)
That day—that day you picked the first sweet-pea,—
And brought it in to show me! I recall
With terrible distinctness how the smell
Of your cool gardens drifted in with you.
I know, you held it up for me to see
And flushed because I looked not at the flower,
But at your face; and when behind my look
You saw such unmistakable intent
You laughed and brushed your flower against my lips.

(You were the fairest thing God ever made,
I think.) And then your hands above my heart
Drew down its stem into a fastening,
And while your head was bent I kissed your hair.
I wonder if you knew. (Beloved hands!
Somehow I cannot seem to see them still.
Somehow I cannot seem to see the dust
In your bright hair.) What is the need of Heaven
When earth can be so sweet?—If only God
Had let us love,—and show the world the way!
Strange cancellings must ink th' eternal books
When love-crossed-out will bring the answer right!
That first sweet-pea! I wonder where it is.
It seems to me I laid it down somewhere,
And yet,—I am not sure. I am not sure,
Even, if it was white or pink; for then
'Twas much like any other flower to me,
Save that it was the first. I did not know,
Then, that it was the last. If I had known—
But then, it does not matter. Strange how few,
After all's said and done, the things that are
Of moment.
Few indeed! When I can make
Of ten small words a rope to hang the world!
"I had you and I have you now no more."
There, there it dangles,—where's the little truth
That can for long keep footing under that
When its slack syllables tighten to a thought?
Here, let me write it down! I wish to see
Just how a thing like that will look on paper!

"I had you and I have you now no more."

O little words, how can you run so straight
Across the page, beneath the weight you bear?
How can you fall apart, whom such a theme
Has bound together, and hereafter aid
In trivial expression, that have been
So hideously dignified?—Would God
That tearing you apart would tear the thread
I strung you on! Would God—O God, my mind
Stretches asunder on this merciless rack
Of imagery! O, let me sleep a while!
Would I could sleep, and wake to find me back
In that sweet summer afternoon with you.

Covering the Campus

Summer? 'Tis summer still by the calendar!
How easily could God, if He so willed,
Set back the world a little turn or two!
Correct its griefs, and bring its joys again!

We were so wholly one I had not thought
That we could die apart. I had not thought
That I could move,—and you be stiff and still!
That I could speak,—and you perforce be dumb!
I think our heart-strings were, like warp and woof

In some firm fabric, woven in and out;
Your golden filaments in fair design
Across my duller fibre. And to-day
The shining strip is rent; the exquisite
Fine pattern is destroyed; part of your heart
Aches in my breast; part of my heart lies chilled
In the damp earth with you. I have been torn
In two, and suffer for the rest of me.
What is my life to me? And what am I
To life,—a ship whose star has guttered out?
A Fear that in the deep night starts awake
Perpetually, to find its senses strained
Against the taut strings of the quivering air,
Awaiting the return of some dread chord?

Dark, Dark, is all I find for metaphor;
All else were contrast,—save that contrast's wall
Is down, and all opposed things flow together
Into a vast monotony, where night
And day, and frost and thaw, and death and life,
Are synonyms. What now—what now to me
Are all the jabbering birds and foolish flowers
That clutter up the world? You were my song!
Now, let discord scream! You were my flower!
Now let the world grow weeds! For I shall not
Plant things above your grave—(the common balm
Of the conventional woe for its own wound!)
Amid sensations rendered negative
By your elimination stands to-day,
Certain, unmixed, the element of grief;
I sorrow; and I shall not mock my truth
With travesties of suffering, nor seek
To effigy its incorporeal bulk
In little wry-faced images of woe.

230

I cannot call you back; and I desire
No utterance of my immaterial voice.
I cannot even turn my face this way
Or that, and say, "My face is turned to you";
I know not where you are, I do not know
If heaven hold you or if earth transmute,
Body and soul, you into earth again;
But this I know:—not for one second's space
Shall I insult my sight with visionings
Such as the credulous crowd so eager-eyed
Beholds, self-conjured in the empty air.
Let the world wail! Let drip its easy tears!
My sorrow shall be dumb!

—What do I say?
God! God!—God pity me! Am I gone mad
That I should spit upon a rosary?
Am I become so shrunken? Would to God
I too might feel that frenzied faith whose touch
Makes temporal the most enduring grief;
Though it must walk awhile, as is its wont,
With wild lamenting! Would I too might weep
Where weeps the world and hangs its piteous wreaths
For its new dead! Not Truth, but Faith, it is
That keeps the world alive. If all at once
Faith were to slacken,—that unconscious faith
Which must, I know, yet be the corner-stone
Of all believing,—birds now flying fearless
Across would drop in terror to the earth;
Fishes would drown; and the all-governing reins
Would tangle in the frantic hands of God
And the worlds gallop headlong to destruction!

O God, I see it now, and my sick brain
Staggers and swoons! How often over me
Flashes this breathlessness of sudden sight
In which I see the universe unrolled
Before me like a scroll and read thereon
Chaos and Doom, where helpless planets whirl
Dizzily round and round and round and round,
Like tops across a table, gathering speed
With every spin, to waver on the edge
One instant—looking over—and the next
To shudder and lurch forward out of sight—

231

Ah, I am worn out—I am wearied out—
It is too much—I am but flesh and blood,
And I must sleep. Though you were dead again,
I am but flesh and blood, and I must sleep.[297]

Millay grew up in a working class family; although her mother had to work two jobs, she found the time to teach her young daughter to write at the age of five. Millay wrote poetry throughout her primary and secondary education, impressing her teachers. She made her college debut in a variety of short-lived literary magazines, until she finally began submitting to the *Miscellany* during her sophomore year. In her junior year, she applied for an editorship. Besides her poetry, her plays were also met with campus acclaim. Vassar students performed her play *The Princess Marries the Page* during her senior year. Her talent seemed to have been well known on campus. Indeed, she was quite popular with the female students, with whom she allegedly had numerous sexual affairs. "People fall in love with me," she once wrote in her characteristically mysterious style, "and annoy me and distress me and flatter me and excite me."[298]

After graduation she moved to New York City and settled in Greenwich Village, where she met many prominent artists, writers and political radicals, including the poet Wallace Stevens, the playwright Eugene O'Neil, and the leftist journalist John Reed. Though Millay's personal life was unconventional, she used traditional verse forms such as ballads and sonnets, and her love poems describing her affairs were not especially erotic. Millay's poetical voice was intense but simultaneously controlled. Her subjects ranged from meditations on nature to feminism to stark reflections on death. Like her younger contemporary Dorothy Parker, she was a keen observer of human relationships. "We all wandered in after Miss Millay," Parker once wrote. "We were all being dashing and gallant, declaring that we weren't virgins, whether we were or not."[299]

In 1929, Millay was elected to the National Institute of Arts and Letters and then to the American Academy of Arts and Letters in 1940. Three years later she was awarded the gold medal of the Poetry Society of America. In 1943, she earned the Frost Medal for her lifetime contribution to poetry.

Interestingly, though, Millay was never celebrated on Vassar's campus the way that she was outside of it. Decades later, it took a fellow *Miscellany* staffer—Sherry Corlan Chayat '65—to advocate for her rightful place in the College's pantheon of notable graduates. "I remember thinking it was very strange that Vassar seemed, for a time at least, to scorn its most famous poet," Chayat recalled. In her memory, Millay was ignored by the mostly male English Department. Chayat became friendly with Norma Millay, Edna's sister, who dedicated her life to preserving the poet's papers and memory. With Norma's inspiration, Chayat formed the Edna St. Vincent Millay Club at Vassar. "I think Millay's early radicalism really found an audience in the 1960s as the College was itself becoming increasingly liberal," she recalled. "Eventually, she was incorporated into the English curriculum and was even listed as one of Vassar's 'famous' graduates."

Mary McCarthy '33

Orphaned at the age of six, Mary McCarthy was raised by her wealthy grandparents, who provided for her education and sent her to the elite Vassar College. There, she studied literature alongside Elizabeth Bishop, graduating *cum laude*. At Vassar, she became politically and socially active. Joining the *Miscellany* staff within her first month on campus, she reported mostly on national political events. McCarthy was listed as a Senior Reporter, a position that required at least one submission per week. Her politics likely guided her reporting on political and economic issues. During college, she became a zealous Trotskyite and fervent anti-Stalinist. Moving to New York in 1934 with her first husband, she eventually earned teaching positions at a host of prestigious schools, including Bard and Vassar.

Over the next decade, her writing career soared. Her first book, *The Company She Keeps* (1942), was critically acclaimed. The novel was a collection of stories about her social and intellectual life in the city, depicting a failing marriage much like her own. She also included many of her Vassar acquaintances in her writings; *The Group*, her 1963 bestselling novel, followed the experiences of eight sexually liberated Vassar graduates from the 1930s. This novel was much to the chagrin of College President Alan Simpson, who had to cope with the public relations fallout from the book. Though *The Group* was published one year before his arrival on campus, it led to great public fascination with the sexual conduct of Vassar students—a fascination that he had to quash for the sake of older, more conservative alumnae.

Much of her work incorporated the liberal politics that McCarthy had developed at Vassar. Throughout her career, she wrote actively against the American presence in Vietnam and published essays on nuclear proliferation and relations between the sexes. McCarthy was known for her leftist views—views that were likely grown on the liberal Editorial Board of the *Miscellany*.

Elizabeth Bishop '34

Elizabeth Bishop is considered one of the greatest American poets of the 20th century. Bishop wrote for the paper in 1931 and 1932, and became a full editor during her junior year in 1933. During her time on the paper, she wrote "sparse and witty" pieces for the Campus Chat column. Bishop remembered herself as a "mysterious figure" in the *Miscellany* office, and one staff member recalled her as a "quiet gray presence" always in a gray sweater and skirt "at a slight remove from the rest of us."[300] In 1933, she co-founded the radical literary magazine *Con Spirito* with fellow *Miscellany* writers Mary McCarthy and Eleanor Clark.

One of her most significant moments on the *Miscellany* was an interview she conducted with the famed poet and dramatist T.S. Elliot in the spring of 1933. Elliot had come to Vassar to see the premiere production of his play *Sweeney Agonistes*. After the performance, he read part of *The Waste Land*—his acclaimed modernist poem—and sat down with Bishop.[301] In Bishop's classically terse and eloquent style, the following report appeared in the newspaper the next week:

> Before reading selections from *The Waste Land*, Mr. Elliot declined to explain it, saying that he had read explanations of it which were much better than his own intention. Critics have called it a "criticism of the contemporary world," but "to me," he confessed, "it was just a piece of rhythmical grumbling."[302]

During her last semester at Vassar, the College librarian introduced her to the poet Marianne Moore, initiating a friendship that would prove instrumental for Bishop. In the next few years, Moore gave her professional advice and criticism. After Bishop's graduation in 1934, she traveled all over the country and the world to New York, Boston

Key West, Mexico and Brazil. She eventually settled in Massachusetts, where she went on to become Poetry Editor of the *Nation*. She then became a successful editor at Houghton Mifflin, while continuing to publish her poems.

Much of her poetry is defined by household objects or everyday occurrences, to which she attaches symbolic meaning. Travel and internationalism is another strong current of her work. Bishop went on to receive a host of accolades for her poems and anthologies. In 1949, she was named Poet Laureate of the United States. While living in Brazil in 1956, Bishop received the Pulitzer Prize for her collection of poetry, *North & South — A Cold Spring*. Between 1970 and 1977, she taught poetry at Harvard University, while also writing numerous pieces for the *New Yorker*.

Vassar College is the principle repository of Bishop's original papers, which include her personal correspondence, working papers, notebooks, and diaries. Among the collection are over 3,500 pages of drafts of poems and prose.

Katharine Meyer Graham '38

Before becoming one of the nation's most powerful media mavericks and 1988 Pulitzer Prize winner, Katharine Meyer Graham '38 was a writer for the *Miscellany News*. Graham attended Vassar for two years before transferring to the University of Chicago. During that time, she was a member of the 1936 Daisy Chain, and was active in political organizations, becoming a delegate to the American Student Union. Her *Miscellany* articles were written on a variety of topics, from national politics to curricular policies. One of her colleagues on the paper, Betty Frank '38, speculated that Graham feared that she would never be asked to join the Editorial Board, no matter how hard she worked at her reporting. This, Frank believes, was one of her primary motivations for transferring. "I don't think [she] was a very gung-ho, creative reporter," said Frank.[303] "She was terribly shy. I don't know whether she would have actually gotten... a slot on that Editorial Board." Actually, Graham *was* asked to join the Board at the end of her sophomore year, but she had already committed to the University of Chicago.

Her greatest notoriety after Vassar came after the death of her husband in 1963. Graham took over his position as publisher of the *Washington Post*, one of the nation's oldest daily newspapers. Graham was essentially the first woman to hold such a powerful position in publishing or journalism, and wrote extensively in her autobiography about her initial lack of confidence. Nonetheless, Graham saw the *Washington Post* through its most famous and successful era—the Watergate scandal. Under her leadership, reporters Bob Woodward and Carl Bernstein broke the story in 1972, leading the paper to a Pulitzer Prize and national fame.[304]

Graham returned to the Hudson Valley in 1997 to receive the Four Freedom's Medal at the Franklin D. Roosevelt Presidential Library in Hyde Park for her contribution to the freedom of speech. Her memoir *Personal History* earned her a Pulitzer of her own in 1998.

Anne Armstrong '49

During her first two years at Vassar, Anne Legendre became an increasingly regular contributor to the *Miscellany*. Writing mostly on Vassar's student government, she was given the job of Managing Editor in her junior year. However, she left the paper in September of 1948 to join an organization with even more political intrigue—Harry Truman's presidential campaign. She served as a dedicated volunteer, throwing herself into the political grassroots process. After working briefly for *Harper's Bazaar* after graduation, she married Tobin Armstrong, whom she met while visiting a fellow Vassar alumna and *Miscellany* editor in Texas.

By the 1952 presidential race, Armstrong had switched political parties. She started working as a precinct worker and "sort of branched out," as she told The *New York Times* in 1976.[305] She soon became vice chair of the Republican Party from 1966 to 1968, and then a member of the Republican National Committee (RNC) from 1968 to 1971. She then chaired the RNC until 1973. In that role, she pushed for the Party to become more inclusive of women, minorities and younger voters. Armstrong was the keynote speaker at the 1972 Convention—the first woman in either party to deliver a convention keynote.

In 1980, she served as chair of Ronald Reagan's presidential campaign, and then became chair of the President's Foreign Intelligence Advisory Board. Reagan awarded her the Presidential Medal of Freedom in 1987.

Lucinda Franks '68

Lucinda Franks wrote for the *Miscellany News* during the late 1960s, one of the most successful periods in the paper's history. After her graduation from Vassar, she moved to London to become a reporter for the *United Press International*. She won the 1971 Pulitzer Prize for National Reporting for her five-part documentary on the life of the 28-year-old revolutionary Diana Oughton, entitled "The Making of a Terrorist." The documentary examined The Weatherman, a radical anti-Vietnam group who staged bombings and riots. Franks was the first woman to win the Pulitzer Prize for National reporting, and the second *Miscellany* Pulitzer winner—Edna St. Vincent Millay '17 won the Pulitzer Prize for Poetry in 1922. Katherine Meyer Graham would win the award for The *Washington Post*'s Watergate coverage in 1998.

After her award, she became a staff writer for the *New York Times* and has since become a regular contributor to the *New York Times Magazine*, the *New Yorker* and the *Atlantic*. She is also the author of several books.

Michael Specter '77

Michael Specter was never an editor for the *Miscellany News*, but he was a sporadic contributing writer throughout his Vassar years. Since graduation, he has enjoyed a prestigous career in writing and journalism. Between 1985 and 1991, he wrote for the *Washington Post*, serving as the paper's national science reporter. Eventually he was promoted to New York bureau chief. Switching gears, he was appointed co-chief of the *New York Times* Moscow bureau in 1995. While in Russia, he covered topics including the war in Chechnya, healthcare and the Russian presidential elections. In 1998, he moved to the *New Yorker*, where he is a staff writer. He continues to write about issues related to science and society.

Specter has received much acclaim for his work, winning the American Association for Advancement of Science Journalism Award in 2002, and twice receiving the Global Health Council's Annual Excellence in Media Award.

"Hell! It's in Latin!"

Not all graduates appear to be as well informed as those who served on the *Miscellany. Anne Cleveland, Vassar: A Second Glance*

Elizabeth Sporkin '78

Not all experiences with the *Miscellany News* were positive for alumnae/i, who nevertheless managed to achieve fame in writing and publishing. Elizabeth Sporkin is one such example. Sporkin wanted to be a journalist since she was a little girl, but her parents insisted that she receive a complete liberal arts education first. "When I arrived [at Vassar] as a freshman, I made a beeline for the *Miscellany News*," she recalled.

Her first assignment was to cover the student government elections—always a complex and arcane process involving countless candidates, rules and regulations. "I thought it was weird to give a story like that to an incoming freshman who knew nothing about campus politics, but I made an attempt. Naturally my story was completely rewritten and the editors handled the situation by avoiding me." Sporkin was not pleased. "I found [the editors] to be mean and cliquish, and that was the end of my Vassar journalism experience. I said to myself, 'Screw them. I'll just put journalism on hold and begin my career after I graduate.' And that's what I did."[306]

Twenty-five years later, Sporkin is the Executive Editor of *PEOPLE Magazine*, with a weekly circulation of 3.75 million and annual revenue in excess of $1.5 billion.

Rick Lazio '80

Rick Lazio, who represented New York's Second Congressional District for eight years, began his career in politics by covering the student government for the *Miscellany News*. Unlike Sporkin, Lazio was inspired by his experience. After writing detailed features about the student leaders, he was moved to run for the Student Senate himself. By his senior year, he chaired the Student Advisory Committee, which he recalled as his most memorable involvement at the College. "Being in a room with people of authority and often being in the position to challenge that authority, ultimately coming to a consensus, was very useful in the work of my later life," he said.[307] Of his experiences on the *Miscellany* and in the student government, he once told a writer for the Vassar's Office of College Relations, "I learned how to work within the system. I learned how to respect and at the same time confront authority, to challenge authority when I thought that the answer was not satisfactory, or that we could do better."[308]

After graduating from Vassar, Lazio attended the American University School of Law.[309] He worked as an Assistant District Attorney in Suffolk County for several years, and then was elected as a Suffolk County Legislator in 1989. He soon turned his eyes to Washington, running for Congress in 1992. Lazio won by a wide margin, defeating an 18-year incumbent. He served four terms from 1993 to 2001, becoming the Deputy Majority Whip in 1994 and later the Assistant Majority Leader. As a moderate Republican, Lazio focused on issues ranging from the environment and criminal justice to health care and Federal housing programs. During his time in Congress, he served on the Banking and Financial Services Committee, the Commerce Committees and the Subcommittee on Health and Environment.

Lazio began his political career as a news reporter for the *Miscellany* and then a member of the student government. The *Vassar Quarterly*.

During the last four years of his tenure in Congress, Lazio was the only member to serve on both the Commerce and Banking Committees, and was thus instrumental in passing the Gramm-Leach-Bliley Financial Services Modernization Act of 1999. As chairman of the House Financial Services Committee's Subcommittee on Housing, Lazio authored and negotiated legislation enacting reform of public housing, and expanded homeownership for low-income families. He also introduced the Work Incentives Improvement Act, which maintains the security of health care insurance through Medicare and Medcaid.

In 2000, five months before Election Day, Lazio entered the race for Senate to succeed Daniel Patrick Moynihan, but was defeated by Hillary Clinton. His late entry into the race followed Republican New York City Mayor Rudolph Giuliani's decision not to run. Many of Lazio's personal papers rest in Vassar's Archives and Special Collections Library. This sweeping collection includes many of his campaign materials, speeches, legislation and personal correspondences.

Peter Cummings '83

After leaving Vassar with a degree in Art History, former *Miscellany* Editor in Chief Peter Cummings decided to pursue his lifelong passion of journalism. He attended Northwestern University, where he earned his master's degree in journalism, and since then has worked for several prestigious publications, including the *Chronicle of Higher Education* and the *Advocate*. He also worked for numerous magazines in England, where he lived for almost a decade after graduate school.

In England, Cummings became accustomed to the country's "social and sexual openness," and came to believe that America relegated its gay community to the outskirts of its mainstream society. Using his experience in writing, Cummings decided to create a publication that would promote gay pride and openness in the United States. From this idea, *XY Magazine* was born. "People are scared of *XY Magazine*," Cummings said in a 2002 interview with the *Vassar Quarterly*, "because it takes on important issues no one else will touch, and it tells the truth. Whenever necessary, *XY* is also willing to criticize itself, the gay community, and American society to make its point."[310] The magazine, which features a broad range of cultural, politics and social issues, has a circulation of about 40,000 across the United States and Europe.

Matthew Kauffman '83

Editor in Chief of the *Miscellany News* in 1981, Matthew Kauffman began his work on the paper immediately after he arrived at Vassar in 1979. He ran with several investigative stories, including one about sexual assault and another about lax security on campus. After graduating with a degree in Political Science, Kauffman moved to Connecticut where he now writes for the *Hartford Courant*. During his time at the *Courant*, he has written innumerable investigative pieces on legal affairs and business. His 2003 series of articles on drug company scandals garnered much critical acclaim, earning him the paper's distinction of Reporter of the Year. He has since investigated a wide variety of topics, including a scandal at the University of Connecticut involving coaches trading sporting tickets for automobiles. He has also investigated various charity executives, examining the percentage of donations they used for personal gain.

Kauffman is now best known for his four-part series "Mentally Unfit, Forced to Fight," which he researched with Lisa Chedekel. The series of articles broke the story of mentally unstable soldiers, many with post-traumatic stress disorder, who were forced to remain in Iraq. The story won Kauffman the Selden Ring Award for Investigative Reporting, the Worth Bingham Prize and the Heywood Broun Award.

He and Chedekel were also finalists for the 2007 Pulitzer Prize in Journalism. Kauffman has since appeared on numerous television programs, including *The O'Reilly Factor* and *ABC World News*.

Neil Strauss '91

Like many *Miscellany* graduates, Neil Strauss bridged his post-Vassar career between books and newspapers. After his graduation, he wrote for several small magazines before joining the staff of the *Village Voice*. His talents stood out, and he was soon invited to become a music critic for the *New York Times*. He then became a writer and Contributing Editor for *Rolling Stone*, where he penned cover stories on celebrities ranging from Madonna to Tom Cruise to Kurt Cobain. Strauss won the ASCAP Deems Taylor Award for his coverage of Cobain's suicide, and for his profile of Eric Clapton's life and career in the *New York Times*.

Strauss achieved his greatest fame, however, with *The Game*, a nonfiction exposé on the sub-culture of pickup artists. The book remained on the *New York Times* Bestseller List for two months after its 2005 release. He followed that with a controversial graphic novel entitled *How to Live Like a Porn Star* in 2006, before releasing *Rules of The Game*. While *The Game* described Strauss's experience in the community of pickup artists, *Rules of the Game* is a book of strategies for average men seeking women. For his humorously incisive writing, Strauss is regarded as one of the nation's preeminent social critics.

Rachel Simmons '98

Rachel Simmons graduated Phi Beta Kappa from Vassar with a double major in Women's Studies and Political Science, and was chosen as a Rhodes Scholar that same year. The scholarship took her to Oxford, where she earned a master's degree in politics. Active at Vassar, she served as News Editor then Managing Editor of the *Miscellany News*. In her senior year, she served as Student Assistant to the President under Frances Fergusson. Simmons was also an active community volunteer, working as an advocate and caseworker at Dutchess Outreach, the largest human services agency in Dutchess County. In 1995 she was named their Outstanding Volunteer of the Year.

After winning the Julia Flitner Lamb Award for Excellence in Political Science, Rachel completed an Urban Fellowship with the

City of New York where she served as an aide to the Deputy Lawyer for Operations. From there, she became Deputy Finance Director for Charles Schumer's campaign for the United States Senate. Her career switched gears, however, when she wrote *Odd Girl Out: The Hidden Culture of Aggression in Girls*. An instant bestseller, the book discussed aggression and hostility among teenage girls. After Tina Fey (famed writer, actress and director) read the book, she used Simmons as a consultant for her hit movie *Mean Girls* in 2004. Simmons now lectures around the country, and runs the Girls Leadership Institute, a summer program for middle and high school students.

262 "Editor's Note," The *Vassar Miscellany Monthly*, March 1892.

263 Grace Margaret Gallaher, Vassar Stories, (Boston: E.H. Bacon, 1907).

264 "Current Population Survey, 2007 Annual Social and Economic Supplement," U.S. Census Bureau, March 2007.

265 "Hot Off the Presses: New Improved *Miscellany News*," Vassar Quarterly, 2005, Volume 101, Issue 3.

266 *The Fox Journal* of the University of Wisconsin Web site

267 Henry Finck, "College Papers," The New York Post, June 1891.

268 "The Misc's Demise: Take It, It's yours!" The *Misc*, December 2, 1969.

269 "Editorial," The *Vassar Miscellany News* Supplement, December 11, 1914.

270 "Why Not Organize?" The *Vassar Miscellany*, March 27, 1914.

271 "Editorial," The *Vassar Miscellany News*, September 20, 1925.

272 "Return to need-blind rightly prioritizes accessibility," The *Miscellany News*, September 8, 2007.

273 "Prioritizing in tough economic times," The *Miscellany News*, November 6, 2008.

274 "Editorial," The *Miscellany News*, September 21, 2001.

275 Best 368 Colleges, The Princeton Review, 2009.

276 "Obama for president," The *Miscellany News*, October 30, 2008.

277 Mary Mallon, "The *Vassar Miscellany*," The *Vassar Miscellany Monthly*, April, 1915, p. 130.

278 Mary Mallon, "The *Vassar Miscellany*," The *Vassar Miscellany Monthly*, April, 1915, p. 130.

279 "The Clearing House," The *Vassar Quarterly*, January, 1916.

280 James Orton, "Our Obligations to France," The *Vassar Miscellany Monthly*, July, 1872.

281 In 1981, Elizabeth Daniels '41 interviewed Elizabeth Moffat Drouilhet '30, who served as Warden of the College between 1941 and 1976. The Warden was responsible for regulating students' social life under parietal rules as well as the duties discharged today by the Office of Residential Life. When asked in the interview to name the "big four" organizations, she replied, "Philaletheis for dramatics. Athletic Association, Political Association and the religious association that shortly became the Community Church. There were a lot of minor organizations... I should also say the *Miscellany News*... which, while it didn't rate as one of the big four, was the equivalent..." The *Miscellany* seems to have existed parallel to, but outside of, the official organizational structure.

282 Special Collections, Vassar College Archives, comp. "VC Government (1868-1920)." *Subject File* 23.79.

283   Special Collections, Vassar College Archives, comp. "VC Government (1921-1960)." *Subject File* 23.79.

284   Recall from Chapter 1 that in 1893, there were distinct changes to the tone of the poetry and prose in the *Miscellany*. Around that year, the haughty academic language was often replaced with more casual literary pieces about student life.

285   *A Book of Vassar Verse: Reprints from the Vassar Miscellany Monthly, 1894-1916,* Published by the *Vassar Miscellany Monthly*, 1916.

286   Charles Franklin Thwing, "College Journalism," *Scribners Monthly: An Illustrated Magazine for the People*, October 1878: p. 810.

287   The *Vassar Miscellany* Weekly, "Where the Weekly Fails," May 14, 1920.

288   "A Note," The *Vassar Miscellany News*, May 11, 1966.

289   Charles Franklin Thwing, "College Journalism," *Scribners Monthly: An Illustrated Magazine for the People*, October 1878: p. 810.

290   *Ibid.*, 811.

291   The *Vassar Miscellany Monthly*, "Editor's Table," April, 1894.

292   Based on interviews. For researchers interested in correlating participation on student newspapers with career paths, college alumnae/i offices usually maintain running lists of graduates who participated in student publications, as well as running lists of graduates' careers. At Vassar, however, the list of students involved in the *Miscellany* is incomplete, and often gives incorrect designation as to whether the individual was an editor or a writer.

293   Lila Matsumoto, "Jean Webster," edited by Elizabeth Daniels. 2007. http://vcencyclopedia.vassar.edu/index.php/Jean_Webster (accessed May 29, 2008).

294   *Ibid.*

295   Muriel Crane, "Vincent At Vassar Burned Candle But All With Elan and Charm," The *Vassar Miscellany News*, November 19, 1952.

296   "Millay Wins *Misc* content," The *Vassar Miscellany News*, May 14, 1914.

297   Edna St. Vincent Millay, *A Book of Vassar Verse: Reprints from the Vassar Miscellany Monthly, 1894-1916,* Published by the *Vassar Miscellany Monthly*, 1916, p. 81.

298   As quoted by J.D. McClatchy, "Like a Moth to a Flame," The *New York Times*, September 16, 2001.

299   As quoted by John Keats, *You Might as Well Live: The Life and Times of Dorothy Parker,* (New York: Simon and Schuster, 1970), p. 31.

300   Brett Millier, Elizabeth Bishop: Life and the Memory of It, (Los Angeles: University of California Press, 1995), p. 48.

301   James Longenbach, *Modern Poetry After Modernism.* (New York: Oxford University Press, 1997), p. 22.

302 "T.S. Elliot Reads and Comments on His Poetry," Vassar *Miscellany News*, May 10, 1933. Bishop recalled interviewing Elliot in Ashley Brown, "An Interview with Elizabeth Bishop," in *Elizabeth Bishop and Her Art*, ed. Llyod Schwartz and Sybil Estess (Ann Arbor, 1983), p. 293. William Logan, in "The Unbearable Lightness of Elizabeth Bishop," Southwest Review 79, (1994), has suggested that Elliot was "the author of much of Bishop's imaginative circumstance, and his influence was much more deeply absorbed and is therefore… difficult to trace."

303 Carol Flesenthal, *Power, Privilege and the Post: The Katherine Meyer Graham Story,* (New York: Seven Stories Press), p. 75.

304 David Remnick, *Reporting: Writings from The New Yorker.* (New York: Knopf, 2006).

305 William Grimes, "Anne Armstrong, Presidential Adviser and Pioneering Politician, Dies at 80," The *New York Times*, July 31, 2008.

306 Notice that her depiction of the *Miscellany* staff in 1974 very much corresponds to the image developed in Chapter 4.

307 Rachel Wolff, "Congressman Lazio returns to alma mater," The *Miscellany News*, April 8, 2005.

308 "And the Winner Is… the Wellesley Alum," Vassar Quarterly, Winter 2000. http://www.aavc.vassar.edu/vq/articles/lazio_winter00 (accessed November 3, 2008).

309 Biography and description of the Lazio Papers adopted from "Guide to the Rick Lazio Papers," Vassar's Archives and Special Collections Library, http://specialcollections.vassar.edu/findingaids/lazio_rick.html (accessed November 3, 2008).

310 "Persevering Magazine Promotes Gay Pride and Openness," The *Vassar Quarterly*, Spring 2002.

Concluding Thoughts

"What can I say about journalism? It has the greatest virtue and the greatest evil. It is the first thing a dictator controls. It is the mother of literature and the perpetrator of crap. In many cases it is the only history we have and yet it is the tool of the worst men. But over a long period of time and because it is the product of so many men, it is perhaps the purest thing we have. Honesty has a way of creeping into it even when it is not intended."

—John Steinbeck

When Matthew Vassar founded his College in 1861, there were no precedents for an endowed liberal arts college for women.[311] Neither was there a precedent for young women—some as young as 16—writing, editing and publishing their own periodical. And there was surely no precedent for these female students managing financial matters such as advertising sales and subscription revenue. But within a decade of the College's founding, Vassar students exerted an extraordinary amount of editorial and financial control over the *Miscellany*. Their publication was not only *longer* than counterparts at all-male institutions, but in many cases *better*. The 19th century editors put tremendous time and energy into language, as well as stylistic detail. At the beginning of the 20th century, this tradition of excellence transferred from poetry and literature to news writing. Following Vassar's tumultuous shift to coeducation, the paper entered an equally turbulent period with its fortunes rising and falling like the ocean tide. The budget, like the staff itself, grew and shrunk without predictability. On the whole, though, the century ended with a modernized newspaper, clawing its way into the World Wide Web. And by the end of the first decade of the 21st century, the paper had fully embraced the digital age, and once again renewed its commitment to professionalism and excellence.

As the *Miscellany News* approaches its sesquicentennial anniversary, Vassar students and researchers have the opportunity to reflect on the paper's past, present and future. To some, the idea of studying a college newspaper might seem arcane at best, and irrelevant at worst. Why should we pay any heed to student journalism at all, with its inevitable quirks and inaccuracies? More narrowly, can *this* paper—which essentially covers a small 1,000-acre stretch of land in Poughkeepsie—provide any valuable knowledge? Indeed it can.

The *Miscellany News* tells a story that is far from local. Compulsory religion in school. Personal independence. Clashes between students and administrators. Women's suffrage. Anti-war riots. Civil rights.[312] All of these philosophical and political discussions have unfolded through poetry and prose, in letters and articles, on the pages of the *Miscellany*. As I sit here, buried deep in the College's archives, I can hear the debating voices of countless writers and editors. What opinions pieces should be included? What stories should go on page one? What are our rights as students and as citizens? What kind of society do we want to live in, and how can our staff editorial hasten the creation of such a society? Far from being esoteric or insignificant, the *Miscellany News* records the events of a student body against the grand backdrop of American history.

But it also tells a story that is distinctly local. It describes individuals coming of age, learning and growing during their most formative years. The paper captures generations of unique student voices and student experiences. As Charles Thwing put it in 1878, a college newspaper is "a mirror of undergraduate sentiment, and is either scholarly or vulgar, frivolous or dignified, as are the students who edit and publish it."[313] Thwing goes on to recommend that, before any father send his child off to college, he would be wise to "consult a year's file of their fortnightly paper" to better gauge the "moral and intellectual character" of the institution. Unlike a college's promotional brochures, the student paper tells the unfiltered story of life as students actually experience it. Dissatisfactions inevitably find voice in student reporting. "Indeed, the spirit of rebellion among college men often flows out into ink," Thwing wrote. For Vassar, the *Miscellany* is a treasure trove of experiences—an irreplaceable source for tracing achievements, attitudes and "rebellion" over the College's history.

And so the *Miscellany* is at once grand and small, personal and professional, national and local. And as John Steinbeck extols, journalism can be both the "mother of literature and the perpetrator of crap."[314] Newspapers can be misleading and even flat-out wrong. Foolish or malicious editors can control them, and the content can be filtered through an external administrative force. "But over a long period of time and because it is the product of so many men, it is perhaps the purest thing we have," noted Steinbeck. "Honesty has a way of creeping into it even when it is not intended."

As the *Vassar Quarterly* wrote in 2005, "Without the backing of a faculty adviser or the training of a journalism department, the staff manages to weld together a publication each week that straddles a journalistic spectrum."[315] Editors have always considered this independence to be their greatest asset. Indeed, the battle for financial and editorial autonomy unfolded over a century and a half. It is precisely this independence that ensures that the *Miscellany*'s coverage reflects true, lived experiences. To paraphrase Henry Steele Commager, this has allowed for a free press reporting to a free people. It has given us the raw material of Vassar's history, and the story of our own times.

311 Maryann Bruno and Elizabeth Daniels, *Vassar College*, (London: Arcadia, 2001), p. 3.

312 "*Misc* Continues Tradition of Political Commentary," The *Vassar Miscellany News*, February 5, 1964.

313 Charles Franklin Thwing, "College Journalism," *Scribners Monthly: An Illustrated Magazine for the People*, October 1878: p. 810.

314 Cheryl Gibbs, *Getting the Whole Story: Reporting and Writing the News,* (New York: Guilford Press, 2002), p. 8.

315 "Hot Off the Presses: New Improved *Miscellany News*," The *Vassar Quarterly*, 2005, Volume 101, Issue 3.

The Bylaws of the
Miscellany News

As we have seen, the Bylaws of the *Miscellany News* have always been an odd document. In theory, they dictate the operation of the paper and ensure continuity of style, purpose and policies. In practice, the Editorial Board has almost always 'worked ahead' of the Bylaws, revising its procedures in the newsroom and then rewriting the Bylaws to match the new reality. It would drive a strict constitutionalist mad. Yet this method seems to have prevailed since the first regulatory guidebook was developed at the turn of the 20th century.

In addition to the Bylaws, the *Miscellany News* maintains a lengthy style manual. This manual deals with mechanical issues such as capitalization, proper titles for administrators and correct usages for the different sections of the paper. The Bylaws, by contrast, deal with larger operational constructs. These include the paper's mission, the responsibilities of its members and its advertising policies.

Presented here are the unabridged Bylaws as they existed at the beginning of the 2008-2009 academic year. It is worth noting that many of these Bylaws are already obsolete. For example, the cover design that began in 2000-2001 was abolished in Spring 2009, making the older Bylaw procedures for selecting each week's cover story irrelevant. Similarly, section editors no longer design their own layouts; layout is the responsibility of the Design and Production Editor. Also, within a year, the Bylaws are likely to provide significantly more space to the Web site, spelling out policies and procedures for Web development.

Thus, the Bylaws are very much a living document that often reflect theory far more than practice.

Section I: Name and Type of Publication.

A. The official name of this publication is the *Miscellany News*. Founded in 1866 and called the *Vassar Miscellany*, the paper was renamed the *Miscellany News* in 1915. It is the oldest student publication at the College.

B. Although the publication appreciates contributions from all members of the College community–students, administration, faculty, alumnae/alumni, staff, and trustees–it is primarily intended as a service for Vassar's students to inform them of news, arts and sports in and around the college in a timely and complete manner, as an open forum for public dialogue on important issues, and to entertain them through humor and interesting features.

Section II: Membership

A. Staff

1. Any student within the Vassar community may serve on the staff of the paper, regardless of gender, color, creed or sexual orientation, as long as s/he attends the weekly writers' meetings, or otherwise keeps in contact with the section editor and fulfills the responsibilities of a staff writer as outlined in these *Miscellany News* by-laws. Staff members may be removed for general failure to meet their responsibilities to the paper as outlined in Section III, Subsection B.

2. The *Miscellany News* has the responsibility to publicize and hold weekly staff meetings.

3. The *Miscellany News* aims to maintain a diverse staff, adequately reflecting the student body of the College.

4. The *Miscellany News* will advertise and hold a weekly paper critique open to the public.

B. Editorial Board

1. The following positions on Ed. Board should be filled. Editor in Chief, Senior Editor, Design/Production Editor, Copy Editor, Managing Editor (can be left open if a business manager is elected), News Editor, Arts & Entertainment Editor, Features Editor, Opinions Editor, Sports Editor, BackPage Editor, Photography Editor and Information Technology Editor

(can be left open if paid position is filled assuming similar responsibilities). If these positions are not filled, it is the responsibility of the remaining Ed. Board to actively seek a qualified individual(s).

2. It is favorable, though not required, that the position of Contributing Editor be filled as well. This is an Ed. Board position.

3. It is favorable, though not required, that the position of Spread Editor be filled as well. This is an Ed. Board position. It is favorable for him or her to have been a former editor. The Board may choose to allow another editor to fulfill the responsibilities of Spread Editor.

4. Any person who wishes to serve on the Editorial Board must be approved by the Editorial Board (see Section IV, Subsection D).

5. Membership on the Board cannot be rescinded except through resignation or impeachment (see Section IV, Subsection E).

C. Term Limits

1. All Editorial positions must be declared vacant at the end of each school year.

2. The positions of Editor in Chief, Senior Editor and Contributing Editor are one-semester positions. Editors wishing to hold these positions longer must reapply.

Section III: Responsibilities and Powers

A. Exclusivity

1. No staff member should write a news article about any organization, group, or issue with which the individual is involved or connected in any way.

2. Editorial Board members are permitted to be a part of other campus publications as long as it does not cause a conflict with their responsibilities to the *Miscellany News*. Conflicts of interest or possible conflicts of interest should be brought before the Editorial Board.

3. No Editorial Board member or assistant editor may serve on the VSA Council–either appointed or elected.

3.1 Editorial Board members may not proxy at VSA Council meetings

4. No member of the Editorial Board may serve as the Student Assistant to the President.

5. The Editorial Board has the right to review any possible conflicts of interest and make a ruling, as it deems appropriate, either at the election of a new member or during the year. The Board has the right to know of any possible conflicts of interest if it learns of a conflict after an editor is elected, it may ask the editor to cease his or her participation which causes the conflict. Editors who participate in activities that the Board deems to be conflicts of interest must cease participation upon request of two-thirds of the Board or their actions shall constitute dereliction of duty. Violation of conflict of interest rules shall constitute dereliction of duty, and are grounds for immediate impeachment by a vote of the Editorial Board (see Section IV, Subsection E).

6. It is the responsibility of the Editor in Chief to inform all possible candidates, editors, and staff members of these regulations. This may come in the form of the Editor in Chief asking candidates, editors, and staff members to read these by-laws.

B. Staff

1. All members of the staff are directly responsible to an editor, from whom they receive assignments.

2. All members of the staff should maintain weekly contact with an editor to discuss their work.

3. Staff members must meet weekly deadlines.

4. Staff members are responsible for reporting news in the most accurate, fair and honest manner possible, and never publish material with a malicious intent.

4.1 This includes, but is not limited to, quoting sources accurately, reporting all sides of every story as well as possible, checking facts for accuracy, keeping personal opinions and feelings out of news articles.

5. Staff members are expected to maintain ethical conduct and abide by basic journalistic ethics. Questions of what constitutes ethical behavior should be brought to the attention of the Editor in Chief and Senior Editor.

5.1 Ethical conduct includes, but is not limited to, maintaining the confidentiality of anonymous sources, never misrepresenting oneself, never misusing the newspaper for personal purposes, never reporting "off-the-record" remarks.

6. Staff members who do not fulfill their responsibilities to the newspaper as outlined in these by-laws may be impeached for dereliction of duty.

C. Editorial Board

1. The Editorial Board is responsible for the editorial content of the paper. By a two-thirds vote, the board may overturn any decision of the Editor in Chief.

2. The Board shall have the power to impeach any of its members (see Section IV, Subsection E).

3. The Board shall have the power to elect any qualified person to its ranks (see Section IV, Subsection DC).

4. The Board shall have the power to amend and revise these by-laws, as well as the stylebook (see Section IV, Subsection F).

5. The Board shall be the collective author of the staff editorials (see Section IV, Subsection C).

6. The Board does not take responsibility for views expressed in opinions articles.

7. Board members have the responsibility to keep discussions that take place at Editorial Board meetings confidential.

8. Only the Editor in Chief is to act as the official representative of the *Miscellany News*.

9. The individual responsibilities of the Editorial Board members are as follows:

a. **Editor in Chief**: The Editor in Chief is ultimately responsible for the paper's content. S/he has the final say on everything related to the newspaper (including editorial, production, business, and layout), not specified otherwise in these by-laws. The student in this position is a major source for editorial suggestion and editorial policy. The Editor in Chief maintains administrative and student contacts and is the official spokesperson for the paper, representing it in public. S/he presides over meetings and other such events, makes arrangements for meetings, orders office supplies through the Managing Editor, and supervises salaried personnel. This person has the final edit on the staff editorial. This person makes the final proof of the entire paper after the Design/Production Editor(s), Copy Editor(s) and Senior Editor. Should the Senior Editor be absent, this person also assumes the responsibilities of the Senior Editor. The Editor in Chief oversees all aspects of production, and financial matters. S/he places the ads in the paper each week from a list submitted by the Managing Editor. S/he settles any disputes between Editors. It is the responsibility of the Editor in Chief to ensure all members of the Board are aware of these by-laws. It is the responsibility of the Editor in Chief to compile and submit an organization report to the Vassar Student Association Secretary each month. It is the responsibility of the Editor in Chief to attend weekly VSA meetings as a representative of the *Miscellany News*.

b. **Senior Editor**: This position should be filled by someone of comparable skill and experience to the Editor in Chief. The Senior Editor should coordinate, manage, and advise the Design/Production Editor(s), Spread Editor(s), Copy Editor(s), Contributing Editor(s) and section editors as needed, in cooperation with the Editor in Chief. S/he will be responsible for proofreading all of the sections for grammar, clarity, and design aspects. S/he should be responsible for recruiting staff members. Should the Editor in Chief be absent, the Senior Editor assumes the responsibilities of the position for 2 weeks at which time the Editorial Board must review the situation on a weekly basis.

c. **Contributing Editor**: The Contributing Editor shall actively contribute to a specified aspect of the *Miscellany News*, shall have held an editorial position for at least two semesters, and be judged by the Editorial Board to have made significant contributions to the newspaper. The responsibilities of this position will vary according to the needs of the paper and the individuals filling the positions.

Generally, this position is granted to an editor with senior standing on the staff; as such, this editor is a resource and advisor. Upon applying to be a Contributing Editor, applicants must outline what they plan to do for the paper during the semester. Failure to follow through with their proposed plans shall constitute dereliction of duty.

d. **Managing Editor:** The Managing Editor is responsible for the financial management of the paper. It is also his or her duty to evaluate and advise operating procedures of the paper. The Managing Editor is responsible for the soliciting of ads and billing of advertisers. The Managing Editor must maintain close, regular contact with the treasurer of the Vassar Student Association, and will serve as Treasurer of the *Miscellany News*. It is the responsibility of the Managing Editor to present the monthly business reports to the Editorial Board at the first meeting of the Editorial Board each month. The Managing Editor shall be responsible for delegating tasks to the office assistant, archiving papers, keeping accurate and detailed financial records, maintaining a database of advertisers, and creating a list of ads to be published each week. The Managing Editor shall remain in close and constant contact with advertisers and subscribers. If the Editor in Chief and Senior Editor are absent, the Managing Editor, in conjunction with the most senior editor on staff, will assume their responsibilities.

e. **Online Editor:** The Online Editor is responsible for the continued updating, maintenance, design and functionality of the *Miscellany News*'s Web site. The Online Editor reports directly to the Editor in Chief. S/he will work with Section Editors to determine content that should be placed online in between the production of the printed newspaper. S/he will also write and post breaking news stories to the Web site when they occur on campus. Additionally, the Online Editor may work with the Editorial Board to design or redesign certain elements of the Web site.

f. **News Editor:** The News Editor is responsible for covering campus news each week, teaching staff members about news writing, and assigning reporters to cover news events. It is the responsibility of the News Editor to attend weekly VSA meetings, or delegate this responsibility to a writer. The News Editor is to lay out that section of the paper devoted to news. S/he must hold weekly meetings with the News staff. The News Editor is responsible for submitting a list of photos and graphic requests to the appropriate editor each week at Ed. Board as well as nominating a story each week for the cover. The News Editor is responsible for editing news articles for content and grammar before giving their section to the Copy Editor(s).

g. **Arts Editor:** The Arts & Entertainment Editor is responsible for covering dance, art, music, theater, literature, and movies both on and off campus. The Arts & Entertainment Editor is to lay out that section of the paper devoted to arts. S/he must hold weekly meetings with the Arts & Entertainment staff. The Arts & Entertainment Editor is responsible for submitting a list of photos and graphic requests to the appropriate editor each week at Ed. Board as well as nominating a story each week for the cover. The Arts & Entertainment Editor is responsible for editing art & entertainment articles for content and grammar before giving their section to the Copy Editor(s).

h. **Opinions Editor:** The Opinions Editor is responsible for letters, columns and opinion's pieces. The Opinions Editor is to lay out that section of the paper devoted to opinions and letters; The *Miscellany News* does not attempt to verify the authorship or content of letters unless an obvious problem exists. The *Miscellany News* does not take the responsibility for letters or columns, but the Opinions Editor should use discretion to avoid the printing of letters or columns that are obscene, gratuitously offensive, or potentially libelous by bringing any letters which s/he thinks may be problematic to the attention of the Editor in Chief. The Opinions Editor is bound by the letters policy. It is favorable that a summary of the letters policy be printed regularly in the opinions section. Any changes to the letters policy must be made by the Editorial Board on recommendation from the Editor in Chief. The Opinions Editor should be familiar with the rules of libel. S/he must hold weekly meetings with the Opinions staff. The Opinions Editor is responsible for submitting a list of photos and graphic requests to the appropriate editor each week at Ed. Board as well as nominating a story each week for the cover. The Opinions Editor is responsible for editing opinions pieces for content and grammar before giving their section to the Copy Editor(s).

i. **Features Editor:** The Features Editor is responsible for assigning feature stories about people, issues, lectures, and anything pertinent to Vassar students, including off-campus events. The Features Editor is to lay out that section of the paper devoted to features. S/he must hold weekly meetings with the Features staff. The Features Editor is responsible for submitting a list of photos and graphic requests to the appropriate editor each week at Ed. Board as well as nominating a story each week for the cover. The Features Editor is responsible for editing features articles for content and grammar before giving their section to the Copy Editor(s).

j. Sports Editor: The Sports Editor must provide news and feature stories relating to Vassar sports, both men's and women's, and is encouraged to discuss intramural as well as national sports. The Sports Editor is to lay out that section of the paper devoted to sports. S/he must hold weekly meetings with the Sports staff. The Sports Editor is responsible for submitting a list of photos and graphic requests to the appropriate editor each week at Ed. Board as well as nominating a story each week for the cover. The Sports Editor is responsible for editing sports pieces for content and grammar before giving their section to the Copy Editor(s).

k. Photography Editor: The Photography Editor receives photo assignments from all editors, is responsible for developing film and recruits and delegates photographers to cover those assignments. To avoid confusion, a final list of photos must be compiled a week in advance and given to the Photography Editor. However, the Photography Editor should be prepared for late-breaking news requiring coverage. The Photography Editor is responsible for the maintenance, care, and whereabouts of the digital camera.

l. Design/Production Editor: The Design/Production Editor is responsible for setting the production deadlines of the paper in consultation with the Editorial Board. The Design/Production Editor is responsible for the weekly creation of templates, and will maintain and oversee any problems that arise with section templates. The Design/Production Editor oversees the layout, design, and graphical elements of the paper. All section editors should consult with this editor during the lay-out process.

m. Copy Editor: The Copy Editor(s) is responsible for reading each section to check for style, clarity, punctuation, and length. The Copy Editor(s) is responsible for the management of copy staff. All section editors are responsible for giving their completed sections to the Copy Editor to read. While not an official member of senior staff, the copy editor has unique insight into the overall status of the paper. All corrections by the copy editor are to be input by section and assistant editors unless otherwise directed by they senior editor or editor in chief. Also, the copy editor should be present at senior staff meetings.

n. Backpage Editor: S/he is responsible for maintaining a weekly calendar of college community events, for laying out this calendar, and for collection and laying out classified ads. Preferably, the calendar and the Backpage (in tabloid format) should feature humor. The Backpage Editor should advertise and maintain methods of submitting information to the calendar that are open to the entire College community.

   o. **Spread Editor:** The Spread Editor is responsible for assembling, editing and laying out center spreads, special sections and topic-oriented pages for at least three issues per semester. No more than half of the content of the Spread section can be written by the Spread Editor. The Spread Editor must submit an outline of their plans for each spread plan at the beginning of each semester. Upon presentation by the Spread Editor, this plan will be subject to a vote by the Ed. board. The plan may be revised at any point throughout the semester through a majority vote by the Editorial Board.

      10. Section editors have control over their own sections, although the Editor in Chief has final say. They must further respect the recommendations of the Senior Editor, Design/Production Editor, and Copy Editor; any disputes shall be decided by the Editor in Chief.

      11. All section editors must be in close communication with the Photography Editor.

      12. All Editorial Board members are required to attend all Editorial Board meetings unless excused by the Editor in Chief. Continued absence from Ed. Board meetings will be considered a dereliction of duty and grounds for impeachment.

      13. Editorial Board members are responsible for drafting at least one editorial a semester (see Section VI, Subsection D.3).

D. Other positions

   1. **Assistant Editors:** Assistant editors should assist the section editors with fulfilling their responsibilities. Assistant editors are interviewed by and voted on by the Editorial Board as described in Section IV.D. Assistant editors should participate in all aspects of the editorial responsibilities of his or her section with the intent of becoming the editor in the future. Assistant editors are required to write every other week, or weekly if the section editor deems it appropriate. Assistant editors are required to enter a round of corrections each week.

2. **Senior Positions:** Staff writers and photographers who have worked diligently and with distinction for more than one semester may be promoted to Senior Staff Writer or Senior Photographer at the discretion of the Editorial Board as described in Section IV.E.8. A member of the Editorial Board must recommend an individual for promotion to the senior staff position. There is no limit as to how many senior staff members there may be and this position does not necessarily have to be filled.

3. **Circulation Manager:** S/he is responsible for picking up the press run on the morning it is first available, putting copies in the distribution bins and specified locations, and leaving a sufficient number of issues in the office for archival and subscription use.

4. **Office Assistants:** S/he participates in elements of newspaper business and production, including maintaining subscription database, assisting business staff with all aspects of advertising (particularly communications and invoices), maintaining voicemail system, distributing mail, and inputting as well as updating website content. S/he may also work on special projects as needed. This person meets weekly with Managing Editor and/or Senior Staff regarding on-going projects and regular responsibilities.

5. **Business Manager:** When the *Miscellany News* does not have a Managing Editor, it must have a Business Manager. The Business Manager fulfills all of the responsibilities of Managing Editor, but does not sit on the Editorial Board. During times when the Editor in Chief and Senior Editor cannot fulfill their duties, the Business Manager does not assume their responsibilities.

6. **Editor Emeritus:** A former member of the Editorial Board, who has served a minimum of four semesters on the Board, may be elected to fulfill the role of Editor Emeritus. This person acts in an advisory role to the Ed. Board. Although not a voting member of the Board, s/he may be asked to attend Ed. Board meetings upon the members' request. Because this person is limited to an advisory role, his or her name is *not* included in the staff box each week.

7. **Cover Designer:** S/he is responsible for putting together the cover image each week. S/he will be responsible for

providing Senior Staff with two or more images which are
decided at Editorial Board meetings each week.

8. **Public Relations Manager:** Duties include, but are not
limited to, increasing community outreach, management
of subscriptions and graduation ad solicitations and
communication with the community at large. S/he ensures
that the *Miscellany News* is a positive force in the College
community.

9. **Staff Writers:** Staff writers will be responsible for writing an
article every week, with two "off" weeks each semester to be
taken at their discretion. In the case where there are more
writers than assignments, writers are exempt from their
writing requirement for that week. Before becoming a Staff
Writer, all writers must write at least one article credited as
a Guest Writer. For that article, Guest Writers should work
under the close guidance of their respective section editor.
At any point following their first article, writers may then be
nominated at Editorial Board for the Staff Writer position
at the discretion of their section editor, in consultation
with the Copy Editor, Senior Editor and Editor in Chief, as
needed. Applicants can write no more than five articles as a
Guest Writer without being confirmed as Staff Writer by the
Editorial Board. It is preferable that aspiring Staff Writers
meet with one of the Contributing Editors for a writing
workshop before their nomination. Former editors may
automatically assume the position of Staff Writer.

10. **Columnist and Cartoonists:** You must submit 2 samples as
your application. Columnists must also submit a statement
of intent detailing the focus of their column not to exceed
one paragraph in length. Cartoonists must use the pre-sized
templates provided by the *Miscellany News*. Your work
will be reviewed by the editor of your section and/or the
Editor in Chief and then brought to an editorial board
vote. Columnist must interview with their application,
Columnists and cartoonists can choose to print on either
a weekly or bi-weekly basis. If you skip a submission, your
position is immediately open for review by the editorial
board. The position lasts for one semester, at which time
the columnist or cartoonist may reapply by submitting
either: a) one sample from previous semester(s) and one new
sample or b) two new samples. Ed Board members must set
a deadline for applications for Columnists and Cartoonist

at the beginning of each semester. This deadline must be advertised in the paper.

11. **Staff Photographer:** Staff photographers will be responsible for contributing every week, with two "off" weeks each semester to be taken at their discretion. In the case where there are more staff than assignments, staff will be exempt from their requirements for that week. All staff photographers must attend general staff meetings once a week. To apply for staff photographer, one must take photographs for three issues, at which time their name automatically comes to an editorial board vote. If not given the designation as staff, photographers can be re-considered after taking photos for another issue. Former photo editors may automatically assume the staff photographer position.

Section IV: Board Procedure

A. Quorum

1. A quorum on the Editorial Board shall consist of the presence of two-thirds of the members.

2. In the event that a member of the Editorial Board cannot attend the meeting, that member may send their assistant editor as proxy. A proxy can only be sent twice a semester and must be done with permission from the Editor in Chief.

3. Any two members of the board may call a meeting of the Editorial Board; however, those members are responsible for making all the arrangements for that special meeting.

B. Meetings

1. Editorial Board meetings are to be held weekly on a day and time chosen at the beginning of each semester.

2. Editorial Board meetings are closed to the public. Non-members may be admitted by a majority vote of the Board on a meeting-to-meeting basis.

3. The Editor in Chief shall e-mail the agenda for Editorial Board meetings to all Board members 24 hours prior to the meeting.

4. Prior to each Board meeting an advertised critique of the previous week's issue, open to the public, shall be held.

5. If an Editor misses more than 2 Editorial Board meetings, their standing on Ed. Board will be reviewed by the Ed. Board.

C. Voting

1. Each Board member shall have one vote.

2. Upon the request of at least one Board member, a closed ballot vote will be taken.

3. Approval by a simple majority vote of a quorum of the Editorial Board shall constitute passage of any item before that Board, except where specified otherwise in these by-laws.

4. If two editors ask for a vote to be postponed because they cannot attend a meeting for emergency reasons then it must be postponed.

5. Absentee voting shall not be allowed without the designation of a proxy; absent editors will be counted as abstentions.

6. If a matter is not on the aforementioned agenda, the vote must be postponed if there are absent editors.

D. Editorials

1. Editorials represent a two-thirds' majority opinion of the Editorial Board.

2. Two editorials may be written, should the Board deem it necessary.

3. Any member of the Editorial Board has the right to request that a pro-con editorial be written.

4. Editorials should be the combined effort of the Board. A member, or multiple members will compose a draft, then distribute it among the Board. Any member is allowed to make suggestions. Each editor is required to draft at least

one editorial each semester, alone or in conjuncture with another Board member.

5. Because s/he represents the paper to the community, the Editor in Chief is responsible for the final edit of the staff editorial. It is therefore necessary for the Editor in Chief to be a part of the voting majority.

E. Elections

1. Advertisements for the election of the Editor in Chief should be published in time for the newly elected Editor in Chief to run the final two issues of the semester, not including the graduation issue. Elections for all other positions shall be held so that new editors can work on the final issue of the year that is not the graduation issue.

1.1 A full-page advertisement should be devoted to open positions in the fourth-to-last week and the second-to-last week of the paper's run.

2. Applications for the Editorial Board positions must be submitted to the Editor in Chief by a publicized date.

3. Each applicant has the right to an interview.

3.1 The Editorial Board has the responsibility of conducting fair and equal interviews for each applicant. Any discrepancy in the nature of an interview should be brought to the attention of the Editor in Chief.

4. A majority of the Board shall elect a person, with abstentions not being counted in the total.

5. Elected editors share the position with the outgoing editors for at least one week, and then run the section themselves in the final issue of that year.

6. In the event that a position is not filled in spring elections, that current editor is responsible for finishing any obligations required of them for the remainder of the year.

7. No more than two people may be elected to a single position without an Editorial Board vote to allow more than two in special situations.

8. There is only to be one Editor in Chief, except in special circumstances discussed and approved by the Editorial Board. There is also to be only one Senior Editor, except in special circumstances when the Editorial Board deems it necessary to have two.

9. A member of the Editorial Board running for a position before the Board must leave before discussion of the vote begins and while other candidates for that position are being interviewed.

10. Any violation this procedure should be brought to the attention of the Editorial Board, who shall then review the applications.

11. Any staff member may be promoted to senior staff member by a majority vote of the Editorial Board.

12. The Editor in Chief (or the head of the electoral board who shall be decided on in advance of elections, should the Editor in Chief be seeking re-election) shall notify all candidates of the results.

13. The electoral board is made up of the Editorial Board members voting to fill positions, excluding those running for each specific position.

F. Impeachment

1. At the request of at least one Board member, which must be seconded by at least one other member, an impeachment hearing must be held. All members of the Board must be present at any impeachment hearing. At the request of any Board member who cannot attend an impeachment hearing, the hearing must be postponed.

2. Any vote for impeachment must be approved by a two-thirds' majority of the Editorial Board.

2.1 The impeachment hearing shall be run by the Editor in Chief. If the party in question is Editor in Chief, the hearing shall be conducted by the Senior Editor. If no Senior Editor is on staff, the responsibility falls to the most senior editor on staff.

3. One may be impeached on the following grounds:
   a. Dereliction of duty, including misrepresentation of the paper and failure to meet basic responsibilities.
   b. Flagrant and repeated violation of these by-laws.
   c. Financial misconduct.

4. The accused has the following rights:
   a. To be presumed innocent until proven guilty.
   b. To know the accuser.
   c. To know the grounds of impeachment.
   d. To resign before a vote is taken
   e. To have anyone present a defense on behalf of the accused.

G. Amendment

1. These by-laws should be reviewed periodically and revised and/or amended as needed.

2. Any member of the Editorial Board may propose to the Board a revision of amendment of these by-laws or the stylebook.

3. A simple majority of the Executive Board is necessary to amend or waive these by-laws.

Section V: Business

A. Business Issues

1. Business, advertising revenue, and other financial matters will be the immediate responsibility of the Managing Editor and his or her assistants, in frequent consultation with the Editor in Chief.

1.1 The Managing Editor shall compose a written budget at the beginning of each semester, in frequent consultation with both the Editor in Chief and the VSA Treasurer.

1.2 Major purchases (single items over $100) must be made with the approval of a simple majority of the Editorial Board.

2. Managing Editor(s) shall give monthly written reports to the Editorial Board. The Managing Editor shall submit a financial report to the Editorial Board at the beginning of each month and should keep in close contact with the Editor in Chief about any financial issues.

2.1 All business transactions should be carefully detailed and recorded in the monthly written reports, for audit purposes.

3. The *Miscellany News* may not donate or give any of its funds to other individuals or organizations on or off campus. While it respects the need for organizations to share funds and assist each other, it believes that the funds of the *Miscellany News* must be spent on the improvement of the *Miscellany News*.

A. Advertising Policy

1. The *Miscellany News*, in the interests of the financial solvency, attempts to print all ads it receives. The Editorial Board has the right to reject any advertisement. The appearance of an ad in the paper does not imply the paper's endorsement.

2. It is the responsibility of the Managing Editor, Editor in Chief and Senior Editor to read all ads printed in the paper prior to going to press.

3. Should an advertisement appear to conflict with state or federal law or Vassar College regulations, it is the responsibility of the Managing Editor to bring it before the Editorial Board for discussion and review. If an ad is deemed to violate state of federal law or if it conflicts with Vassar College regulations, the ad may not be printed.

4. The Managing Editor is further responsible for bringing ads of a potentially controversial nature before the Editorial Board for discussion and review. To print potentially controversial ads that do not conflict with state or federal law or Vassar College regulations, the approval of two-thirds of the entire Board is required. Criteria for determining whether or not an ad should be run:

4.1 To what extent the ad is content-based and resembles a supplement created by the staff. A good way to determine its reliability on content is to ask whether it could be run as a letter to the editor.

4.2 If the ad is soliciting a service or product.

4.3 If the ad has a clear signatory and/or contact information.

5. The *Miscellany News* may not print advertisements publicizing candidates for any VSA position. The paper does reserve the right to print official candidates' statements when all candidates for an office are included.

Guardians of
the *Miscellany News*

The following table shows the names and approximate tenures of the Editors in Chief of the *Miscellany News* from the beginning of weekly publication in February 1914 through the present. Editors of the *Vassar Miscellany*, which began as a quarterly in 1872 and continued through 1924 (running concurrently with the *Weekly* for a decade), are not included here because the publication often had multiple editors at once. As a result, this list covers only the leaders of the more traditionally formatted newspaper. The names of those earlier editors are listed, however, in the *Vassarion*, Vassar's yearbook.

The dates given below are rough for several reasons. First, they are listed in terms of academic semesters. Hence, "Spring 2003" would reflect the period between January 2003 and June 2003. However, the academic calendar has shifted over the past century. Even then, within certain semesters, two or more individuals have served as Editor in Chief concurrently. Certain editors have served as acting Editor in Chief for brief periods, often without being recorded. It is also worth noting that Editors in Chief have historically begun their term by working alongside the outgoing editor, without their name on the masthead. Even if a term is listed below as having begun in the spring semester, that editor likely served as acting Editor in Chief for the last few issues of the preceding fall semester. In short, this table is meant only as an approximate chronological reference.

Editor in Chief	Dates Served
Mary Peinberton Nourse	Spring 1914—Spring 1915
Mary Mallon ✳	Fall 1915—Spring 1916 *diary*
Elizabeth Heath	Fall 1916—Spring 1917
Mary Fox	Spring 1917
Alice Campbell	Spring 1917
Julia Coburn	Fall 1917—Spring 1918
Edith Wetmore	Fall 1919
Alice Stoehr	Fall 1919
Clara Marburg	Fall 1919—Fall 1920
Emily Burke	Spring 1921—Fall 1921
Margaret Bliss	Spring 1922—Fall 1922
Lucia Sherman	Spring 1923—Fall 1923
Mary McCall, Jr.	Spring 1924—Fall 1924
Elizabeth Wadleigh	Spring 1925—Spring 1926
Nancy Houghton	Fall 1926—Spring 1927
Molly Day Thatcher	Fall 1927—Spring 1928
Caroline Mercer	Fall 1928—Spring 1929
Katrina Hincks	Fall 1929—Spring 1930
Carroll Angell	Fall 1930—Spring 1931
Barbara Bailey	Fall 1931
Eunice Clark	Spring 1932—Spring 1933
Mary St. John	Fall 1933—Spring 1934
Harriet Tompkins	Spring 1934—Spring 1935
Jane Whitbread	Fall 1935—Spring 1935
Anna DeCormis	Fall 1936—Spring 1937
Vivian Liebman	Fall 1937—Spring 1938
Barbara Allen	Fall 1938—Spring 1939
Nancy McInery	Fall 1939
Charlotte Feldman	Spring 1940—Spring 1941

Barbara Gair	Fall 1941—Spring 1942
Georgianna Flather	Spring 1942—Fall 1943
June Wollen	Spring 1944
Irene Hay	Fall 1944
Betty MacMorran	Fall 1944
Roberta Hodes	Fall 1945—Spring 1946
Anne Ross	Fall 1946—Spring 1947
Rose Friedman	Fall 1947—Spring 1948
Marilyn Lammert	Fall 1948
Ethel Silver	Spring 1949—Fall 1949
Marty Smith	Spring 1950—Fall 1950
Emily Weston	Spring 1951—Fall 1951
Dorris Caplan	Spring 1952—Fall 1952
Janet Binder	Spring 1953
Natalie Becker	Fall 1953—Spring 1954
Nancy Schatz	Fall 1954
Ellen Silver	Fall 1954—Fall 1955
Marilyn Blatt	Spring 1956—Fall 1956
Jean Sonkin	Spring 1957—Fall 1957
Carol Sheingorn	Spring 1958
Pauline Morrison	Fall 1958
Mary Davis	Spring 1959—Fall 1959
Rosalind Friedman	Spring 1960—Fall 1960
Judith Wells	Spring 1961—Fall 1961
Judy Levin	Spring 1962—Fall 1962
Jessica Bonnie Bascal	Spring 1963
Sherry Corlan Chayat	Fall 1963—Spring 1964
Ruth Welch	Fall 1964
Sara Linnie Slocum	Spring 1965—Fall 1966
Jennifer Read	Spring 1966
Beth Dunlop	Fall 1966—Spring 1968

Wendy Knickerbocker	Spring 1968
Laura Jones	Fall 1968—Spring 1969
Susan Casteras	Fall 1969—Spring 1970
Dale Mezzacappa	Fall 1970—Spring 1971
Margaret Sandbord	Fall 1971—Spring 1972
Nancy Borland	Fall 1972
Carol Miegel	Spring 1973—Fall 1973
Deborah Seaman	Spring 1974
Jason Isaacson	Fall 1974
Marian Lindberg	Spring 1975—Spring 1977
Cynthia Sheps	Fall 1977—Spring 1978
Carol Belkin	Fall 1978—Spring 1979
Laura Wimmer	Fall 1979—Spring 1980
Jay Delorey	Fall 1980
Catherine Shumate	Fall 1980
Matthew Kauffman	Spring 1981—Fall 1981
Peter Cummings	Spring 1982—Spring 1983
Steven Kauderer	Fall 1983—Spring 1984
Nick Katz	Fall 1984—Spring 1985
Nicholas Platt	Fall 1985—Spring 1986
Josh Weiss	Fall 1986—Spring 1987
Rosalind Olden	Fall 1987
Jennifer Harriton	Spring 1988—Fall 1988
Beth Saulnier	Spring 1989—Fall 1989
Carol Ann Davis	Spring 1990—Fall 1990
David Gallagher	Spring 1991—Spring 1992
Laura Buzard	Fall 1992
Alicia Dougherty	Spring 1993—Fall 1993
John Griffith	Spring 1994
Jonathan Kang	Fall 1994
Jessica Ellen Thaler	Spring 1995—Fall 1995

Jessica Barron	Spring 1996
Amanda Spielman	Fall 1996
Joe Goldman	Spring 1997
Hill Anderson	Spring 1997
Jen Higgenbotham	Fall 1997
Gabe Anderson	Spring 1998
Melissa Walker	Fall 1998
Ken Archibold	Spring 1999—Fall 1999
Joe Dickson	Spring 2000
Kevin Murtaugh	Fall 2000
Hilary Shroyer	Spring 2001
Katie Pontius	Fall 2001
Marcie Braden	Spring 2002
Mike Healy	Fall 2002
Wolfe Gleitsman	Fall 2002
Emma White	Spring 2003
Aaron Biberstein	Fall 2003—Spring 2004
Larrisa Pahomov	
Aaron Biberstein	Fall 2004
Aaron Biberstein	Spring 2005
Judy Jarvis	
Rachel Wolff	Fall 2005
Anita Varma	Spring 2006
Aaron Biberstein	
Anita Varma	Fall 2006
Amanda Melillo	Spring 2007
Samuel Rosen-Amy	Spring 2007
Lauren Sutherland	Fall 2007
Acacia O'Connor	Spring 2008
Brian Farkas	Spring 2008—Present

Bibliography

The material for this project was derived primarily from two vital sources. The first has been the print and microfilm archives of the *Miscellany News* in the Vassar College Libraries; the second has been conversations with dozens upon dozens of Vassar alumnae/i who served as editors, writers and photographers for the paper. The editors extend from the 1930s through the present. Though I went to the greatest lengths to track down former Editors in Chief, I also tried to hear the reflections of average reporters and photographers. Interviews are cited within the text, and direct references to the *Miscellany*'s archives are made in chapter endnotes.

In addition to archives and interviews, I have consulted a variety of other sources to give useful historical context to Vassar's newspaper. These sources tend to be histories of journalism, histories of Vassar, or biographies of eminent *Miscellany* alumnae/i. Of particular help has been the work of Vassar's own institutional historian Elizabeth Daniels '41. The *Vassar Encyclopedia*, which she founded, has been invaluable in guiding me through Vassar's past, as have the specific articles on campus publications by Sarah Riane Harper '09.

A word of caution to those interested in perusing the archives of the *Miscellany*: Vassar's microfilm holdings of the paper extend only between 1914 and 2005. Even within that range, some reels of film are incomplete—perhaps most significantly, the period during the Second World War. For these missing date ranges, researchers must make an appointment in the Archives and Special Collections Library in order to view bound copies of the original paper. The precursor publications to the *Miscellany*, the *Vassariana* and the *Transcript*, exist only in Special Collections as hard copies. The *Vassar Miscellany* between 1872 and 1924 does not exist on microfilm; however, the Library has bound copies available in circulation, in addition to supplemental copies in Special Collections.

Archives and Special Collections, Vassar College Libraries, comp. "Vassar Student Association Records."

Baltzell, E. Digby. *Judgment and Sensibility: Religion and Stratification.* Transaction Publishers, 1994.

Bouslog, Elba Huffman. *Letters from Old-Time Vassar, 1869.* Poughkeepsie, NY: Vassar College, 1915.

Bruno, Maryann, and Elizabeth A. Daniels. *Vassar College.* London: Arcadia, 2001.

Burstyn, Joan. *Victorian Education and the Ideal of Womanhood.* London: Croom Helm, 1980.

Cleveland, Anne, and Jeane Anderson. *Vassar: A Second Glance.* Boston, MA: Thomas Todd Company, 1942.

Cohen, Robert. *When the Old Left was Young: Student Radicals and America's First Mass Student Movement, 1929-1941.* New York: Oxford University Press, 1993.

Colburn, David. "Govenor Alfred E. Smith and the Red Scare, 1919-20." *Political Science Quarterly*, September 1973.

Coolidge, John Calvin. "Enemies of the Republic: Are the 'Reds' Stalking Our College Women?" The *Delineator*, June 1921: 4-5, 66-67.

Daniels, Elizabeth A. *Bridges to the World: Henry Noble MacCracken and Vassar College.* Clifton Corners, NY: College Avenue Press, 1994.

—. *Main to Mudd: An Informal History of Vassar College Buildings.* Poughkeepsie, NY: Vassar College, 1996.

Daniels, Elizabeth A., and Clyde Griffen. *Full Steam Ahead in Poughkeepsie: The Story of Coeducation at Vassar, 1966-1974.* Poughkeepsie, NY: Vassar College, 2000.

Edward, Linner. *Vassar: The Remarkable Growth of a Man and His College.* Edited by Elizabeth A. Daniels. Poughkeepsie, NY: Vassar College, 1984.

Felsenthal, Carol. *Power, Privilege and The Post: The Katharine Graham Story.* Washington, D.C.: Seven Stories Press, 1999.

Gallaher, Grace Margaret. *Vassar Stories.* Boston, MA: E.H. Bacon, 1907.

Gibbs, Cheryl. *Getting the Whole Story: Reporting and Writing the News.* New York: Guilford Press, 2002.

Goodsell, Willystine. *Pioneers of Women's Education in the United States: Emma Willard, Catherine Beecher, Mary Lyon.* New York: McGraw-Hill, 1831.

Goodwin, Lorine Swainston. *The Pure Food, Drink, and Drug Crusaders, 1879-1914.* Jefferson, NC: McFarland, 1999.

Gordon, Eleanor. *Public Lives: Women, Family and Society in Victorian Britain.* New Haven: Yale University Press, 2003.

Goudy, Frances, ed. *Published Diaries, Reminiscences, Journals and Autobiographies by American Women.* Poughkeepsie, NY: Vassar College, 1984.

Haeussler Bohan, Chara. *Go to the Sources: Lucy Maynard Salmon and the Teaching of History.* New York, NY: Lang, Peter Publishing Inc., 2004.

Harper, Sarah Riane. *The Chronicle.* Edited by Elizabeth Daniels. 2007. http://vcencyclopedia.vassar.edu/index.php/The_Chronicle (accessed June 17, 2008).

—. *The Chronicle of the 1970s.* Edited by Elizabeth Daniels. 2007. http://vcencyclopedia.vassar.edu/index.php/The_Chronicle_of_the_1970s (accessed July 9, 2008).

—. *The Miscellany Monthly.* Edited by Elizabeth Daniels. 2006. http://vcencyclopedia.vassar.edu/index.php/The_Miscellany_Monthly (accessed April 8, 2008).

—. *The Modern Miscellany News.* Edited by Elizabeth Daniels. 2006. http://vcencyclopedia.vassar.edu/index.php/The_modern_Vassar_Miscellany_News (accessed May 3, 2008).

—. *Vassar Newspapers Tackle Pressing Concern: Which College Men are Best for the "Vassar Girl?".* 2007. http://vcencyclopedia.vassar.edu/index.php/Vassar_Newspapers_Tackle_Pressing_Concern:_Which_College_Men_are_Best_for_the_%22Vassar_Girl%3F%22 (accessed May 19, 2008).

Johnson, Joan Marie, ed. *Southern Women at Vassar: The Poppenheim Family Letters, 1882–1916.* Columbia, SC: Johnson University of South Carolina Press, 2002.

Johnson, Joan, ed. *Southern Women at Vassar: The Poppenheim Family Letters, 1882-1916.* Columbia, SC: University of South Carolina Press, 2002.

Kiernan, Frances. *Seeing Mary Plain: A Life of Mary McCarthy.* New York, NY: W.W. Norton & Company.

Kosner, Edward, and Peter Hamill. *It's News to Me: The Making and Unmaking of an Editor.* Thunder's Mouth Press, 2006.

Lange, Helene. *The Higher Education of Women in Europe.* Ann Arbor: A. Strahan, 1890.

Longenbach, James. *Modern Poetry After Modernism.* New York, NY: Oxford University Press, 1997.

MacKinnon, Alison. "Educated Doubt: Women, Religion and the Challenge of Higher Education, c.1870-1920." *Women's History Review.* 241-259. 1998.

Mallon, Mary. "The *Vassar Miscellany*." The *Vassar Miscellany Monthly,* April 1915.

Marchalonis, Shirley. *College Girls: A Century of Fiction.* Piscataway, NJ: Rutgers University Press, 1995.

Matsumoto, Lila. *Sarah Gibson Blanding.* Edited by Elizabeth A. Daniels. 2005. http://vcencyclopedia.vassar.edu/index.php/Sarah_Gibson_Blanding (accessed June 3, 2008).

McCarthy, Mary. *The Group.* New York, NY: Harcourt Press, 1991.

Milford, Nancy. *Savage Beauty: The Life of Edna St. Vincent Millay.* New York, NY: Random House, 2002.

Millier, Brett C. *Elizabeth Bishop: Life and the Memory of It.* Berkeley, CA: University of California Press, 1993.

Mott, Frank Luther. *A History of American Magazines.* Cambridge, MA: Harvard University Press, 1968.

Negri, Paul. *English Victorian Poetry: An Anthology.* New York: Dover Publications, 1999.

New York Times Company. *The New York Times: The Complete Front Pages: 1851-2008.* New York: Black Dog & Leventhal Publishers, 2008.

Nielsen, Kim E. *Un-American Womanhood: Antiradicalism, Antifeminism, and the First Red Scare.* Cleveland, OH: Ohio State University Press, 2001.

Peraza-Baker, Maya. *Vassar Encyclopedia.* Edited by Elizabeth A Daniels. June 11, 2008. http://vcencyclopedia.vassar.edu/index.php/The_Telephone.

Poulson, Susan L, and Leslie Miller-Bernal. *Challenged by Coeducation: Women's Colleges Since the 1960s.* Memphis, TN: Vanderbuilt University Press, 2006.

Reilly, Lisa, Karen Lengen, and Will Faller. *Vassar College: An Architectural Tour.* Princeton, NJ: Princeton Architectural Press, 2003.

Remnick, David. *Reporting: Writings from The New Yorker.* New York, NY: Knopf, 2006.

Rosenberg, Rosalind. "The Limits of Access: The History Of Coeducation in America." *Women and Higher Education: Essays from the Mount Holyoke College Sesquicentennial Symposia.* Ed. John Mack Faragher and Florence Howe. New York: Norton, 1988.

Rudikoff, Lisa Breskin. *Women in the Popular Front: Student Peace Movement at Vassar College, 1935-1941.* Ann Arbor, MI: University of Michigan Dissertation Services, 2007.

Rudolph, Frederick and John Thelin. *The American College and University: A History.* Atlanta: University of Georgia Press, 1990

Sims, Norman. *Literary Journalism in the Twentieth Century.* Evanston, IL: Northwestern University Press, 2008.

Special Collections, Vassar College Archives, comp. "VC Government (1967-1979)" *Subject File 23.79.*

Stanton, Richard. *All News is Local: The Failure of the Media to Reflect World Events in a Globalized Age.* Jefferson, N.C.: McFarland & Co., 2007.

Stephen, Barbara. *Emily Davies and Girton College.* London: Constable & Co., 1927.

Stephens, Mitchell. *The History of News: From the Drum to the Satellite.* New York: Viking, 1988.

Taylor, James Monroe, and Elizabeth Hazelton Haight. *Vassar.* New York, NY: Oxford University Press, 1915.

The Bowdoin Orient. *About the Orient.* 2008. http://orient.bowdoin.edu/orient/about.php (accessed July 20, 2008).

The Colgate Maroon-News. *General Information.* 2008. http://www.maroon-news.com/home/generalinformation/ (accessed July 20, 2008).

Thwing, Charles Franklin. "College Journalism." *Scribners Monthly: An Illustrated Magazine for the People* (Scribner and Son) 16, no. 6 (October 1878): 808-812.

Vassar College. *Guide to the Vassar Student Association Records, 1868-2004.* 2006. http://specialcollections.vassar.edu/findingaids/vc_student_assoc.html (accessed June 1, 2008).

Whitt, Jan. *Women in American Journalism: A New History.* Urbana: University of Illinois Press, 2008.

Zimmer, Troy A. "The Views of College Newspaper Editors on their Readers, Newspapers, and News Priorities." *The Journal of Higher Education* (Ohio State University Press) 46, no. 4 (August 1975): 451-459.

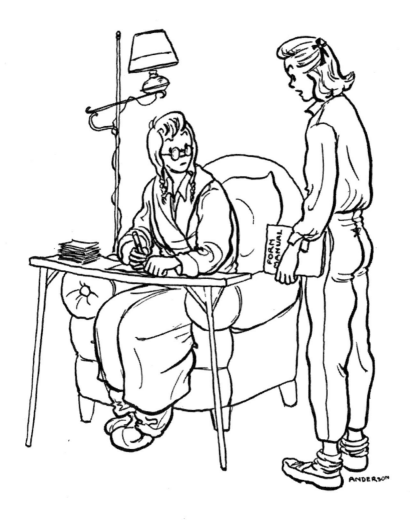

"A Senior told me if you have less than thirty footnotes it's plagiarism."

Jean Anderson, Vassar: A Second Glance

Index